"A must-read for anyone who wants to make the future better than the past—and that's just about all of us."
Anne Fisher, Ask Annie columnist,
Fortune Magazine

■

"Dr. Frankel develops organizations by focusing on the fundamentals: effective personal performance by fully functioning people. Her critical insights and tools for shaping complete capability offer personal and organizational tool kits for people and their managers. Individual inefficiency and personal barriers to success are the frightening cost issues of twenty-first-century companies. Lois offers useful means to avoid those costs beginning now!"
John Hofmeister, president,
Shell Oil Company

■

"A must-read for coaches working with corporate employees. Each chapter is a mini-workshop, and the author's generous use of client stories and coaching examples makes for an interesting read. This is the perfect gift for the client who's ready to get back on track."
Cheryl Richardson, founding president,
International Coach Federation

Also by Lois P. Frankel, PhD

SEE JANE LEAD:
99 Ways for Women to Take Charge at Work

NICE GIRLS DON'T GET RICH:
75 Avoidable Mistakes Women Make with Money

NICE GIRLS DON'T GET THE CORNER OFFICE
101 Unconscious Mistakes Women Make That
Sabotage Their Careers

KINDLING THE SPIRIT:
Acts of Kindness and Words of Courage for Women

WOMEN, ANGER AND DEPRESSION:
Strategies for Self-Empowerment

STOP SABOTAGING YOUR CAREER

8 Proven Strategies to Succeed— In Spite of Yourself

Lois P. Frankel, PhD

WARNER
BUSINESS
BOOKS™

NEW YORK   BOSTON

Copyright © 1998, 2007 by Lois P. Frankel
Originally published by Crown as *Jump-Start Your Career*.

Warner Business Books
Hachette Book Group USA
237 Park Avenue
New York, NY 10169

Visit our Web site at www.HachetteBookGroupUSA.com.

Warner Business Books is an imprint of Warner Books.

Printed in the United States of America

First Warner Edition: April 2007
10 9 8 7 6 5 4 3 2 1

Warner Business Books is a trademark of Time Warner Inc. or an affiliated company. Used under license by Hachette Book Group USA, which is not affiliated with Time Warner Inc.

Library of Congress Cataloging-in-Publication Data
Frankel, Lois P.
    Stop sabotaging your career : 8 proven strategies to succeed in spite of yourself / Lois P. Frankel.—1st Warner ed.
      p. cm.
    Rev. ed. of: Jump-start your career. 1998.
    Includes index.
    ISBN-13: 978-0-446-69785-9
    ISBN-10: 0-446-69785-0
    1. Self-defeating behavior. 2. Success—Psychological aspects. 3. Work—Psychological aspects. I. Frankel, Lois P. Jump-start your career. II. Title.
    BF637.S37F73 2007
    158—dc22   2006036971

Book design by Giorgetta Bell McRee

I once read, "Entrance to another's soul is a sacred honor." This book is dedicated to the men and women who, for more than two decades, have allowed me the privilege of entering their personal and professional lives, trusted me enough to make the leap of faith required to follow my coaching suggestions, and provided me with the opportunity to learn from them as much as I hope they learned from me.

Contents

Preface *ix*

Introduction: The Dynamics of Career Self-Sabotage **1**

Success Strategy 1:   *Build Strong 360-Degree Relationships* **37**

Success Strategy 2:   *Be an Integral Member of Your Team* **74**

Success Strategy 3:   *Capitalize on the Power of Perception* **107**

Success Strategy 4:   *Develop Your Emotional Intelligence and Likability Quotients* **151**

Success Strategy 5:   *Manage Up* **189**

Success Strategy 6:   *Balance Detail Orientation with Strategic Thinking* **221**

Success Strategy 7:   *Develop Your Value-Added Brand* **251**

Success Strategy 8:   *Network for Success* **290**

Personal Development Planning **323**

Acknowledgments **335**

Index **337**

About the Author **347**

Preface

I'm delighted that Diana Baroni at Warner Books acquiesced to two years of my nagging by giving me the opportunity to update and re-release a book I wrote a number of years ago titled *Overcoming Your Strengths: 8 Reasons Why Successful People Derail and How to Remain on Track* (called *Jump Start Your Career* in the paperback version). One reason it was so important to me was that I wanted to respond to all the *men* who have asked me to write a book that's not exclusively for women so they can read it without embarrassment. But the primary reason I kept pursuing it was that the world and the workplace are so different than they were a decade ago. Back then, terrorism and natural disasters on an epic scale were things that happened in other countries, not ours. WorldCom and Enron were well-respected companies with trusted leaders. *The Apprentice* was not a television show but rather someone who learned a trade under the tutelage of a more experienced craftsperson. And Martha Stewart was a domestic diva, not a convicted felon.

In the intervening decade, business has become increasingly competitive, and many workplace mores have fallen to the wayside. Work formerly done by Americans is now outsourced to foreign countries, and laws have been enacted that circumscribe and regulate corporate governance. A new generation of savvy, swift, and smart workers who bring a set of values and a work ethic far different from their predecessors' is poised to take over where the baby boomers leave off. Work–life balance has become an increasingly hot topic of concern to workers of all ages. Yet some things haven't changed. People who rise to the top aren't always those with the highest IQs. They aren't the people who work the hardest or make the biggest sacrifices for the sake of their careers. And they certainly aren't the people who keep their noses to the grindstone with their mouths shut. They're the people who understand that nontechnical capability (often referred to as the soft skills) is every bit as important—if not more important—as technical capability when it comes to reaching their maximum career potential.

How, then, do some folks always seem to do and say the right thing, while others can't quite figure out what it takes to achieve and, more important, *maintain* successful careers? Regardless of career path or position, most of us have experienced that sinking feeling of being on the sidelines watching as less qualified colleagues get the choice assignments, promotions, or developmental opportunities that are intended to groom them for the next rung of the corporate ladder. We may grumble about the injustice of being overlooked for opportunities we feel we deserve, but rarely do we take the time to examine why this happens and what we can do to make ourselves more competitive.

Three decades as a human resource professional, management consultant, and executive coach working inside some of the largest and most respected organizations worldwide have given me the opportunity to learn firsthand why some people surpass their professional peers indefinitely while others spin their wheels in what are at times lucrative but dead-end jobs. One principal reason why companies bring in business coaches to work with executives is that they know even the most talented professionals can have Achilles' heels or blind spots that preclude them from achieving their full potential. Savvy companies, like sports teams, turn good players into great ones through coaching. They understand that the cost of turnover is too high to let them fail. My access to the best and the brightest was as a consultant and business coach committed to helping organizations achieve extraordinary results through maximization of their *human* resources.

If you're reading this book, it's likely that your profile resembles that of many of my clients: You are good at what you do, and may even be recognized for one or more particular strengths, but are somehow stalled and unknowingly sabotaging your best professional efforts. This phenomenon, whereby fast-trackers are displaced from successful career paths by over-relying on the skills that helped them achieve past success, is called derailment. Researchers from the Center for Creative Leadership in Greensboro, North Carolina, estimate that 30 to 50 percent of high-potential managers and executives derail. In my own practice, I've found that such derailment occurs at *every level* of the workplace with just about the same frequency as it does among executives—and always for the same reasons. That's why this book provides a broad context for understanding workplace behavior geared toward anyone at any professional level who wants to stop sabotaging his or her career and learn the essential strategies for becoming and staying competitive in the workplace.

I define *derailment* as "any unexpected change in career momentum." Successful people find that their careers begin to stall or fall off track entirely for seemingly inexplicable reasons. People who work hard and have been rewarded for their contributions to a firm through promotions, choice job assignments, or special perks and incentives find themselves suddenly being overlooked for further recognition for no apparent reason. Their opinions may no longer be solicited, they may not be included in meetings with key people, or they may be given more routine, low-profile assignments than in the past. These people suddenly feel invisible.

When I first started out as a business coach, the profession was just emerging, so I had to develop my own models for understanding workplace success and helping people become more competitive in the world of work. My experience as a human resource professional with a doctoral degree in counseling psychology proved an invaluable combination as I became one of the pioneers in business coaching. It helped me determine that people who experienced career setbacks almost always behaved in ways consistent with childhood expectations and relied almost exclusively on these behaviors for continued success. Typically, these are employees who have no history of job-related performance problems. In fact, they have frequently been identified as high-potential candidates targeted for upward mobility.

Looking inside organizations that downsized, I realized that the survivors of layoffs were frequently not the most technically proficient, best educated, or most productive employees. As corporations cut more closely to the bone, there appeared to be few notable differences between those who were given their pink slips and those who remained. As I examined the situation more closely, however, a pattern emerged: The people kept on staff had the *widest array of technical and interpersonal capabilities,* rather than very specific but more limited ones. This is what has become known as the best-player approach to downsizing: *keeping those people who can function successfully in a wide variety of areas and with a diverse group of people.*

Managers are forced every day to make choices about who will be promoted, given a larger raise, or provided with a developmental assignment among people who, on the face of it, appear to be equally qualified. How, then, do they choose one over another? The answer lies in infrequently commented on, less tangible aspects of workplace behavior. Remarks such as "Steve's a great worker, cranks out the work like no one else, but he doesn't get the big picture" or "Ann is one of our most talented engineers, but she doesn't get along with people" give us our greatest clues as to why some people are recognized and rewarded while others languish in roles for which they may be overqualified. Career setbacks don't always equate to automatic layoff, termination, or demotion. Less extreme, yet equally damaging to your career, is when you are simply overlooked again and again. Your input may be ignored, or you may be overlooked for further growth opportunities. Whether you are laid off, ignored, or overlooked, the result is the same: career stagnation.

The common thread for people who don't progress in their careers to a degree consistent with their intelligence or capability is that they often exhibit superior skill in a particular area *to the exclusion of developing complementary behaviors.* Even when a change in job assignment requires them to apply a different skill set, or when they see people around them develop in diverse areas, they fail to notice that they themselves have limited skill sets. Instead, they turn up the volume on those behaviors that they already do well, hoping that doing more of the same will save them! How do intelligent people neglect to notice something as important as their own lack of a diversified approach to other people and problem solving? The answer to this question requires an understanding of how their strengths were developed and reinforced in response to early-childhood expectations.

Let me give you an example. Jamie comes from a home where her mother was an alcoholic and her father, partially in response to her mother, was a workaholic. Jamie grew up knowing that her survival depended on taking good care of herself, because there was no one else to do it for her. She learned to be independent and self-sufficient. Initially, she was a terrific employee. She was self-motivated and required little coaxing or direction. Eventually, however, Jamie began missing deadlines because she became overextended and failed to ask for assistance. Paradoxically, Jamie's strengths were what ultimately caused her to fail. She must learn to overcome her strengths, through the development of complementary skills, if she is to remain successful over the long term.

The truth is, we all have a little of Jamie in us. Maybe we didn't grow up in the same type of household, but we did grow up in environments that placed certain expectations and restrictions on our development. Whether we learned by word or deed that *Children are to be seen and not heard,* or *You must do things yourself because no one else is to be trusted,* or *Never disagree with authority,* those internalized past messages affect our present behavior in the workplace. Our subconscious tells us that if childhood survival depended on being quiet, independent, or compliant, then our adult well-being must certainly also be contingent on exhibiting those same behaviors. People like Jamie need to be coached to add complementary skills to their existing strengths to help them stay on the track to professional success.

Starting out as a business coach in 1987 with no models for how to do it was probably a good thing for me. It enabled me to use my experience and education to develop a process that would focus not on what people were doing *wrong*, but rather on what they were doing *right* and how this was actually impeding their career progress. The coaching philosophy I developed is simple: *People should not stop engaging in behaviors that work for them, but rather identify the gaps in their repertoire of skills and fill them in with complementary behaviors.* People should remain essentially the same while adding new skills. It's a bit like learning a sport. When the golf coach suggests that the student change his grip, the coach isn't asking him to fundamentally change who he is. She's only giving a tip for how to be more successful on the golf course. If the student incorporates this tip into his game, he's rewarded with better scores.

Much has been written lately about allowing people to succeed from a place of their strengths rather than focusing on development areas. I had quite a heated discussion with an audience member at a keynote speech I was delivering who espoused this philosophy and totally disagreed with my model for developing a broad skill set. Nonetheless, I stand by it, because I've seen it work for hundreds of people over two decades. As I told this woman, change is difficult. We would all like to think that we can simply beef up our strengths and come out as winners, but all we end up with is overdeveloped strengths—and we haven't addressed our performance gaps.

The process of learning how to achieve your career goals by balancing old skills with new ones needn't involve a lot of time or money. It isn't always necessary to hire an outside coach or spend countless years in psychotherapy. You can coach yourself to success by taking the eight proactive steps I describe in this book needed to make yourself an invaluable member of any work environment. The book is designed for anyone who ever wondered why his or her career has gotten off track—and everyone who wants to prevent that from happening in the future. The Career Status Check in the first chapter will help you objectively assess possible blind spots that may be causing you to unknowingly sabotage your career. Suggestions throughout the book offer specific ways that you can enhance your existing skill set to become more competitive and recognized as a winner in your workplace. The key to using this book effectively lies in your willingness to critically assess your background, your behavior, and the direction of your career.

Throughout this book, you'll find inspiring stories of how top professionals—some famous, some not—both avoided and came back from dramatic career setbacks to become leaders in their fields. Specific suggestions for building your career muscle are contained at the end of each chapter. As you read, it's likely you'll discover you have more in common with Bill Clinton, Margaret Thatcher, or Bobby Knight than you realized—because even people who achieve great things must never stop looking for ways to succeed in spite of themselves.

Lois P. Frankel, PhD

STOP SABOTAGING
YOUR CAREER

Introduction:

The Dynamics of Career Self-Sabotage

Success isn't permanent and failure isn't fatal.
Coach Mike Ditka

Dan was a senior accountant with an outstanding record of achievement in his midsize manufacturing firm. He had worked his way up through the ranks and was targeted as a high-potential employee expected to go far and fast—until he was promoted to manager of his department, that is. Although he'd been able to produce high-quality results as an individual contributor, he foundered in his role as a leader. He thought he had to have all the answers. Not only did he exclude others from the decision-making process, but he also failed to delegate, thereby becoming too involved with day-to-day minutiae. It appeared that the skills that enabled him to accomplish so much at lower levels in the organization were no longer sufficient to ensure success. Through coaching, Dan learned new behaviors that complemented his existing strengths and enabled him to not only add more value to his company but achieve his career aspirations as well.

Whether you're an administrative assistant or a senior executive and whether you've been on the job one year or ten years, you're equally susceptible to unexpected changes in career momentum. The phenomenon cuts across all ages and stages of careers as well as gender, ethnicity, and career field. When you least expect it, your career trajectory suddenly slows and causes you to question all that you've accomplished to date and how you achieved it. One day, you're on top of your game—and the next it seems you can't do anything right.

As a business coach for the past twenty years, I've been called on to assist employees such as Dan with overcoming obstacles to long-term career success. Coaching typically begins with a phone call from a senior-level manager or human resource professional who wants to find a coach for someone who is technically capable but foundering in one or more other areas required to be considered fully competent in his or her role. The descriptions are astonishingly similar: "I've got this employee who does really great work but is creating problems in her department. No one wants to work with her. I don't want to lose her, but I'll have no choice about letting her go unless something changes." When asked for a more detailed description of what the employee is doing wrong, the manager continues, "She's like a bull in a china shop. She runs roughshod over people and embarrasses them in front of their peers. She gets the job done, but she leaves a trail of bodies in her wake. She can't seem to understand that what it takes to be successful in our company is a collaborative effort, not just meeting the goals assigned to her."

Frequently, people such as this woman and Dan fail to achieve their career goals without ever understanding why. Unfortunately, they often go on to other jobs and make the same mistakes again. They don't understand that the skills, characteristics, and qualities that contributed to success early in their careers are the same ones that will ultimately serve to derail them once they reach higher levels of an organization or later stages of their careers. That's because, paradoxically, the behaviors that contribute to your early career success are often learned early in childhood as defense mechanisms. That is, they enabled you to survive what might have been a difficult, traumatic, or demanding childhood and have worked in the past, but at some point they fail to ensure *future* success.

THE REPETITION COMPULSION

Whether the description is of someone who runs roughshod over his or her peers, does all the work instead of delegating, sees only the pieces of the puzzle instead of the bigger picture, has difficulty with authority, or is so easygoing that people walk all over him or her, it's a variation on the same theme: *failure to develop new skills that will provide balance to those that contributed to early career success.* If you're someone who continues to rely on behaviors that enabled you to survive childhood, despite the fact that those behaviors have outlived their usefulness, then unfortunately you may be sabotaging your career.

Although I'm no fan of Sigmund Freud, there is one theory that I think he was right about: *the repetition compulsion*—the tendency of human beings to return to past states. It seems we repeat acts over and over, even when they no longer work, until we understand what purpose they serve. We can all cite examples of people we know who marry several times, each time selecting the same type of partner and each time wondering why it doesn't work. For those of us on the outside looking in, it's abundantly clear why it doesn't work, but for the person making the choices it's Freud's repetition compulsion in action.

The choice of a life partner is a good example to use, because it so often reflects the early-childhood experience. That is, if Dad was an alcoholic, a woman may choose a husband who is either an alcoholic or in some similar way incapacitated. If Mom was depressed, her son may choose a depressed wife. This is not to say that these choices are conscious, because they most frequently aren't. We make choices because they're familiar, and this familiarity enables us to know how to act in a given situation. Choosing a partner who is in some way familiar enables us to repeat the childhood behaviors we learned to survive—even though those behaviors are no longer functional!

I've been talking about developing survival skills in response to dysfunctional family behavior, but don't get the impression that people from these families are the only ones who develop such skills. Research suggests that nine out of ten people come from families of origin in which there is some type of dysfunction, but these are not the only families for which survival skills are needed. You may come from that one-in-ten functional family where everyone is a high achiever with advanced degrees in rocket science. Survival skills in your family may *look* different but can still have the effect of obscuring necessary, complementary behaviors. If you're supposed to get straight A's and it doesn't really matter if you have any friends or extracurricular activities, survival skills exclusively in the area of academic achievement can be just as limiting.

I also don't want you to think I'm suggesting that defense mechanisms and survival skills are bad things—because they're not. We all learned early on which behaviors pleased or satisfied our childhood primary caretakers, whether they were parents, nannies, grandparents, favorite teachers, or child care workers. Even preverbal children subconsciously know that their survival depends on the caretaker. Therefore, if repeating pleasing behavior was critical to survival, it is only logical that we would assume those behaviors that pleased the caretaker would also please others later in our lives. Most of us want to be loved and accepted, and often our behavior is motivated by this desire rather than an objective assessment of what the situation requires. Because the caretaker is also the first authority figure in our lives, we think that behaviors that pleased him or her will also please another authority figure—and in the workplace, that authority figure is called "the boss."

So what does all this psychological jargon mean in today's workplace? Let's go back to Dan for a moment. He's an outstanding individual contributor, but he can't quite empower others. Dan's direct reports complain about him grandstanding (keeping the high-profile projects for himself), about not trusting them with an entire project, and about micromanaging their work. To understand these behaviors, we need to look at how they developed and what functional purpose they served in the past. As it turns out, Dan was the oldest of six children. Both parents worked, and he had responsibility for taking care of his younger siblings after school, babysitting during summer vacations, and so on. He learned early in life that his survival— approval from his parents—was dependent on taking responsibility for whatever needed to be done without being asked. In order to juggle school and his chores at home, Dan had to be organized, plan his activities in advance, and keep a close eye on his siblings.

In college, Dan was the ideal student. He not only had his papers done on time, but had them done in advance. He remained current with his studies while holding a part-time job from the second semester of his freshman year on. As a young accountant, Dan was every boss's dream. He showed initiative by anticipating what needed to be done and doing it thoroughly, paying close attention to detail, and requiring little supervision. His performance reviews were, as might be expected, outstanding. The reward for his accomplishments as a superb worker was a promotion to a management position. As in most corporations, good individual performance in Dan's company led to being promoted to leader of a team of employees. The problem inherent to this common practice is that the skills needed to lead a team are substantially different from those needed to succeed independently.

The repetition compulsion suggests that to ensure success in his new assignment, Dan would naturally rely on the same skills that made him successful up to this point—and he did. What was perceived as grandstanding, not trusting others, and micromanaging was merely the repetition of the same childhood behaviors that contributed to his survival. He wasn't consciously keeping the high-profile projects to himself; nor was he intentionally trying to impede the growth of his staff by giving them only small pieces of projects. Given an assignment from upper management, he would simply plan out what had to be done and diligently go about doing it. He was more than happy to assist his direct reports with their routine tasks, in much the same way as he would help his younger siblings with their homework, but they perceived it as micromanaging. Dan had no inkling that his behavior was unusual or inappropriate. It's almost as though he thought, *If it got me to this point, I should do more of it.* And herein lies the problem for so many employees at all levels: not *only* doing what has worked in the past, but doing *more* of it.

Turning Up the Volume

When faced with the prospect of failure, the child part of the adult psyche kicks into gear and *turns up the volume* on the same old behaviors, then wonders why there is static on the new station. The old station didn't have static! If controlling, planning, and doing the work himself worked for Dan in the past, then certainly doing more of the same should work, too. As Dan met with resistance from his staff in the form of missing deadlines, withholding critical information, or doing work that wasn't up to acceptable standards, his survival instincts told him that he needed to engage *more* in the behaviors that contributed to past success.

The obvious problem is that these were the same behaviors that were now contributing to poor morale, low productivity, and lack of cooperation within his department. Doing more of the same only served to escalate the problem. It never occurred to Dan that he exacerbated the problem by controlling and directing even more. In fact, because he had no alternative skills in his repertoire, he thought that he wasn't doing these things enough!

Promotions aren't the only situations that can cause you to stumble along your career path. The inability to recognize and make the shift to changing requirements of the organizational culture or movement from one company to another, one department to another, or one boss to another are but a few others. Clearly, behaviors that are appropriate in one situation can become potential derailers when applied in a different situation. If the culture of Dan's company was more hierarchical—one in which people expected close supervision and little responsibility for entire projects—then his behavior would not have been considered problematic. In fact, he could most likely continue to succeed using the behaviors he learned early in life.

Margaret Thatcher provides a familiar example of someone who did not sustain her stature as one of the world's most powerful women as long as she could have due to her failure to balance strengths with complementary skills when the situation called for it. As prime minister of England, Thatcher had a clear vision of where she wanted to take her country and how that should be accomplished. She was willing to take on tough and, at times, controversial issues. Her strengths earned her the nickname "the Iron Lady." Early in her tenure as prime minister, she was welcomed by many citizens as one who stood by her convictions and who could lead the nation through a difficult period of social and economic decline. She never faltered during the Falklands War and is characterized by her statement during the poll tax controversy, "You turn if you want to. The lady's not for turning."

So what went wrong? Thatcher relied almost exclusively on behaviors learned early in childhood. Her independent, self-sufficient behaviors required complementary skills in consensus building and succeeding through cooperative efforts—skills that she never developed and, in fact, openly eschewed. Shortly after her election, she proclaimed, "I am not a consensus politician. I am a conviction politician." And when the going got tough, Thatcher got tougher. She turned up the volume on her convictions. Throughout her tenure, she relied on the same skills she learned and relied on in childhood, and they ultimately failed her.

As with many of the examples I include in this book of high-profile people who unknowingly sabotaged their careers, I wanted to see if my theory that over-reliance on childhood survival skills contributes to unexpected changes in career momentum holds true. So I went back to their biographies, autobiographies, or other reports of their life stories. By all accounts, Thatcher grew up in a joyless household. Outsiders report that there was never much gaiety or laughter in the home. Her mother was competent but remote. Thatcher never really forged a relationship with her and rarely makes mention of her. It was her strict, work-oriented, and devoutly religious father with whom Thatcher aligned and to whom she credits her success. When she went to school and realized that other children actually had fun in their families, she asked him why their family never went on picnics, rode bicycles, or played games. His reply was "Margaret, never do things or want to do things just because other people do them. Make up your own mind about what you are going to do and persuade people to go your way." Clearly, she learned that lesson well. So well that she was alienated from her peers during her school years and throughout her lifetime claimed no close friends with the exception of her late husband.

In the workplace, an example of an employee turning up the volume on old behaviors is one who moves from a department that places high value on teamwork, collaboration, and consensus to another department in the same organization that requires independent decision making, quick turnaround, and minimal interaction among team members. Because the employee came from a family where harmony was the norm, we'd expect him to be successful in the first department; its requirements match his behavioral schemata. Moving to the latter department, however, he'll be unsure of what behaviors are expected and will, most likely, rely on the people skills that secured career success thus far. When at first they don't work, he will likely engage in the behaviors to an even greater degree. The employee will founder if he doesn't recognize the need to engage in alternative, situationally expected behavior. As he tries to reach consensus and build collaborative relationships, he may meet with resistance from his new co-workers. The likely method for dealing with this resistance is to turn up the volume even farther on the affiliative skills—and wonder why there's static on the line!

High Tolerance Levels

Another aspect of relying on early-childhood behaviors involves the ability to tolerate bad employment situations or poor leadership. When confronted with a boss who is unreasonable (or downright impossible), employees will tolerate those behaviors that are congruent with their primary family experience. Let me give you an example. At the end of a leadership workshop, Tim took me aside and asked how to cope with a boss who made unreasonable demands, embarrassed him in front of others, and never gave any praise. When I asked, "Does he remind you of anyone?" Tim hesitated for a moment while thinking and finally replied, "My father." Tim had come to expect this behavior from people in authority and tolerated it more than someone who was raised in a more nurturing environment. Like many people, he couldn't see that there was anything wrong with the boss's behavior and instead blamed himself. Similar to the child who engages in magical thinking, the employee believes working harder or staying under the radar screen will change the boss's behavior toward him.

Let me give you one more example from a slightly different perspective. Rita worked for a boss who confided in her about myriad personal problems with her children, parents, and spouse. On some occasions, the boss would go into Rita's office, close the door, and break down sobbing. Rita said she was uncomfortable being used as a confidante in this manner because it made her hesitant to go to the boss with her own work-related problems. She felt sorry for her boss and didn't want to burden her any more than necessary. As a result, Rita was left having to figure out for herself how to resolve problems and create programs for which she had little experience. Because she grew up with a mother who needed excessive attention and was histrionic, Rita felt as responsible for her boss as she had for her mother. She turned up the volume on her listening and caretaking behaviors in an effort to soothe the boss. *The child inside Rita needed to make things better, never expecting that she was entitled to leadership and direction from her boss.*

The tolerance levels both Tim and Rita showed were higher than those of their peers because the situations were familiar to them and they possessed the coping skills to survive. However, their performance and self-esteem suffered from lack of mentoring and the absence of growth opportunities that should have been provided to them from people in management positions. Both employees eventually left their positions and their companies once they understood the dynamics and decided not to be controlled by old behaviors that had outlived their usefulness.

You may find that you have a high level of tolerance for inappropriate behaviors that are familiar to you, especially if feelings about being treated in a particular way haven't been worked through in psychotherapy or other developmental opportunities, such as attending workshops, taking classes, or reading self-help books. You may seek approval from authority, be unable to see when you're being treated unfairly or inappropriately, and therefore assume responsibility for making the situation better. If you think your early-childhood relationships are getting in the way of your success, I encourage you to read *Your Boss Is Not Your Mother: Eight Steps to Eliminating Office Drama and Creating Positive Relationships at Work* by Debra Mandel.

THE CORPORATE PLAYING FIELD

One of the models I developed early in my coaching career has proved invaluable in helping people understand how they misread the requirements for workplace success in a variety of changing conditions and corporate cultures. Consider your workplace the same as any competitive sport. It has a playing field, boundaries, rules, and strategies. The boundaries mark the area in which you must operate if you want to succeed. When you go out of bounds in sports, you are either called out, fouled, lose a point, or lose control of the ball. There is typically some type of penalty for going out of bounds. The same holds true in companies. Understanding the boundaries of the workplace playing field is essential to winning the game.

A major difference that presents a unique problem is that the bounds and rules of the corporate playing field aren't quite as clearly defined as in a sport. The boundaries change when you move from one company to another, from department to department within the same company, from boss to boss within a company, and even for different people in the same situation. This phenomenon was unexpectedly hammered home during a keynote presentation I made to employees at a national defense company. On a flip chart, I drew the diagram that follows. I explained that in the area of creativity, the boundaries differ from a defense contractor to the entertainment industry. Whereas a person working in defense can and should be creative in terms of problem solving, devising new systems, or developing new products, his or her boundaries are narrower than those of someone working in entertainment where, on the development side of the business, the boundaries for creativity are practically nonexistent.

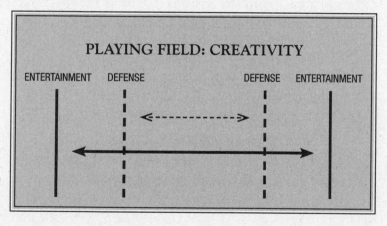

At first, I got some push-back from audience members who thought I was making a value judgment about expectations in the defense field. Fortunately, a young woman raised her hand and exclaimed, "That explains everything!" She went on to describe how she recently transferred to this particular contractor from a Hollywood motion picture company and couldn't figure out why she was having so much difficulty adjusting to the new culture. "Whereas everything I did in my last company was right, everything I do now seems wrong," she said. The diagram enabled her to understand—and enabled everyone else in the audience to understand as well—*that what worked in the past wouldn't necessarily work in the future when the playing field changes.* To be successful in her new corporate culture, the woman had to readjust her behavior to fit within the new boundaries.

The boundaries change not only between companies but also for different people within the same company. Although the corporate playing field clearly denotes the area in which it expects employees to operate, there are a number of inherent dangers. The field may be artificially narrowed based on factors relating to gender, ethnicity, age, or other subjective factors. Ask any woman or person of color and they'll tell you this is true. When the field narrows, it becomes easier to go out of bounds. For example, the playing field for men in the area of emotionality is narrower than it is for women. The range of emotions that they are permitted to express is narrower than that permitted for women. A woman can get away with crying at work; a man usually can't.

Similarly, the playing field for women in the area of assertiveness is narrower than for their male counterparts. Behavior that borders on aggressive may be acceptable— or even preferred—in some businesses and industries, whereas more polite, collegial behavior is expected in others. It's not that simple for women, though. Regardless of a company's boundaries for assertive behavior, a woman's boundaries are typically *narrower* than those of her male counterparts. It's why so many women report that when they say or do the same thing as a man, they get called "the B-word." It's because the boundaries are different, and winning the game is contingent upon playing on the field and in bounds.

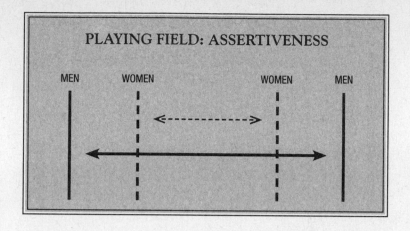

PLAYING FIELD: ASSERTIVENESS

MEN   WOMEN   WOMEN   MEN

Managers and employees alike need to be aware of their own biases that may artificially narrow the playing field for their colleagues and make every effort to create a more even field for everyone. Otherwise, they risk homogenizing the workplace—expecting everyone to look and sound the same. Organizations that fall into this trap miss out on the richness that diversity brings. Similarly, if we all don't work to create an equal playing field, people who don't match the workplace stereotype will play the game too carefully, never taking the kinds of risks that might put them out of bounds. In an environment such as this, creativity and productivity are stifled. As in sports, you must take calculated risks and play the game toward the edge of the bounds, but intentionally decide when the risk of going out of bounds is worth what will potentially be gained by it.

Successful corporate players scope out the playing field and adjust their behavior accordingly. In other words, *they remain in bounds for each given situation*. Those who espouse the Popeye philosophy—"I yam who I yam"—often find they're the odd person out and fail to develop the widest repertoire of skills possible. Once again, it's about balance.

If you pride yourself on constantly going out of bounds, and are even sometimes rewarded for it, don't be surprised if you're eventually called out. On the other hand, if you always play the workplace game safely within bounds, you may not be adding the value required for long-term success. People who win the game of work are those who (1) know where the bounds are and recognize that they narrow and widen with different circumstances, (2) play the corporate game taking calculated risks, and (3) balance the risks with the eight behaviors described in this book.

THE EIGHT MOST COMMON
SELF-SABOTAGING BEHAVIORS

Consider the following workplace conversation:

Al: *Did you hear about Kathy's promotion?*

Barbara: *Did I ever. I've been here three years longer than Kathy and work twice as hard. I should have been the one given that promotion.*

Al: *I thought for sure this one had your name on it. Kathy's only been in her position for eighteen months. She hardly warmed up the chair. She must know people over at corporate.*

Barbara: *Not only does she know them, she spends more time meeting with them than doing her work. She's always going to this committee meeting and that presentation. If she spent half as much time in her* *office working as she does schmoozing, she could get something done.*

Al: *Yeah. It's people like us who keep this place going and people like her who get all the credit. Do you know that she even has time to take her staff members out to lunch for their birthdays?*

Barbara: *That's what I mean. She's so busy getting everyone else to do her work that of course she has time for all that stuff. The HR vice president asked me to be on the personnel review committee, and I turned him down flat. If I don't keep close tabs on my staff, nothing gets done.*

Al: *I know what you mean. I've got my schedule just about where I want it now and I'm not willing to change it for anyone. Those committees take up way too much time.*

Sound familiar? While Barbara and Al are busy micromanaging, doing the work themselves, and sticking close to their offices—behaviors that have worked for them up until now in their careers—people like Kathy are expanding their repertoires of business behavior and spheres of influence. It's the difference between *careerists* and *achievers*. The former manage their careers; the latter get the work done. But you can't simply focus on your career to the exclusion of accomplishing your work, and you can't only accomplish your work without paying attention to your career development. The reality is, you've got to do both—it's a combination of these two factors that ultimately leads to career success.

It should go without saying, but I'll say it anyway to make it abundantly clear: *There is no substitute for technical competence.* It is the foundation upon which all the other behaviors referred to in this book rely. Without technical competence, you build a career on quicksand. It is necessary—but it's also not sufficient. *Most people who sabotage their careers rely on technical competence to the exclusion of all other necessary behaviors.* They think that expertise in their fields should be enough to maintain and further their careers. This may have been true in 1960 or 1970, but it's far from true in today's competitive workplace.

In the workplace sweepstakes, I've consistently seen eight factors that distinguish the winners from the losers. People who possess technical competence but get stuck at some point along their career paths do so because they:

1. Overlook the importance of people.
2. Do not function effectively as part of a team.
3. Fail to focus on image and communication.
4. Possess limited emotional intelligence and likability.
5. Have difficulty working with authority.
6. Have too broad or too narrow a vision.
7. Exhibit indifference to client or constituent needs.
8. Work in isolation.

What makes matters worse is that most people struggling to achieve their full career potential fail to build skills in more than just one area. For example, the inability to function effectively as part of a team may be related to poor emotional intelligence. Likewise, overlooking the importance of people may cause you to work in isolation. The following Career Status Check will help you to determine which specific areas you may need to work on to become more professionally competitive. I urge you to take the inventory and to use it in determining which chapters might have the most meaning for you personally. Also, examine your workplace behaviors in light of the early-childhood experiences outlined in the Childhood Experiences Contributing to Strengths and Developmental Areas chart that begins on page 30 to determine which complementary skills the inventory suggests are required to be a fully functioning adult. If you focus only on the inventory, you'll miss out on the opportunity to understand your behavior in a fuller context. This is the same reason why many business coaches fail to help clients achieve their goals—*they focus on changing behavior, not understanding the purpose the behavior serves and how it has contributed to success in the past.*

CAREER STATUS CHECK

To determine your career strengths and areas for development, use the scale below to answer each of the following questions as candidly as possible. Even if it's difficult to answer a particular item, don't leave it unanswered.

1 = Not descriptive of me or my situation.
2 = Somewhat descriptive of me or my situation.
3 = Descriptive of me or my situation.
4 = Highly descriptive of me or my situation.

_____ 1. Others describe me as a real people person.
_____ 2. I prefer to work as part of a team, rather than working independently from others.
_____ 3. When I speak, I notice people pay close attention to my ideas and opinions.

_____ 4. I don't bring my moods to the office.

_____ 5. When I have a logical reason for it, I don't have a problem with expressing a viewpoint different from my management.

_____ 6. When working on a project, I take time out now and then to reassess its direction and my own method of approaching it.

_____ 7. I can tell you how my contribution to the organization is distinguished from that of others.

_____ 8. I spend at least some portion of each week networking with colleagues.

_____ 9. I spend some part of each workday engaged in small talk with co-workers.

_____ 10. I consciously identify ways to assist my fellow team members with their projects.

_____ 11. I'm known for getting to the point quickly and succinctly.

_____ 12. I'm aware of my areas for development and am currently working to improve them.

_____ 13. If I see managers making decisions that I believe might be harmful to our firm, I offer my opinion about these decisions.

_____ 14. It doesn't bother me when my boss interrupts a project I'm working on to add new and sometimes different elements to it.

_____ 15. I am known throughout the organization for my commitment to customer or client service.

_____ 16. I belong to professional organizations and attend their meetings with enough regularity to know the other members.

_____ 17. I know most of my co-workers on more than just a professional basis.

_____ 18. I enhance the success of my projects by securing input from my peers.

_____ 19. I think before speaking to make certain my comments are presented in the best light possible.

_____ 20. I'm good at reading the nonverbal messages of others.

_____ 21. People would describe me as someone who can independently assess management decisions and offer alternative perspectives when appropriate.

_____ 22. Others describe me as someone with a vision of the future.

_____ 23. It is unusual for me to say no to a request.

_____ 24. A few times each month, I'm invited to join key players on my team or in my organization for lunch.

_____ 25. I am often successful where others fail because of the relationships I have with others.

_____ 26. I enjoy projects that call on people with different perspectives to work together.

_____ 27. I intentionally dress for the job I *want*, not the job I *have*.

_____ 28. *Gracious* is my middle name.

_____ 29. When managers solicit my opinion, they know I'll respond candidly.

_____ 30. I balance task accomplishment with finding new and creative ways of doing things.

_____ 31. I have consciously developed my personal brand in the workplace.

_____ 32. I'm well tuned into my firm's grapevine.

_____ 33. I don't have an inordinate need for everyone to like me.

_____ 34. I'm energized by the exchange of ideas that comes from brainstorming with others.

_____ 35. People have told me that I'm a good public speaker.

_____ 36. I require little outside prodding or motivation to get a job done.

_____ 37. I believe it's more important to be honest with my manager than to placate him or her for the sake of staying in his or her good graces.

_____ 38. It is important to me that things be done with a focus on excellence quality as well as on time.

_____ 39. I love my work.

_____ 40. I have colleagues in positions similar to mine in other divisions within my own firm, or at other firms, with whom I regularly interact to exchange ideas and keep abreast of issues pertinent to my job.

CAREER STATUS CHECK SCORE SHEET

To score your inventory, first transfer your numerical responses from the questionnaire itself to the columns below. Please notice that the item numbers within each column are not in order, so take care to put your response next to the correct item number. After you have transferred your answers and made sure you have answered each question, tally each column separately, then add each of the column subtotals together for an inventory total.

I. People Skills	II. Teamwork	III. Image and Communication	IV. Emotional Intelligence	V. Working with Authority	VI. Detail vs. Big Picture	VII. Value-Added Branding	VIII. Networking
1. ___	2. ___	3. ___	4. ___	5. ___	6. ___	7. ___	8. ___
9. ___	10. ___	11. ___	12. ___	13. ___	14. ___	15. ___	16. ___
17. ___	18. ___	19. ___	20. ___	21. ___	22. ___	23. ___	24. ___
25. ___	26. ___	27. ___	28. ___	29. ___	30. ___	31. ___	32. ___
33. ___	34. ___	35. ___	36. ___	37. ___	38. ___	39. ___	40. ___

Column Subtotal: ___

Inventory Total: I + II + III + IV + V + VI + VII + VIII = ___

(continued)

Interpreting Your Scores

The *subtotal* of each column tells you the area in which you need to expand your complementary skills and where your current strengths lie. The *total* score tells you if your career is on track or if you should be engaging in aggressive career development. It is entirely possible to need development in one or two specific areas and still be on track.

If each column subtotals:	or	Your total score is:	
		5–8	You are seriously sabotaging your career! In addition to following the suggestions in this book, you'll need help (a career coach, mentor, etcetera) to achieve your career goals.
		9–13	*Warning!* You're dangerously close to falling from your career track. It's time to do a serious self-assessment and expand your skill set.
		14–17	Fine-tuning may be needed to stay on track. Review those questions where you gave yourself a 1 or 2 and add those complementary skills to your existing repertoire.
		18–20	You're right on track! Keep up the good work. Examine those areas where you rated yourself a 3 or 4 and consciously try to continue engaging in those specific behaviors.

FACTORS TO CONSIDER IN ASSESSING AND CHANGING BEHAVIOR

Critically examining your behavior is no easy task, but it can have an immense payoff both at work and at home over the long term. In fact, through the years I've heard many clients say that the areas we're working on in coaching are the same ones their spouses complain about. This shouldn't be too surprising. If you're not a great listener at work, you're not likely to be a great listener at home, either. If your tendency is to take a *Ready, fire, aim* approach at home, then you're going to do the same thing in your workplace. We are who we are and we take with us our strengths—and areas for development—everywhere we go. As one woman executive said, "We all have baggage. I just hope to turn mine into a tiny little carry-on."

Keep the following points in mind as you begin to consider how you might complement your strengths with new behaviors.

People Don't Intentionally Behave Inappropriately or Ineffectively

To hear managers tell it, you would think that the behaviors of their employees are intentional attempts to undermine their efforts. As a result, they wind up labeling and blaming employees, and employees internalize these labels as undeniable truths—truths that in turn impede learning alternative behaviors. I don't believe there is a person on this earth who gets up in the morning, pours a cup of coffee, and says, "I think I'll go to work today and make a huge, costly mistake." The vast majority of employees act with the best of intentions. If you knew better, you'd do better. The problem is, you can't know what you don't know!

It is crucial to separate the act from the actor. Those who haven't learned how to build affiliative relationships aren't bad people simply because they haven't learned this skill. Generally, the reason that a particular skill hasn't been learned is that, historically, it wasn't important in the scheme of things. Avoid the tendency to become your own critical parent. Keep in mind that we all have strengths and development areas. Praise yourself for being open to change and allow plenty of room for initially falling short of the mark.

People Do Best the Things for Which They Have Been Rewarded in the Past

What does the Career Status Check indicate are your greatest strengths? Think about these strengths as overdeveloped survival skills, and ask yourself these three questions:

- Who wanted (or needed) me to act in this way?
- How was I rewarded when I did?
- What happened if I didn't?

Use the the Career Status Check Score Sheet to help stimulate your thinking in this area. This exercise will help you demystify the role that your strengths played while you were growing up and enable you to examine why other behaviors weren't as important.

Be Willing to Take Calculated Risks

Examine your scores and look for the items where you rated yourself 1 or 2. These are behaviors that may not come naturally to you or ones that you may even have been discouraged from exhibiting in childhood. Developing complementary skills often means being uncomfortable in the beginning. As people progress through the stages of initial learning, they feel inadequate, impatient, or insecure and revert to more familiar behaviors as a means of coping. Only through the willingness to engage in unfamiliar, uncomfortable behavior, and to stick with it, can complementary skills be developed.

Don't Do Anything Less—Expand Your Skill Set

Competent people don't fail because they're not good at what they do. They fail when they can't see the complementary behaviors that must be developed in response to a new challenge or situation. If, for example, you focus on being less critical or less task-oriented, you'll naturally be uncomfortable with doing less of what you know best. Instead, think about the skills that you need to *add* to your repertoire of workplace behaviors to be more effective. It's about having a *balanced* skill set.

Going back to the case of Dan for a moment, his manager didn't want him to completely stop cranking out the work. He wanted Dan to achieve more balance in his leadership style. Employees frequently leave feedback sessions feeling more confused than when they first went in. They become fearful of exhibiting *any* of what's described as the "problem behavior" and wind up going to the opposite extreme. Continue engaging in those behaviors where you rated yourself a 3 or 4 as you develop comfort and familiarity in those areas where you rated yourself lower.

Successful People Are Good Observers of People and Events

In most cases when people change positions, companies, departments, bosses, or jobs, no one bothers to tell them what's expected of them. It's as though they hear a tape playing over and over, telling them how to behave, and they try harder and harder to act consistently. The only problem is that the tape is usually an old one, developed in response to childhood needs, not present realities. The people who succeed at career transitions are those who observe how others in the new situation are acting and adjust their behavior accordingly. When in Rome, do as the Romans do.

This isn't to say that you should become a chameleon; do anything unethical, illegal, or immoral; or give up the essence of who you are. You should, however, take note of cultural customs such as how people dress, whether they have lunch with co-workers, and the kind of social interactions that go on in the office. A little bit of accommodation can go a long way toward the perception of fitting in.

Assure Success Through a Development Plan and Ongoing Feedback

Just as you wouldn't build a house without a plan, neither should you expect to achieve personal or professional development goals without one. The common theme among motivational success stories is the fact that people had a vision of what they wanted and a plan for attaining it. Success isn't accidental. Based on the Career Status Check, choose the two or three skills that are most important to add to your repertoire and determine how you will achieve them. Be sure to identify the resources you will require in the process: people, classes, books, and experiences.

One tip you might consider is to let others know the changes you're attempting to make. This way, people will actually look for and notice the behavior change, increasing the likelihood that they'll give you positive feedback. Once you have your development plan, ask someone you trust to review it with you and give you feedback as to how you're doing. Let your partner know what you're trying to accomplish and how you'd like to receive your feedback. Then, on a regular basis, sit down and review progress. Discuss where you encountered difficulty, brainstorm methods for overcoming obstacles, revise the plan, and, perhaps most important, reward wins—even small ones—with a mental pat on the back, thumbs-up, or more tangible self-indulgences. Remember, you're most likely to repeat behaviors for which you've been rewarded.

The following chart ties together the eight most common reasons why successful people fail with early-childhood experiences that may be contributing to these learned behaviors. Because people develop strengths in a particular area for any number of reasons, it's impossible to list every combination of experiences contributing to every area of strength. Use the chart as a point of reference to begin thinking about how and why you developed strengths in certain areas and not others. You may even want to add your own unique experiences to those listed.

CHILDHOOD EXPERIENCES CONTRIBUTING TO STRENGTHS AND DEVELOPMENTAL AREAS

SUCCESS FACTOR	WHEN UNDERDEVELOPED THE PERSON MAY	WHEN WELL DEVELOPED THE PERSON IS TYPICALLY	CHILDHOOD EXPERIENCES THAT CAN CONTRIBUTE TO UNDERDEVELOPMENT
1. PEOPLE SKILLS	• Be a loner. • Have a reputation for being socially inept or unfriendly. • Exhibit discomfort in social situations. • Lack insight. • Avoid people contact. • Have an inordinate need to be liked.	• Comfortable interacting at all levels of the organization. • Able to build strong 360-degree relationships. • Appropriately disclosing of personal information. • Concerned with making others comfortable in his or her presence. • Sought out by peers for opinions, friendship, support.	• Value placed on accomplishments. • Rewarded for grades, achievements. • Overly protective parenting. • Intelligence, ostracized by classmates. • Economic status lower than peers. • Physical impairment. • Narcissistic parenting. • Conditional love and acceptance.
2. ABILITY TO WORK AS PART OF A TEAM	• Have difficulty seeing interdependent linkages. • Grandstand.	• Conscious of putting the needs of the team before his or her own. • Willing to freely share information.	• Oldest in family or only child. • Alcoholism in family. • Both parents worked outside the home.

	Behaviors	Desirable Traits	Causes
3. POSITIVE IMAGE AND COMMUNICATION STYLE	• Not include others in decision making. • Hoard information. • Be overly independent. • Not think before speaking. • Wear clothes of a caliber lower than called for by the company's image. • Dress as you would for a party. • Not be able to get to the point. • Be uncomfortable making presentations. • Lack confidence. • Lack credibility.	• Supportive of the ideas of others. • Appropriately participative in team meetings. • Focused on planning his or her message before speaking. • One who dresses in a manner appropriate for each situation. • Well groomed. • Tactful. • One who uses a communication style that suits the situation and person with whom he or she is communicating. • Known as a good public speaker.	• Rewarded for self-reliance. • High-achiever expectations. • Wasn't listened to. • Given little parental guidance. • Neglected. • Limited world exposure.
4. HIGH EMOTIONAL INTELLIGENCE/ LIKABILITY	• Dismiss the needs of others. • Have low impulse control. • Require constant prodding. • Be avoided by peers. • Come across as insincere. • Act like a bull in a china shop. • Lack social graciousness.	• Conscious of his or her own behavior and how it impacts others. • Continually seeking self-improvement. • Empathetic. • A self-starter. • Concerned with managing his or her emotionality in the workplace.	• Critical parental messages. • Parents with emotional problems. • Lack of positive reinforcement. • Conditional love. • High-achiever expectations.

CHILDHOOD EXPERIENCES CONTRIBUTING TO STRENGTHS AND DEVELOPMENTAL AREAS (*continued*)

5. **ABILITY TO MANAGE UP**

- Be combative or argumentative with management.
- Embarrass management in front of others.
- Be afraid to speak up.
- Not be willing to critically assess processes or procedures.

- Supportive of management decisions—even ones with which he or she may not agree.
- One who understands and attempts to help management achieve goals.
- Capable of pushing back without offending management.

- Overly critical or controlling parenting.
- Narcissistic parenting.
- Physical or emotional abuse.

6. **BALANCED VISION AND DETAIL ORIENTATION**

- Be too narrowly focused.
- Have a one-track mind.
- Not be able to juggle multiple priorities.
- Have difficulty with turning ideas into reality.
- Pursue unrealistic ideas or goals.

- Realistic in assessing situations before taking action.
- Adept at combining good ideas with good planning.
- Not one to get stuck in old ways of doing things.
- In search of new and improved methods for achieving corporate goals.

- Ritualistic family behavior.
- Alcoholism or physical abuse.
- Unpredictable or chaotic environment.
- Absence of boundaries or norms.

7.	**WELL-DEVELOPED PERSONAL BRAND**	• Be seen as a naysayer. • Do the job, but not much more. • Identify problems, but not solutions. • Require inordinate supervision. • Be risk-averse. • Be in the wrong job.	• One to seek ways to add value to the company, client, or customer. • Ready to deliver what he or she promises—and often more. • Embracing of change. • Flexible.	• Controlled environment. • Predetermined career path. • Powerless parental attitude.
8.	**NETWORKING SKILLS**	• Not seek opportunities to widen his or her sphere of influence. • Not have necessary contacts in place when needed. • Not keep up professionally. • Overlook the importance of connecting like-minded people.	• Active in participating and at times helping plan company events. • A member of professional associations, and attends their meetings. • One who makes a point of introducing people with professional commonalities.	• Rewarded for self-reliance. • Not encouraged to join clubs or teams. • Overly attached to primary caretaker.

My intention in providing this chart is not to make you an armchair psychologist, but rather to help you to look at your strengths in the context of your experiences and motives. We are not one-dimensional objects. We bring to the workplace a host of multifaceted intentions, which, when developed in light of organizational needs, can contribute significantly to work's synergistic process and the satisfaction we gain from it. When we view ineffective behaviors as overdeveloped, purposeful strengths, they no longer seem like insurmountable obstacles—and we can make conscious choices to succeed in spite of ourselves.

Each of the chapters in this book focuses on the key strategies required to craft a highly regarded and sought-after professional reputation. I use the stories of well-known historical and contemporary figures to illustrate how you can avoid or survive dramatic career setbacks. Also provided are examples of behaviors based on my experiences working with clients around the world and suggestions that I gave them for how to build complementary skills. At the end of each chapter is a list of ways that you can develop skills in the area on which the chapter focuses. Even if many of them may be a stretch for you, I urge you to consider each one as a simple and economical way to begin expanding your repertoire of workplace behaviors.

Give yourself plenty of time to change. To go from being unconsciously *incompetent* to being unconsciously *competent* in the areas where you want to grow requires patience and practice. Once you arrive at Phase Four (see the following chart), you'll find yourself effortlessly meeting your career challenges and well on your way to achieving the recognition and rewards you've worked so hard to earn.

THE PROCESS OF ADDING NEW SKILLS TO YOUR REPERTOIRE

C
O
M
P
E
T
E
N
C
E

PHASE FOUR UNCONSCIOUS COMPETENCE	PHASE THREE CONSCIOUS COMPETENCE
You've practiced the new behavior, incorporated it into your regular repertoire of skills, and engage in the behavior naturally without having to think about it.	You've read books, taken workshops, and maybe even gotten some coaching. You're focusing on exhibiting new behavior to the point where you're self-conscious about what you're doing and how you're doing it (which isn't a bad thing).
PHASE ONE UNCONSCIOUS INCOMPETENCE	PHASE TWO CONSCIOUS INCOMPETENCE
You can't know what you don't know! Until you get feedback that change is needed, this is a blind spot for you.	You've gotten the feedback—you know you need to take action—but what do you do?

CONSCIOUSNESS

SUCCESS STRATEGY 1

Build Strong 360-Degree Relationships

People wish to be confirmed in their being by others.
Secretly and bashfully we watch for a yes that
comes from another human being.

Martin Buber, philosopher and educator

If you're like so many clients who have told me, "I'm not here to win a popularity contest. I'm here to do my job," this chapter has your name written all over it. Like it or not, *you can't be effective in the long run without strong 360-degree relationships.* Even more important, *when you need a relationship, it's too late to build it.* Consider the fates of two equally capable but temperamentally different world leaders: former US President Bill Clinton and former Israeli Prime Minister Benjamin Netanyahu. Both are intelligent men, politically driven, and charismatic in their own rights, but both encountered serious challenges at the height of their careers.

Despite his many transgressions, both before and during his term of office, Clinton reminded many people of the kid brother who was always getting into mischief but whom they loved anyway. Those who have met him consistently describe him in similar ways: "When he talks to you, he makes you feel like you're the most important person in the room"; "He talks to you in a way that draws you in"; "He asks you questions about yourself—and actually remembers the answers." I firmly believe the primary reason why Clinton wasn't run out of office for behavior that some would describe as improper and others might call immoral (but most would agree was unbecoming the leader of the free world) was that he was a master at building relationships. He possessed a high likability quotient—something that I address in a later chapter.

To understand how such a bright guy could end up in such hot water, you have only to go back and study his childhood. Young William Jefferson Clinton grew up not knowing his biological father and watching his alcoholic stepfather abuse his younger brother, Roger, and his beloved mother, Virginia. He lived on the wrong side of the tracks, a chubby but intelligent kid. His survival depended on, in part, his ability to be charming and likable. But overdeveloped skill in these arenas became double-edged swords. The same charm that caused Americans to twice elect him president was also used to sexually exploit women. Just as he was elected through the power of his personality, his presidency was tarnished by the behaviors of a man acting much like an emotionally impoverished little boy. Of course, the factors contributing to Clinton's or anyone else's behavior are far more complex than this, but it does give you an idea of how early-childhood experiences contribute to career success—and potential self-sabotage.

Benjamin Netanyahu's political fate was determined by just the opposite phenomenon: the *failure* to build relationships. Elected prime minister of Israel in 1996 by a victory margin of less than 1 percent, he served only one term before being ousted by an opposing political party. Despite the fact that his policies were met with overwhelming approval from the Israeli people, he was never able to build the kinds of relationships that would support him in the longer term. And in retrospect, he *knew* that this was a major factor in his downfall. In a January 1999 interview with *Time* magazine, when asked what he would do differently if he had a second term in office, he replied, "I wouldn't do anything differently on the political side. Where I would do things differently is in the management of egos . . . the maintenance, shall we say, of, ah, personal relationships." A look at his more recent forays back into Israeli politics suggest this is a lesson he has yet to master.

This simple truth is one that many people refuse to understand until it's too late: *The ability to do your job is contingent upon having relationships in place that will support your efforts, provide you with what you need when you need it, cut you slack when you make a mistake, and act in your best interests during good times and bad.* Taking time to build relationships is the best investment of time and energy you can make in your career for the long haul. It may not seem like it when you have to stay late because you took the time to listen to someone who needed an ear or went out of your way to do someone a favor, but believe me, it will pay dividends when you least expect it.

One of my very first coaching clients was a man whom I'll call Sam. He was the director of sales at a large manufacturing company. When the vice president of human resources called me about Sam, she told me that he was an outstanding and valued employee. No fault could be found with the quality of his work. The problem was that his peers didn't want to work with him. They found Sam to be aloof, standoffish, and difficult to work with. Despite the fact that he was *technically competent*, he would soon become persona non grata if he didn't stop creating problems within the sales department.

Sam arrived at our first coaching session looking every bit the executive. Neatly groomed and impeccably dressed, he appeared to be the very model of professionalism. As we became acquainted with each other through initial superficial conversation, I noted that he spoke with a clarity and confidence that belied his age (he was in his late twenties). When I asked him what skills he thought his management wanted him to develop via coaching, he didn't have a clue. He said he just wanted to do the best job possible and tried to do everything asked of him perfectly so as to make his boss and the department look good. That's when a light went on for me.

The package that Sam presented was indeed one of perfection. On the surface, his image and communication skills were excellent, but my hunch—and it later proved accurate—was that he strived so hard to be perfect for the boss that he overlooked other critical workplace behaviors. I explored this with him by changing tack. I asked what he did for fun outside work. In other words, what was he like when he wasn't being perfect? Unexpectedly, this unleashed a flood of emotion. Sam held back tears as he said that he didn't have much of a life outside work. He was going through a difficult divorce and had three children he rarely got to see because he arrived at work early and left late. By the time he made the hour-long commute home, he was exhausted, grabbing something to eat and then falling into bed. Weekends were spent working; he had little time to pursue activities and friendships he'd once enjoyed.

After carefully listening to him, I asked if perhaps his

need for affiliation was fulfilled at work with friends and colleagues. His answer was no. He worked through lunch hours and didn't want to waste the company's time and money on idle chat or gossip with co-workers. He did notice that his peers seemed to spend time engaged in casual conversation—which he felt was fine for them, but he didn't have the time to spare for chitchat. He wanted to model appropriate behavior for his staff, so he worked at a steady, energetic pace throughout the workday and often into the night.

What others interpreted as standoffishness, or being difficult to deal with, was really just Sam's need to be the perfect employee. Having grown up with strict German parents, he developed the defense mechanism of striving for perfection early in life so as to ward off critical comments from his parents and older siblings. The need to be perfect underscored not only his workplace relationships, but his personal ones as well. One reason his marriage had failed was that he felt his wife didn't understand his high standards. Even though he never said anything to his colleagues, they picked up on the fact that he was critically assessing them. He found their personal conversations self-indulgent and didn't feel that anyone else worked as hard as he did—which was in fact true. No one else shared his compulsive need for perfection.

WHEN TECHNICAL EXPERTISE CEASES TO BE ENOUGH

Sam is an ideal example of someone who, despite technical competence and genuine desire to be of service, was on the verge of causing serious damage to his career. An infrequently talked about fact of business life is that *at some point in most people's careers, technical expertise ceases to be the key factor contributing to success.* We *build* our reputations early in our careers on competence. We *remain* successful, however, based on a combination of competence and the eight factors described in this book. Once you have proven your technical abilities in your field, competence becomes a given—something that others depend and rely on, but not something that necessarily will continue to move you forward. It's as though your competence reaches the point of diminishing returns. If you continue to focus exclusively on gaining increased technical skill to the exclusion of developing complementary behaviors, you'll become professionally unbalanced. If a prizefighter has a killer right uppercut but can't move deftly on his feet, it will do him no good to continue to develop that uppercut. He needs complementary strengths that will help him win bouts, not just rounds.

Review the checklist on page 43 to see how well you build one-on-one relationships. Ideally, you would check every item here (as well as with each checklist contained in subsequent chapters). The fewer items you check, the greater the likelihood that this is a potential developmental area for you.

INTERPERSONAL SKILLS: DIFFERENTIATING YOURSELF FROM THE PACK

In a competitive job market, employers are careful to choose people for their past experience, education, and previous on-the-job success. In other words, they select people who are good at what they do. Once on the job, however, when the playing field is level with equally qualified employees,

_____ I know the names of the people on my floor.

_____ I notice when something is troubling a colleague and inquire about it.

_____ I schedule time throughout the day for small talk with co-workers.

_____ I meet socially with co-workers outside the workplace.

_____ I tend to go out of my way for colleagues—even if I see no immediate benefit.

_____ I see building relationships as equally important to accomplishing my job tasks.

_____ Other people describe me as a good listener.

_____ I know the names of the husbands, wives, significant others, and children of my co-workers.

_____ I share personal information and discuss topics of common interest with my co-workers.

_____ I treat administrative professionals the same as I treat executive management.

_____ I have lunch several times a week with co-workers.

it's the subtler behaviors that distinguish the fast-trackers from those who remain stagnant or are overlooked for new opportunities. Those with superior interpersonal skills, combined with technical capability, are perceived as a more valuable asset than those who exhibit only technical competence. It is through positive working relationships that we secure the cooperation of the people we need to accomplish our tasks and further the organization's goals. These interpersonal skills also help us to develop the goodwill of clients and customers and a network of people on whom we can rely for the skills and information required to function effectively.

In Sam's case, coaching alone wasn't sufficient to help him remain relevant and competitive in his work environment. The presence of a deep-seated need for perfection suggests intrapersonal conflicts that required professional counseling. Fortunately, when this was recommended to Sam, he was open to the idea and followed up on it. His coaching sessions then focused on several specific things that he could do immediately to change the impression others had of him. He is a good example of someone who had several overlapping areas of development. Sam needed not only to do a better job of building one-on-one relationships, but also to be perceived as a better team player and to begin thinking about the importance of networking. My work with him addressed all three areas.

His first assignment was to spend no less than fifteen minutes each day engaged in casual conversation with a different co-worker—even if he had to force himself to do it or put it on his calendar as a reminder to get up and do it. I wanted him to get to know his colleagues personally— to find out what outside interests and hobbies they had, the names of their children, and what made them tick.

If you're anything like Sam, your heart is beating a little faster at just reading this—or you may be making mental excuses why it's not possible. Suggesting they do this makes some people feel as if they are robbing the company coffers, when in reality they are investing in relationships that have a long-term benefit to the company. Building such relationships enables the work to be done more efficiently, with less sabotage and higher team morale. That *saves* the company money, it doesn't waste it.

Similarly, I recommended that initially Sam take a lunch break at least once a week and use the time for something he enjoyed. The adage *All work and no play makes Jack a dull boy* was certainly true in this case. Part of what made it so difficult for Sam to talk to others was that he felt he had nothing to say. He had become so immersed in his work that he was oblivious to outside interests. Sam decided to make use of the company gym to work out. At the gym, he met several co-workers with whom he shared common interests and eventually became friends; he started to have lunch and socialize with them after work. He began to expand his network.

In an effort to coach him to be a better team player, I recommended that Sam listen to the concerns co-workers expressed at team meetings and later offer to help resolve some of these concerns rather than use his time to perfect and fail-safe his already good work. He could put his compulsive work behaviors to good use by extending himself to those who needed his assistance. In other words, he could win back their regard by making not only his boss look good, but his colleagues as well. In the process, he was building what is described as *network reciprocity*—the exchange of services and favors within formal and informal networks. The importance of networks is discussed in detail in a later chapter, but for now suffice it to say that Sam had to identify and participate in the quid pro quo of his workplace relationships.

It wasn't easy for him, but Sam worked hard to change the perceptions of others as he successfully learned how to overcome his strengths. It also wasn't always two steps forward. As with most people learning a new skill, it was sometimes one step forward, two steps back. As a result of his effort, however, Sam was promoted to a new position in a different division of the company, started spending more time with his children, and now reports that the quality of his life is better than he has ever known it to be.

UNDERSTANDING THE QUID PRO QUO

Inherent to *every* relationship there is a *quid pro quo*— something given in exchange for something else. Without realizing it, you exchange things with people all the time. When relationships fail or falter, it's typically because the quid pro quo isn't recognized, or it changes without the consent or acknowledgment of one or both of the parties involved. I remember working with one woman who was concerned with her troubled employment history. It seemed that she had no trouble *getting* a job. In fact, she was never without one for long. She was technically competent, physically attractive, and interpersonally capable. Clearly, she presented well in interviews and secured most of the jobs for which she interviewed. The problem was that once she was *in* the job, she became quickly dissatisfied and disillusioned. Her employers wouldn't give her challenging assignments or recognize her technical capability.

In an effort to uncover what the cause of the problem

really was, I asked her to role-play an interview with me. Much to my surprise, I found this professional woman turned into a femme fatale! The normally assertive demeanor that I had come to associate with her was replaced by what I would describe as an intentionally sweet disposition. The slight Southern accent with which she normally spoke became more pronounced. She was coy, acquiescent, and charming. It was almost as if she were flirting.

The role play made it apparent that the woman secured the job based on one set of behaviors but unwittingly changed them once she was inside the company. In other words, the quid pro quo changed. Her employer expected one thing based on the interview and, instead, got something else. She didn't present as, nor was she selected for being, an assertive, upwardly mobile career woman in the interview. Her employers selected her for the behavior she presented, not what she became once employed. This created a chasm between what *they* wanted and what *she* wanted. There was obviously nothing wrong with what she wanted, but it wasn't the message she gave during her interviews. When the quid pro quo changed, unbeknownst to the parties involved, it created turmoil and unfulfilled expectations for both.

Part of building successful relationships at work involves identifying the quid pro quo between you and everyone with whom you interact, and working to assure that everyone's needs—including your own—are met. Some people tell me that this business of quid pro quo sounds awfully manipulative. On the contrary! It's an honest, businesslike assessment of what you have to offer others and what you need from them. We trade on relationships all day long without ever realizing or discussing it. Say, a month ago you asked me to cover for you at a meeting so that you could attend to a problem with one of your children, and I willingly agreed. A few weeks later, I needed some research done that only you know how to do, and you gladly obliged. Neither of us was counting the chips we had collected with each trade, but they had accumulated in our accounts. The trick is to always have more chips in your account than you need—and this can't be done manipulatively; it can only be done through a generosity of spirit. To do otherwise would soil the integrity of the relationship.

The value of the quid pro quo was apparent during a training program I conducted when a small group working on an assignment decided that they needed an LCD projector to make a presentation to the larger group. One participant said that she thought she could arrange it and excused herself to make a call. I mentally noted that there was little chance of getting the equipment on time—their presentation was just a few hours away. Ninety minutes later, a man entered the room with the LCD in hand. He also took the time to set it up and make certain it was working properly before he left. At the break, I asked the woman how she'd managed to get it so quickly. She smiled and said, "I've done a lot of favors for this guy. He owed me one." Without ever saying, *You owe me,* she successfully traded on the quid pro quo.

My own life has been profoundly impacted by this concept of the quid pro quo. When I first started my consulting business more than twenty years ago, I received a call from an administrative assistant I once helped while I worked at the oil company ARCO (now BP). At the time, her boss had delegated to her the responsibility for preparing the department's affirmative action plans. If you've ever prepared one, you know they're quite complex and not a lot of fun to do. She knew that I had experience developing these plans, so she asked for my assistance. As much as I, too, hated preparing affirmative action plans, I was happy to help her complete the assignment and didn't give it a second thought. For several subsequent years, she would call me when it came time to complete the plan, and each year I helped her get it done. When I left the company, I never expected our paths would cross again—until a call came in from her.

As we chatted, I learned that she was now working in the international training department at ARCO. The training director from ARCO Indonesia was coming into town and was looking for someone to conduct management training programs from a Western perspective. My former colleague wanted to know if I would be interested in meeting with him to discuss the training programs I had developed. Her call came at a time when I was struggling to get my business off the ground and having difficulty meeting my financial objectives. I wound up meeting with the man, and within a few weeks I was in the exotic city of Jakarta conducting training. Over the years I developed a clientele in Indonesia with several multinational firms that have provided me with a steady stream of business, income, and friendships—and all because I took the time to do a favor for one administrative assistant with no expectation that it would ever be returned.

Besides covering at meetings, conducting research, or referral to potential clients, what else gets traded in the workplace? You would be surprised. Here's a list that participants in one workshop came up with in less than five minutes:

- *Information*
- *Lunch*
- *Quality service*
- *Friendship*
- *Promotions*
- *Quick turnaround time*

- Gossip
- Priority
- Muscle/brawn
- Gifts
- Heads-up
  (advance notice)

- Technical
  know-how
- Raises
- Influence
- Public praise

- A listening ear
- Help
- Feedback
- Personal concern

It's important to remember that *once you need a relationship, it's too late to build it.* This is what makes building relationships on an ongoing basis so important. Again, it can't be done simply for the purpose of knowing that you might have to call on it at some time. It must be done because you value people and your relationships with them. Absent this, others will detect a lack of genuineness, and perhaps a bit of manipulation, and never fully engage in a healthy and productive professional relationship with you.

Every so often, I hear someone claim that he or she just doesn't care about building relationships. It always strikes me as oddly incongruous. The same people who claim not to care frequently exhibit behaviors that indicate they care very much. I've come to learn that it's simply their defense mechanisms speaking. After years of being hurt by others or not having much success in building relationships, they build impenetrable walls that they dare others to break through. In other cases, people who claim not to care about others are the same ones who don't care much about themselves. They don't pay attention to their own needs and certainly don't expect others to fulfill them. Whatever the reason, it is *critical* to overcome real or perceived indifference to the people with whom you interact. Once technical competence has become a given, the foundation on which successful careers are built is genuine, mutually rewarding relationships.

Look at the person at the very top of your own organization. It's unlikely that he's a rocket scientist or that she could find a cure for cancer. In fact, there are probably many people smarter, and perhaps more technically capable, than your CEO. Despite this lack of genius, he or she found the way to the top—most likely due to basic competence combined with the relationships that were built throughout a career.

Then there are those who build good relationships—but only with people at levels in the organization that are higher than their own. It's a clever move, but one that usually proves a fatal mistake in the long term. You can probably identify people like this in your own organization. They're like heat-seeking missiles. Watch them in a room full of people—they'll gravitate toward those with the most power. The only problem is that power shifts. Those in power today may be out tomorrow. Or the person in power may delegate day-to-day operational responsibility and decision making to a direct report. If you stepped on the toes of this direct report on your way to the power source, it's going to be a lot harder to get your needs met.

I once worked with a woman who built her career on relationships with people in power. She managed up quite successfully, but she overlooked the importance of gaining the commitment of colleagues and staff. Because of her relationships with senior management, she traded favors to become exempt from the grunt work the rest of us had to do. It worked for a while, but then, as in most corporations, the power shifted. Her protectors were out, and a new wave of power brokers swept in. Many of the new people in power had, at one time, been this woman's colleagues. They had long memories and short tolerance for what she had put them through over the years. Within months, the situation was so uncomfortable for her that she was out looking for another job.

Fear of losing your job should not be the primary reason for building relationships with people at all levels of the organization, however. A wealth of information resides within the rank and file, and at some point you will have a need for it. It's a lot easier to gain access to information when you already have a relationship in place at the time you need the information, rather than trying to pry it loose from someone with whom you never took the time to speak in the hallway or the coffee room. Besides, you spend nearly a third of your life at work—building warm, collegial relationships can make it even more fulfilling.

Once you have achieved technical competence, building relationships is the most important thing that you can do to continue along your successful career path. How do you do it? The remainder of this chapter tells you, but if initially in your life or career you received more reinforcement for task accomplishment than for relationship building, you won't find it particularly easy or comfortable. Like Sam, whom you read about earlier in this chapter, you may have to take some risks and be willing to stop hiding behind your technical competence. One thing is for certain, though: The profit will outweigh the risk in the long term.

LISTENING WITH A THIRD EAR

The late John F. Kennedy Jr. was once asked what made his father such a beloved figure in American history. He replied that he thought it was because his father was such a good listener. Others had shared with him stories about how the late president could make people feel comfortable and empowered by simply listening. Anne Morrow Lindbergh, author and wife of the aviator Charles Lindbergh, underscores the importance of this trait: "It is not possible to talk wholeheartedly to more than one person at a time. You can't really talk to a person unless you surrender to them for the moment (all other talk is futile). You can't surrender to more than one person a moment."

Listening is the most important thing that you can do to build and maintain relationships. Most people spend the greatest part of their days hearing what others say, but few people really listen. They don't take the time to fully understand what other people think, what problems they may be encountering, or how they feel. You've probably heard the maxim, *People are given two ears and only one mouth so that they'll listen twice as much as they speak.* But do you adhere to it? There are myriad reasons why it's difficult to surrender to another, and the reasons differ from person to person. Decide which reasons on this list are your greatest obstacles to listening:

• **Rehearsing.** Mentally practicing what you're going to say before the speaker stops talking is rehearsing. The moment you start rehearsing, you stop listening.

• **The halo effect.** This is thinking that you already know what someone is going to say, or putting a positive or negative slant on the message, based on your previous relationship with the person. For example, if every time Bob comes into my office he gives me bad news, before long, when I see Bob, I cast a negative halo around all his messages, regardless of actual content. Conversely, if Ingrid and I have a great relationship, then I tend to perceive her messages positively no matter what the content.

• **Pseudo-listening.** Pretending to listen (and even

looking like you are) when in fact you're thinking about something other than the message is pseudo-listening. You know that you've been busted for pseudo-listening when the speaker asks, "So what do you think?" and you don't have a clue what's just been said.

- **Distractions.** When you're preoccupied with other thoughts or problems, you become distracted and unable to listen to the message. Interruptions or noise (phones ringing, people coming in and out of your office, noise from the hallway) make it difficult to concentrate on the speaker's message and are common workplace distractions.

- **Listening for a point of disagreement.** We all know people who wait for one point with which they disagree so that they can look intelligent, one-up the speaker, or impress others in the conversation. If you listen for a point of disagreement, you're potentially missing lots of points on which you could agree and build.

- **Nervousness.** Anxiety about the situation, the message, or upcoming responsibilities impedes being able to fully listen to the message.

- **Disinterest.** It's difficult to listen to the subject or the speaker if the topic is of no interest to you.

- **Poor speaker.** A speaker who is boring, has difficulty making his or her point, or who makes the subject dry and tedious is someone to whom you may be unlikely to listen.

You will have to ascertain for yourself the reasons you fail to completely surrender yourself to others when they speak. Once you do, you'll be able to overcome some of your difficulties by engaging in the technique of active listening developed by the psychologist Carl Rogers. He coined the term *unconditional positive regard* to refer to the process by which you enter into a relationship believing the best about another person. Without strings attached or qualification, you hold another person in high esteem. To really listen to someone, you first must have unconditional positive regard for him or her. Otherwise, the halo effect overshadows the message. Rogers said that once you have unconditional positive regard, active listening, rather than the passive taking in of information, can help you to assure that you've actually heard not only the message but also what the speaker may *not* be saying.

Active listening involves three steps.

Step 1: Paraphrasing

This is the act of repeating (in your own words) what you think the speaker has just said. If you haven't really listened, then you can't do it. If you haven't surrendered yourself to the speaker, paraphrasing isn't as easy as it sounds. You needn't worry about repeating the message verbatim. When you paraphrase, the other person will let you know if you correctly heard the message. Paraphrasing also has the secondary benefit of allowing the speaker to hear his or her message played back. After a paraphrase, it's not unusual to hear someone say, "That's what I said, but it's not what I meant." It allows clarification for both the speaker and the listener.

Here's an example of a paraphrase:

Speaker: *Whew! I'm glad that presentation is over. Every member of the board of directors was there, and every one of them had questions. What was supposed to be a fifteen-minute presentation turned*

> *into an hour of picking apart every last detail of the proposed new building site.*

Listener: *Sounds like your audience really raked you over the coals.*

Speaker: *And how. I never knew there could be so many differences of opinion about what I thought was a done deal. At least I was able to answer every question.*

When you paraphrase, the speaker feels heard and is encouraged to continue. Done to the extreme without using other active listening techniques, however, paraphrasing gives the impression of simply parroting the speaker. The next step is asking questions that provide for further clarification and full understanding.

Step 2: Asking Appropriate Questions

By asking questions, both you and the speaker delve more deeply into the content of the message. An appropriate question is always one that is *based on what has just been said*. All too often the listener changes the direction of the conversation by asking a question unrelated to what the speaker is saying. On the surface, it may appear appropriate, but closer examination reveals that it's really just a polite way to change the subject. An example of an inappropriate question based on what the speaker above said would be, "What did you think about the guy from ABC Company who sits on the board? I'm going to have to meet with him next week." Active listening for the purpose of building relationships is designed to help you to hear and understand another person, not get your needs met at that particular moment. If the listener wants to build a relationship with the speaker, then the focus has to remain with the *speaker*. Here's how the conversation might continue:

Listener: *Are you worried that the project might be stalled?*

Speaker: *Not really. It's just that everyone was trying to one-up everyone else, and the only way they could really do it was by showing how much they knew about the building site and proposal. I just got caught in the cross fire. I guess I thought that the presentation was pro forma, when in fact I see now that it was a political decision to put me on the agenda.*

Now the listener has even more information about what happened, why the speaker thinks it happened, and—without anything being said directly—how he or she might feel. Here is where the third part of active listening comes in—the ability to extrapolate the speaker's feelings from the spoken message by reading between the lines.

Step 3: Reflecting Feelings

This is the toughest part of active listening. It involves taking a guess about how you think the other person must *feel*. It brings the relationship to an even deeper level of understanding. People who have difficulty expressing their own feelings have difficulty with listening to and reflecting the feelings of others. If you reflect feelings and they're ignored, or the conversation comes to a grinding halt, it's best to drop this step. Part of being an active listener and listening with a third ear includes the ability to respond to the needs of the speaker. If talking about feelings makes him or her uncomfortable, don't push. Not everyone wants his or her feelings reflected, but those who do will appreciate a well-timed reflection.

The same conversation might continue with this reflection and additional paraphrasing and questions:

Listener: *You must have felt as though you were ambushed.*

Speaker: *Yeah, I was pretty mad. I wished that someone had let me know what the real agenda was instead of my having to figure it out for myself. I guess I felt a little foolish.*

Listener: *I don't blame you for feeling as you do. What are you going to do about it?*

Speaker: *I'm not sure yet. I do know that I don't want to be put in that situation again—or at least I want to be forewarned about it.*

Listener: *How do you think you might prevent it from happening in the future?*

Speaker: *I guess I should talk to the boss. She's usually open to hearing me out. I think I'll sleep on it and decide tomorrow what to do.*

Listener: *Sounds like a good idea. Let me know if I can help in any way.*

Speaker: *You already have.*

This conversation could have gone in any number of directions—and all away from the speaker's feelings. Active listening helps you stay focused on the topic and not be distracted by tangential issues or personal needs. As you can see, it requires surrendering to the speaker and putting your own opinion on hold for the moment. The speaker walks away feeling as if he or she has really been heard, and the listener benefits from understanding the full context of the message—both content and emotion.

USING DOORWAY CONVERSATIONS TO BUILD RELATIONSHIPS

Now that you know how to listen, the next question is: To what degree are you comfortable taking the time to do it? If relationships are the cornerstone of ongoing career success, then doorway conversations are the cornerstone of workplace relationships. The term *doorway conversations* comes from a client who uses it to describe those moments when someone appears in your doorway and stands there talking about the latest headline, the previous night's baseball game, or a problem he or she is encountering with a child. In the scheme of things, it may seem trivial to spend time talking about these subjects, but in the long term these are the very things on which relationships are built. As Dale Carnegie once said, "You can make more friends in two months by becoming interested in other people than you can in two years by trying to get other people interested in you."

Relationships that are valuable and meaningful have three essential ingredients: trust, reciprocity, and genuine caring. There's no faking these three elements. They are what distinguish a casual encounter from a real relationship. This is not to say that every workplace relationship must be of the same caliber as the relationships you have with your best friends, but rather that both relationships share common elements. People who fail to build solid workplace relationships frequently fail to build solid friendships. The same childhood defense mechanisms get in the way of both growing close to a friend and knowing a colleague on more than a superficial level. People who have no trouble building relationships may at this point be saying, *But all of this is so obvious!* It may be obvious for you, but for people who have never built mutually rewarding relationships, especially in the workplace, the next section is critical.

Trust

How do you develop trust? Why do we trust some people more than others? Why are certain people everyone's trusted friend whereas others have difficulty getting people to confide in them? The answer lies in the degree to which you act *consistently* and *honestly*. Consistency is the key to enabling others to know what to expect from you. Honesty lets them know that you do what you say you will. Combined, these qualities are very powerful in building trust in the workplace.

One of the more bizarre cases that I investigated when I was an equal employment opportunity specialist involved a woman who'd filed a sex discrimination charge with the California Department of Fair Employment and Housing claiming that her boss was rude, condescending, and treated her unfairly. She believed that this was because she was a woman and that the men in her department were not treated similarly. When I interviewed both male and female co-workers, it turned out that they did not share her opinion that women were treated unfairly; in fact, they trusted their boss very much. How could there be such disparate opinions of the same boss? Each of the people interviewed admitted that the boss was difficult and could be rude and obnoxious. He would yell at them in front of colleagues and embarrass them at meetings, but they watched him do this to everyone, not any one individual. "It's just the way he is" was a common remark.

The irony in this situation was that they trusted him because he acted consistently with everyone. They knew exactly what to expect from him, even if it was inappropriate behavior, and therefore always knew where they stood. Winning this case for the company relied on men in the department being willing to state that they were treated the same as the woman filing the claim. There was no unlawful discrimination—just one very bad manager, which is exactly what the commission eventually determined.

I don't recommend that you show everyone the same terrible treatment that this man did, but there is a lesson here. Even in the face of adversity, people will trust if there is consistency. Now, imagine the kind of trusting relationships that could be built with positive behaviors! Think of the people you trust. It's likely that you're willing to go the extra mile for them, because you know that they are true to their words and can anticipate how they will react in most situations.

Reciprocity

Reciprocity involves not only the quid pro quo exchange described earlier in this chapter, but also a mutuality of sharing. In a solid workplace relationship, both people know that the other has similar feelings about the nature of the friendship. They know this because there is a mutual sharing of personal information, allowing the human side to emerge. Too many of us have been taught that there's no place at work for personal problems or personal information to be shared. Because we spend the largest part of our day at work, however, it's only natural to disclose personal information there. In instances in which people may be good listeners but don't share personal information, they'll soon set themselves apart from everyone else.

Adults who come from narcissistic parents are particularly vulnerable to this dilemma. They learned early in life that they are merely reflections of their parents and, therefore, should not think that their own needs deserve consideration. They go through life listening, but not sharing their own thoughts and feelings. In a workplace relationship, the person who is always doing the talking may begin to feel uncomfortable about continuing to share information when he or she knows nothing about the other person in return. In reality, it takes very little self-disclosure to create a sense of mutuality. It must simply be enough to illuminate the human side of your character.

At a workshop that I was conducting, I mentioned a personal experience that demonstrated what happens when paraphrasing and asking questions are needed but not done. I was collaborating in the design of a new training program with a client who could talk endlessly about ideas and possibilities without ever putting closure on them. Getting impatient and running short on time, I didn't delve deeply into what he was really thinking. Instead, I took what he said at face value and spent quite a bit of time designing the program I thought he wanted. When I presented the outline and materials to him, it was clear this wasn't what he wanted at all.

After mentioning this obvious mistake to the group, a woman came up to me and, somewhat critically, asked why I'd felt the need to make myself look bad in front of the group. She believed the comment was unnecessary and made me look less than perfect. I explained that I wanted program participants to see me as human and that even though I teach these methods for listening, I, too, have to constantly work at them. Her question was really directed more at herself than at me. It unwittingly revealed that she feared appearing vulnerable and didn't want others to know about her human foibles. Whereas most people in the group got my meta-message, it served only to push one of her fear buttons.

Often, as with this woman, the fear that many people have that they will be seen as less competent or somehow imperfect precludes them from being genuine with others. However, honest self-disclosure can be a valuable tool in letting others see the human side of you, and most people do not take advantage of it. The willingness to be seen and heard can actually be quite a liberating experience.

Genuine Caring

The last of the three ingredients for successful relationships, genuine caring, is the hardest of all to coach. It's something that comes from deep inside the heart and transcends logic and intellect. The absence of caring is a lot easier to explain than how to care, because the absence suggests the lack of caring in your own life. With the exception of perhaps sociopaths, who truly lack the ability to care about their fellow human beings, most people have a deep and profound capacity to care. Women tend to have an easier time showing that they care, but it doesn't mean that men don't. Men have simply been socialized to hide it better. Therefore, the question is not *How can I show that I care?* but rather *Why don't I show that I care?* When you have the answer to this, you'll have the answer for how to genuinely care.

Chris appeared not to care at all about her staff of twenty salespeople. Her single-minded devotion was to provide the best service possible to the company's customers. Her natural energy and enthusiasm made her want to storm every hill she encountered. She was always coming up with unique and creative ways to better serve the customer and overcome existing obstacles to superior service. There's nothing wrong with all this, of course, but Chris failed to take into account the fact that she could successfully do this only if her staff followed her into battle. While she was charging up the hill, she failed to look behind her to see that her followers were lingering at the bottom, deciding whether or not they wanted the hill.

My first contact with Chris was through a team-building session that she requested to find ways for her staff to be more effective. When it came time to assess the team's strengths and developmental areas, the staff bravely pointed at Chris as being the primary obstacle to their success. They felt she was so self-absorbed that she either didn't care or couldn't see whether they had the time, resources, or interest to pursue the projects to which she committed them. So when it came time to deliver, Chris was often left holding the bag and trying to figure out why things weren't done as she directed or expected. Chris neglected the human needs of her team, and they responded (very humanly) by resisting her efforts.

Chris was hired because it was clear that she could bring value-added service to this company. Her past achievements in former employment situations pointed to this fact. Chris saw herself as someone who could do anything she put her mind to, and she typically did—provided that she could do it *alone*. When it came to gaining the cooperation of others, she couldn't quite figure out why she never really got it. Heretofore, Chris had been a tremendous individual contributor, but to maintain momentum she would have to learn how to accomplish the goal through others.

Fortunately for this team, Chris *did* care about other people. She just had a hard time showing it. She told me about her military father, who expected high achievement but seldom rewarded it. She realized that, in some ways, she had become her father. She expected a lot from her team, but she didn't see them as people, only as objects there to assist her with meeting her goals. When she understood how this behavior actually impeded her reaching the goal, she was distraught. She had vowed never to do to others what her father had done to her, and yet she now found herself displaying the same behavior. Chris had to learn to complement her already good task-oriented behaviors with skills for building relationships with each team member and creating a cohesive team. Drawing on her teenage experience as a member of a tennis team reminded her of the value of teamwork and became an important point of reference for just how interdependence works.

Chris began trying to win the cooperation of her team with doorway conversations—just dropping by to say hello to people and to find out how, not what, they were doing. As you might imagine, the team at first regarded her with skepticism. They wondered what ulterior motives she had. This discouraged Chris initially, but she was determined to win them over. She approached building relationships in much the same way as she approached her other "projects"—with vigor and enthusiasm. Pretty soon the individuals on her team began responding to her friendly overtures and expressions of interest. Chris didn't do it to get more work out of her team, but to get to know them as unique and valuable individuals. She learned the hard way the true meaning of Chinese philosopher Lao-tzu's saying "Fail to honor people, they fail to honor you." It took her a while, but she finally succeeded in building trust, reciprocity, and caring into workplace relationships. That's what made team members want to work for Chris in the long term and helped keep her on an upwardly mobile career path.

YOU LIKE ME! YOU REALLY LIKE ME!

So far I've been focusing on how to build strong 360-degree relationships. But perhaps you're already good at it—maybe even *too* good. The "You Like Me" acceptance speech that Sally Field made when she won an Academy Award a number of years ago speaks to a unique issue in building relationships. It reveals why she was typically cast in "cute" roles rather than more mature ones. She had an inordinate need to be liked, and that need was typified over and over in her behavior and the roles she received. Thus, a word of caution about building positive relationships: There is a difference between taking the time to build positive relationships and making it the focal point of every activity and decision because you're afraid people won't like you. An inordinate need to be liked interferes with your ability to make difficult decisions, be direct with people, get your own needs met, and be perceived as someone who can perform well even when the chips are down.

THE LIKABILITY CONTINUUM

| Don't care what people think | Healthy combination of concern for others while getting your own needs met | Need everyone to like you |

Although both men and women suffer from this problem, it seems to be more prevalent among women—and for good reason. Women have been socialized to be the nurturers, caretakers, and accommodators in society. They are expected to be good relationship builders. When women act in a manner counter to that expectation, they are often called overly aggressive, bitchy, or some other choice terms. So they go out of their way to be pleasant and try to win support for their ideas by making others like them. It's one of the self-sabotaging behaviors I talk about in my book *Nice Girls Don't Get the Corner Office*. Overutilization of this particular strength can create situations where others don't take you seriously. Ironically, it's the people, both men and women, who have established good workplace relationships who can afford to err on the side of being more assertive or direct. Their accounts are full of chips that can be cashed in at the appropriate time.

Maria is the perfect example of someone whose strength in building relationships interfered with her ability to achieve her career goals. She is the coordinator of outreach efforts for a nonprofit organization. Technically, she knows her job and is respected for her ability to perform it effectively. But when the department manager position opened up on several occasions, she was consistently overlooked as a viable candidate to fill it. When she asked why, she was told that she "wasn't ready" to take this next step.

If you were to meet Maria, you would like her—as does everyone in her office. She's warm, affable, and a good listener. She makes you feel as if what you have to say is important to her. If you spend any length of time with her, however, you realize that her strength in this arena stems from the need to be liked and is not balanced with the ability to be direct and straightforward. If she has an opinion different from yours, she won't tell you. She'll embrace yours as if it were her own. She won't take a stand on any issue if she thinks it might offend you. If you correct something that she does wrong, she becomes overly apologetic and tries to make up for the mistake by bringing you home-baked cookies or some other small gift the next day. Maria will never be considered management material until she overcomes this particular strength by balancing it with more assertive behaviors.

Relationships will never take the place of technical competence; they complement and support it. The ability to see and be seen is an essential ingredient for all good relationships, workplace and otherwise. Beyond making an individual contribution and building one-on-one relationships, you have to work effectively as part of a team. The next chapter provides suggestions for how you can be an effective team member and contribute to your team's success.

COACHING TIPS TO BUILD STRONG 360-DEGREE RELATIONSHIPS

Put a check mark in the box of two or three coaching tips you commit to doing.

❑ **At least once a week, have lunch with one or more colleagues.** Don't just wait for it to happen—*schedule* it at the beginning of each week. Use it as an opportunity to get to know your co-workers, clients, or direct reports and to allow them to get to know you on a personal level by not just talking about work, but also finding areas of common interest outside the job.

❑ **Drop by one person's office per day for ten minutes of casual doorway conversation.** Put a recurring alarm on your desktop calendar to serve as a reminder that it's time to get up and get out of your office or cubicle. Ask questions: "I know you're a gourmet, and I was wondering if you could recommend a good restaurant to take my mother-in-law to this weekend?" or "I heard your daughter is going off to Harvard in the fall. What's she going to be studying?" The question itself doesn't matter as much as showing genuine interest in the other person.

❑ **Smile at people as you walk past them in the hall.** There is no better way to increase your likability quotient than to smile. Don't look away or look preoccupied as you pass others—seize the opportunity to craft your reputation as a warm and friendly human being.

❑ **Keep your office door open** unless you are conducting confidential business or trying to meet a tight deadline and don't want distractions (but never more than a few times each month). If hallway noises are distracting to you, buy a white-noise machine to mute them—it's better than sitting in a closed office all day and giving the impression you don't want to talk to anyone.

❑ **When people talk to you, surrender yourself for the moment.** Develop a mental mantra that will enable you to shift from whatever might preoccupy you to being able to listen to what's being said. My own is, *There is nothing more important than that I be fully present in this moment.* It will eventually become the segue from whatever you're doing to being in the moment.

❑ **Open up to people to let them get to know you by disclosing personal information with which you're comfortable.** This isn't to say you have to reveal your deepest, darkest secrets. Talk about a good movie you saw over the weekend, a particular event on a recent vacation that brought you joy, or something a child did that made you a proud parent.

❑ **Accept co-workers' invitations for lunch or dinner and extend your own.** If you think you don't have time in your busy schedule to break bread with a colleague, think again. Working through lunch makes it look as if you can't handle your workload. Similarly, socializing outside the office enables you to build warmer, more collegial relationships at work.

❑ **Attend company-sponsored social events.** You don't have to be the life of the party or even stay until the event is over—but you do have to show up. Spending a little bit of your own time at these events contributes to the notion that you care about your fellow workers as human beings—not just humans doing.

❑ **Learn the names of co-workers' husbands, wives, significant others, and children.** Having a bad memory is no excuse. Write the information down in your contact file along with the person's phone number and address. It's just another way to humanize your interactions.

❑ **Remember birthdays by keeping a list or marking them on your calendar.** Although it's not necessary to buy a gift or a card, being able to wish people a happy birthday makes them feel special and helps you to build a relationship you might need in the future.

❑ **Follow up on information that has been previously shared with you, particularly personal information.** You won't be able to do this if you haven't really listened or if you're preoccupied with your own activities. If someone tells you her father is in the hospital with terminal cancer—don't forget about it. Periodically ask how he's doing or if there's anything you can do to help.

❑ **Interact with everyone equally, regardless of level in the organization.** From the person who cleans your office to the one who signs your paycheck and everyone in between—they all deserve to be treated with unconditional positive regard.

❑ **Begin every conversation with small talk** (unless past experience tells you the other person doesn't like it). Before delving into the business at hand, ask other people how they're doing or what's new in their lives—and listen to the answers. Small talk cements good professional relationships.

❑ **Enroll in a Dale Carnegie course** (www.dalecarnegie training.com). Many of us remember Dale Carnegie's former slogan: *Win friends and influence people*. Dale Carnegie courses, offered at various locations around the world, are designed to provide you with the skills and confidence needed to communicate effectively, deal with problem solving, and inspire co-workers. Course objectives include developing more self-confidence, controlling your fear of an audience, improving your memory, developing a more effective personality, and widening your personal horizons. Additionally, the firm offers both college credit and continuing education credits (CEUs) to anyone participating in its programs.

❑ **Don't allow an inordinate need for others to like you to get in the way of being direct and straightforward.** Take more risks around developing your own voice without necessarily ignoring or overlooking the opinions of others. You can do this by paraphrasing what you've heard and adding your thoughts to the mix.

❏ **Do favors for people even if you don't anticipate needing them returned.** That's what the quid pro quo is all about. You will find the world a much more abundant place when you act with abundance. Good deeds may not be returned from the person you did a favor for, but they will be returned.

❏ **See beyond the task to the human being who is performing it.** It has become too easy to see people as merely functionaries carrying out duties and responsibilities. Others are not accountants, engineers, waiters, or teachers—they are mothers, brothers, aunts, and grandparents with feelings and needs. You don't build relationships with roles—you build relationships with people.

SUCCESS STRATEGY 2

———

Be an Integral Member of Your Team

Teamwork is not a matter of persuading yourself and your colleagues to set aside personal ambitions for the greater good. It's a matter of recognizing that your personal ambitions and the ambitions of the team are one and the same.

Coach Pat Summitt

If you're a football fan, the name *Terrell Owens* probably rings a bell and you know why I started this chapter talking about him. If you're not, his story is one from which you can learn. In November 2005, Owens was in the second season of a seven-year contract playing for the Philadelphia Eagles. There's no question that as a wide receiver, he was talented and added value to the team. But Owens constantly complained about his forty-nine-million-dollar contract and suggested that the team would be better off without its quarterback Donovan McNabb. Owens also voiced his disappointment that the team's management didn't do more to recognize his one hundredth touchdown catch, and was generally a nuisance to coaches, fellow players, and other teams. When team management finally had enough and asked that he apologize to his teammates, Owens declined to do so, resulting in his ultimate separation from the team. Although he later did apologize, most people involved in the high drama of his self-induced fiasco agreed it was too little, too late.

It's a fact that Owens went on to be picked up by the Dallas Cowboys at a lucrative salary, but his reputation was irreparably tarnished. His name is now synonymous with controversy and poor sportsmanship. Only time will tell whether he will stop sabotaging his career, but when I visited his Web site I heard a song he recorded that gave me doubts. It was Owens rapping about his new team (the Dallas Cowboys) and dissing his old team. Not only does Owens have a problem functioning as a member of a team, but he also could be the poster child for lack of emotional intelligence—a subject I'll talk more about in a later chapter.

Although you may not play for a team on a par with the Philadelphia Eagles, the dynamics of teamwork are nearly identical from the athletic field to the corporate playing field. Individual players come together in an effort to achieve success through synergistic teamwork. Senior management will put up with prima donnas for just so long; then they take action to protect the best interests of the team and the people who depend on that team to produce results. The ability to build strong personal relationships with *individuals* does not always translate into being a strong team player. I'm sure you know people who are charming, charismatic, and influential on a one-to-one basis. But put them in a group where they're not in charge and they don't have a clue how to use those skills to benefit the team.

Conversely, there are terrific team players who are unable to forge deeper, more intimate one-to-one relationships. Depending on the size of the group, teamwork can allow for anonymity, whereas effective interpersonal relationships do not. It's easier to hide personally in a group than it is an individual relationship, provided you pull your fair share of the weight related to task accomplishment. Such people do quite well one-on-one, but somehow become lost in a group. The ability to work effectively as a team member isn't simply an extension of good interpersonal skills, but a separate and unique skill set.

Even if building relationships is one of your strengths, the checklist on the opposite page might reveal a very different area for development.

THE VALUE OF TEAMWORK

The fact that most corporate cultures reward competitiveness and individualism with money and recognition causes some people to question the value of developing cooperative team abilities. There are those who prefer to be individual contributors and in fact work more effectively in this way. They tend to avoid opportunities to work collaboratively. The efficacy of teamwork, however, is well documented through sports analogies, war and peace efforts, and medical triage. The world witnessed the power of teamwork immediately following the tragic events of September 11. Every individual on the emergency service teams that responded to the crisis was superbly trained to do his or her job. But not one of these professionals *alone* could have made the difference made by their respective teams. The magnitude of the event required teams of people who could work collaboratively to rescue those who were still alive, provide medical care to those in need, and recover the remains of those who perished.

_____ I've received feedback that I'm a good team player.

_____ Even when the topic doesn't interest me, isn't pertinent to my function, or leaves me with nothing to add, I stay engaged in team discussions by looking for ways to contribute to the outcome.

_____ I believe that the final product of a group typically exceeds the quality of something that I produce alone.

_____ I freely share information with teammates without questioning their need to know.

_____ I don't mind if a team process slows down because of differences of opinion: I know they add value to, rather than simply delay, outcomes.

_____ I pay equal attention to the task and the process functions of teams on which I participate.

_____ I'm a good follower when someone else takes the lead.

_____ I do not display impatience with the lengthy discussions that are often part of a group's process because I know that they will contribute positively to the outcome.

_____ I volunteer for team-based projects.

_____ Getting individual recognition is not as important to me as my team's success.

_____ I publicly acknowledge others who have worked with me on a successful project.

An inspiring example of how individuals pooled their collective talents to avert a potential catastrophe is the story of the men and women involved with *Apollo 13*. On April 14, 1970, an oxygen tank exploded on this manned mission to the moon, threatening the lives of the crew. The collaboration, ingenuity, and expertise of the crew and flight controllers combined to safely return the ship to earth, but not before a harrowing ordeal, played out in public, made it clear that no one person alone could save the ship and its crew. The unique skills and abilities of each person involved with the *Apollo 13* mission were needed if there was to be any hope of success, but they had to be performed as a team.

Let's bring it even closer to home with another example, this time taken from the routine training exercise that flight attendants undergo to learn techniques for aircraft crash survival at sea. You may not realize it, but these men and women are taught to look for passengers at the beginning of each flight who are most likely to survive on a raft and contribute to the survival of others. The key to ensuring successful survival is in choosing people who can play all kinds of roles at sea. A leader is needed who can inspire others to maintain the vision of being rescued. That person must keep people optimistic about their chances of staying alive by remaining calm as well as seeing and having faith in the big picture, whether this is called faith in God or a higher power. Beyond this role, technical competence is required to survive—to desalinate salt water, repair a tear in the raft, read a compass, or administer first aid. In the end, survival depends not on any single skill set, but rather on taking advantage of the fact that the whole is greater than the sum of the parts. The chances of survival increase with the synergistic effect of teamwork. Paradoxically, as people pool their resources, instead of focusing exclusively on their own survival, the likelihood of survival for *everyone* increases exponentially.

The same is true in organizations. Individuals come to the workplace with unique skill sets that contribute to their own success and the success of their teams. Each of us is endowed with things that we do well and for which people rely on us. Some of these skills are learned, others are developed with practice, and still others are the result of our natural proclivity for them. We aren't expected to do everything equally well, but we are expected to use the resources around us, including the *human* resources, to accomplish our tasks effectively. Much like the survivors of an airplane crash or a space mission gone awry, business survivors must have the ability to perform tasks not only independently but collaboratively in group settings as well.

Over the past decade, team-based projects have become increasingly popular, as have matrixed teams. These make it increasingly important that you be able to work effectively not only with individuals—and not only with members of your immediate team—but also with people from teams other than your own. Whereas some people are able to forge good one-to-one workplace relationships, others excel at and find satisfaction in participating as members of a group committed to a common goal.

The term *good individual contributor* is often used to refer to someone who does his or her job well working independently, but doesn't play particularly nicely in the sandbox with others. It's frequently used to describe someone with good technical skills but poor interpersonal ones, so don't take it as a compliment if someone tells you that you're a terrific individual contributor or if you're moved into an individual-contributor role. The message may be that you are not perceived as a good team player. Even jobs that appear on the surface to be perfect for individual contributors later turn out to require integrated teamwork. As a matter of fact, it is difficult to think of one job in most workplaces today that doesn't require integrated teamwork. Teams accomplish significantly more through the synergistic process of sharing information, technology, or skills than would a group of individual contributors working on pieces of the same project.

The shift in how manufacturers make cars is testament to this fact. Historically, the industrial revolution led to narrowly defined jobs in which workers performed various aspects of the manufacturing operation. This translated into carmakers putting people into assembly-line jobs where each worker was responsible for one part of the car. The belief was that efficiency would increase with people performing repetitive tasks. But the frequent occurrence of production mistakes forced management to examine inefficiencies and find ways of overcoming them. Productivity experts discovered that by increasing the scope of each person's position and creating teams of people who had overall responsibility for the car's assembly, rather than each person being responsible for only one piece, the quality of the automobiles produced actually increased.

In the competitive hospitality business, the Ritz-Carlton hotel chain stresses teamwork in addition to excellence in individual performance during new-employee orientation at each facility. A stay at any one of the hotels is likely to make you realize that the Ritz-Carlton has redefined *customer service* in its broadest sense. Each employee is taught that he or she is personally responsible for the satisfaction of the hotel's guests. Employees are not taught to do just one job well; they are taught to work as a part of the overall hotel team of staff members and to accept responsibility for any request that a guest might make.

During a leadership workshop at the Huntington Ritz-Carlton in Pasadena, California, I decided to put the hotel's philosophy to the test to see whether it worked in practice. Several times during our stay, I asked staff members for items or services that were clearly outside the domain of their responsibility. Each time the request was promptly met. In an effort to make a point to the managers in this workshop about the value of teamwork, I asked a man from the catering staff, who came in to refresh the coffee, whether he knew where I could get a particular color of marking pen. He said that he would take care of it—and sure enough, he returned with the marker in hand.

After thanking him in front of the group, I asked how he liked working at this hotel. He said that it was one of the best jobs that he ever had. When I asked why, he said it was because he was trained to do his job properly *and* felt like an important part of the hotel team. Each morning, he told us, management held team meetings to talk about the guests and their particular needs so that everyone would have all the information required to meet the demands. It was a valuable lesson to workshops participants about the efficacy of teamwork and how it can enhance both customer and employee satisfaction.

Another example of the value of teamwork is provided by the restaurant chain California Pizza Kitchen. With a main fare of individual gourmet pizza and pasta, the restaurants first opened in California in the mid-1980s. Since that time, the chain has expanded to 180 restaurants in twenty-seven states and five foreign countries. Besides serving food that is consistently good across locations (showing that they are technically competent), these restaurants also offer a pleasant dining experience. Their waiters and waitresses have been taught how to treat customers and work as a team. There are no fixed table assignments for servers—everyone is responsible for every table. When I inquired how this worked with regard to tips, I was told by one young man that it wasn't a problem. Peer pressure virtually eliminated those staff people who brought down the tip average for the others due to substandard performance and customer dissatisfaction.

The sports arena offers the greatest source for understanding the importance of teamwork. Sports teams consist of groups of outstanding individual contributors who know that they can't win the game alone—and if they think they can, they don't get the cooperation of their teammates for long. Head Coach Phil Jackson of the Los Angeles Lakers had this lesson emphasized for him the hard way early in his career. In his book *Sacred Hoops: Spiritual Lessons of a Hardwood Warrior,* Jackson shares an experience from an early stint as coach with the Albany Patroons. Despite the fact that he had no formal training as a coach, he did have a coaching vision: "to create a team in which selflessness— not the me-first mentality that had come to dominate professional basketball—was the primary driving force." Part of his method for accomplishing the vision was to assure that everyone on the team be paid the same amount and be given equal playing time.

His strategy worked. Within two years, the Patroons moved from an 8–17 season to the second best record in the league, with Jackson named Coach of the Year. His achievement began to unravel, however, when he allowed one player, Frankie J. Sanders, to dominate the game and compromise his principles. Sanders first convinced Jackson to move him from second slot to starting player, then successfully lobbied management for a sizable raise. Combined with his superior playing skills, these factors gave Sanders (and his teammates) the impression that he was first among equals. Following a series of incidents that included Jackson's suspending Sanders for what amounted to insubordination and then implicitly supporting management's decision to reinstate him (it was felt that he was needed to win games), the team was never the same. "The solidarity that had taken so long to build had suddenly evaporated," writes Jackson. "Not only did we lose the series, we were lost as a team."

Jackson went on to coach other good, but not winning, teams with the same formula for success. First, with the Chicago Bulls during the 1980s and 1990s, he turned a team that was built around one outstanding player (this time Michael Jordan) into six-time NBA champions. More recently, Jackson sold the Lakers on his team-based philosophies and coached the team to three NBA championship titles after a decade with none. He did it, in part, by capitalizing on but not over-relying on star players such as Kobe Bryant and Shaquille O'Neal.

OVERCOMING RESISTANCE TO TEAMWORK

Clearly, teamwork pays huge dividends for both individuals and groups of people. Why, then, do so many people have difficulty being seen as true team players? The answer lies partially in how jobs have recently been defined. As mentioned earlier, the industrial revolution narrowly circumscribed worker responsibilities, but from a broader historical perspective human beings have always worked collaboratively to assure their survival. Clans, tribes, and families can be viewed as the earliest teams. Even in prehistoric time, our predecessors pooled resources by allowing those with the best vision to sight their prey, those with the best dexterity to kill it, and those with the greatest strength to haul it back to the cave. Consciously or otherwise, they realized that their survival depended on a collaborative effort.

Today, in an age where rugged individualism and an *everyone-for-themselves* attitude prevail, teamwork seems like a revolutionary concept. The irony is that people resist having to depend on others for their success when in fact they would fare so much better if they worked collaboratively. In their wonderfully written and enlightening book *The Wisdom of Teams,* Jon Katzenbach and Douglas Smith recognize that there exists a natural resistance to moving from individual contributor to team player. "Our natural instincts, family upbringing, formal education, and employment experience all stress the primary importance of individual responsibility as measured by our own standards and those to whom we report," Katzenbach and Smith write. "We are more comfortable doing our own jobs and having our performance measured by our boss than we are working and jointly being assessed as peers."

The story of a man whom I met during a team-building session in Germany provides insight into how and why some people resist teamwork. Erik was raised in a small village about eighty miles outside Berlin. Throughout the program, he arrived late to each session, sat on the outside of the small group to which he was assigned, and spoke very quietly, which led to him often being ignored—after which he would shut down completely. Combined, his behavior and body language indicated that he was resisting this team's effort to coalesce.

After one particularly intense group exercise where several members of the team received some pretty difficult feedback about their behavior, Erik raised his hand and said that people never change anyway and we shouldn't expect them to. I took that to mean he was putting us all on notice that *he* wasn't going to change. Whereas his teammates were doing their best to overcome cultural and personal obstacles to teamwork, Erik threw a monkey wrench into this painstaking process. Democracy in what was formerly East Germany is a relatively new system, and the remnants of communism were reflected in the hesitance that many of the participants had in speaking openly and honestly. Erik's resistance wasn't making it any easier.

One evening I arrived late to dinner and found only Erik left in the dining room. We made small talk about our families and upbringing while I waited for my meal to arrive. Much to my surprise, he began telling me about his childhood with a cruel father and timid mother. In broken English, he conveyed perfectly that although his father was well intentioned (he wanted Erik to be more than the truck driver that he himself was), he was nonetheless abusive, both physically and emotionally. Erik's mother was ineffectual in preventing the damage her husband did to his children's psyches. As a result, Erik said, he always tried to do his best and worked hard to achieve his goals, never relying on anyone else for assistance.

Erik's lesson from childhood was to be strong and independent, always giving his personal best in an effort to deflect his father's constant criticism and verbal abuse. His survival, and the survival of all of the children in his family, was dependent on each person fending for him- or herself. Neither could he rely on his mother, who had her own problems in the abusive atmosphere created by Erik's father. His resistance to my efforts to help this group become a high-performing team was now understandable to me. I no longer viewed Erik as an impediment to the process, but rather as a human being struggling for survival in an unknown and changing world. Erik had no idea that his long-term success would be dependent on overcoming his greatest strengths. It was a concept as alien to him as democracy once had been.

An interesting side note since the first edition of this book is that one day, out of the blue, I received a call from Erik. He wanted to tell me that he finally realized what I was talking about in terms of the ability of people to change, because he changed. We've stayed in touch since then, and although he still struggles with forgoing individual recognition for team success, he consciously works on it—and his management notices.

The ingredient essential to teamwork, trust, is missing from those most reluctant to embrace it. Somewhere along the line, they learned that they could rely only on themselves. To be a fully productive member of a team requires the ability to make a leap of faith that you will actually be better off by relinquishing some of the need to work independently. In order to do so, you must first believe that other people have something valuable to offer and that together you can accomplish great things.

UNDERSTANDING AND VALUING
"GIFTS DIFFERING"

One invaluable tool that I use in conjunction with individual coaching and team-building programs is the Myers-Briggs Type Indicator (MBTI®) personality inventory. The title of a lovely companion book, *Gifts Differing*, helps us all understand that we each bring unique gifts to the workplace. The challenge of working as part of a team is to understand the gifts that you bring *as well* as those brought by fellow team members. All too often, we come to believe that the gift we bring is the *only* gift needed by the team. Success as a team member depends on your being able to value and use the gifts of others as effectively as you use your own.

The MBTI measures individual preferences on four separate scales: what energizes or takes energy away from a person, what a person likes to pay attention to, how a person makes decisions, and how a person likes to live life. On each of the four scales shown on the following chart, you exhibit a preference for one set of behaviors over the other. Knowing these four things about yourself and your teammates can help you to contribute your own personal best and bring the best out in others as well. Similarly, failure to understand personality types can lead to an enormous amount of frustration and misunderstanding.

Here's an example. At a team-building session in Jakarta, Indonesia, that involved a lot of work in small groups and pairs of people, a woman, Sarinah, came up to me and whispered, "Whatever you do, don't pair me with Malu," then hurried away. Naturally, this was a red flag to me that she probably *needed* to be paired with Malu. Then, a little while later, Malu came up to me and—you can already guess what she wanted—asked not to be paired with Sarinah. I was pondering how best to handle the situation when knowledge of type preferences helped me to solve this dilemma.

I typically do an exercise where people who are opposite types on the MBTI are asked to pair up together to discuss ways in which they have difficulty working as teammates and how those difficulties could be turned into opportunities. Sarinah and Malu scored as opposite profiles. Whereas Sarinah was an Extrovert / Senser / Thinker / Judger, Malu was an Introvert / Intuitor / Feeler / Perceiver. Sarinah was outgoing, practical, results-oriented, in-your-face. Malu was more introspective, attuned to possibilities instead of reality, and sensitive to people and processes. As frequently happens when these two particular types work together without understanding how to capitalize on their differences, ongoing communication problems and misunderstandings existed between them. Malu viewed Sarinah as too blunt, unconcerned with how people felt about things, and so concerned with the bottom line that new and innovative ways of doing things were ignored. Conversely, Sarinah thought Malu was too slow to reach decisions, concerned herself overly with people's opinions, and withheld information.

MBTI® PREFERENCES CHART

ENERGIZING (HOW A PERSON IS ENERGIZED)

EXTROVERT (E)	INTROVERT (I)
external	internal
outside thrust	inside pull
blurt it out	keep it in
breadth	depth
involved with people, things	work with ideas, thoughts

action	reflection
do–think–do	think–do–think

ATTENDING (WHAT A PERSON PAYS ATTENTION TO)

SENSING (S)	**INTUITION (I)**
the five senses	sixth sense, hunches
what is real	what could be
practical	theoretical
present orientation	future possibilities
facts	insights
using established skill	learning new skills
utility	novelty
step-by-step	leap around

DECIDING (HOW A PERSON MAKES DECISIONS)

THINKING (T)	**FEELING (F)**
head	heart
logical system	value system
objective	subjective
justice	mercy
critique	compliment
principles	harmony
reason	empathy
firm but fair	compassionate

LIVING (LIFESTYLE A PERSON ADOPTS)

JUDGMENT (J)	**PERCEPTION (P)**
planful	spontaneous
regulate	flow
control	adapt
settled	tentative
run one's life	let life happen
set goals	gather information
decisive	open
organized	flexible

Copyright © 1990 by Consulting Psychologists Press, Inc.

Given my instructions, they reluctantly paired up together. Once they began talking about the problems between them based on their types, each realized that she saw the world through a set of lenses that was uniquely hers. Instead of each thinking the other was just trying to make her life miserable, both learned that these differences could be used to help the other be more effective. As a result of their discussion, they decided to use each other's strengths to complement their own and as a means of learning alternative skills. Although I don't think that Malu and Sarinah will ever be best friends, they did begin to work more effectively as teammates and overcome the barriers that existed to a collaborative working relationship.

Herein lies one of the secrets to being a successful team player: the ability to move outside the scope of your own preferences and limited worldview to a broader understanding of the complementary nature of team relationships. We get so stuck in our own paradigms that we fail to see how other paradigms add value. Our way of doing things becomes *the* way, thereby limiting the possibilities that result from synergistic teamwork. And the more we learned in childhood that we had to be staunchly independent and self-sufficient, the harder it is to shift our paradigms.

The importance of being able to shift paradigms is made abundantly clear in the works of futurist Joel Barker. His book *Paradigms: The Business of Discovering the Future* and his video *The Business of Paradigms* provide examples of how the failure to move from your own comfort zone to a new, different, and perhaps unexplored sphere of possibilities can limit your future and sabotage your success. I like to tell the story of one Thanksgiving when I learned a lesson about shifting paradigms and teamwork.

It was the first year that I decided to invite a large group of relatives and friends for Thanksgiving dinner. Being the independent woman that I am, I wanted to prepare and serve the meal by myself. As more people came into the kitchen to help, I became increasingly frustrated with my inability to maintain control of the situation. My mother was telling me to do one thing to the turkey, a friend was telling me to do another to the stuffing, and still someone else was telling me how to cook the vegetables. Finally, heeding my own guidance to others that the paradox of control is *The more control you have, the more you give away,* I decided to let everyone do what they wanted. I was just positive, however, that this meal would wind up a disaster.

When we finally sat down to dinner, I held my breath. I would assume no responsibility for how the food tasted. No one was more surprised than I was when it turned out to be one of the best Thanksgiving dinners ever to come out of my kitchen. Too many cooks hadn't spoiled the meal; they had made it even better than I could have prepared alone. There was no better way for me personally to learn the lesson that I already knew to be true for professional teams—collaboration yields a better product if you only allow the process to flow. In retrospect, I realized that my resistance to teamwork in the kitchen was no different from the resistance to teamwork in the workplace. Each person came with skills different from mine, but complementary. If I had been smarter from the beginning, I would have used those skills to my advantage, rather than resisting them.

It's been more than four decades since Lakers coach Phil Jackson vowed to trust his instincts when it comes to teamwork. During that time, he's used Zen philosophy to hone his techniques for convincing individual team members about the importance and value of teamwork. In the process, he's become one of the most successful coaches in the history of the National Basketball Association. In a December 1995 interview with *Fortune* magazine, he explained his approach:

> *Back in the late eighties I used to remind Michael Jordan that no matter how many great scoring games he had, he still sometimes ended up coming out on the losing end, because he would try to beat the other team by himself. Even though he could pull it off occasionally, we weren't going to win consistently until the other players on our team started helping us. . . . Even for people who don't consider themselves spiritual in a traditional, religious way, you need to convince them that creating any kind of team is a spiritual act. People have to surrender their own egos so that the end result is bigger than the sum of its parts.*

Jackson is right. Once you realize that you can't possibly do it all yourself, you can begin to reap the benefits that come from teamwork. Although you may be able to win a few games alone, long-term success comes from interdependent team functioning, not grandstanding. It is a leap of faith to move from individual contributor to team member, but one well worth the risk.

THE MATRIXED TEAM

In the years since I wrote the original version of this book, a new model for teamwork has emerged. It's called a *matrixed team*. Unlike the traditional team, the matrixed team often has no formal manager, hierarchy, or clearly defined roles and responsibilities. Instead, groups of people find themselves working on projects with overlapping responsibilities, reporting to several team leaders, and simultaneously serving the needs of the same clients or customers. It presents unique challenges to staff and leaders alike—and as I often say, *God so loved the world that he didn't send a matrixed team!*

Nonetheless, this is the direction taken by many organizations—and learning to be a strong member (or leader) of a matrixed team can actually help develop valuable skills. And what a lesson it was for two team leaders when I was called in to referee an ongoing dispute between them. The scenario was this: Kevin and Ellen were sales directors, each with responsibility for two different product lines offered by a medical device manufacturing company—four products in all. They were both strong managers with positive reputations that were about to be tarnished if they couldn't learn to successfully manage the matrix. Their customer base, large medical centers in major metropolitan areas, was the same. Their staffs had similar backgrounds, skills, and sales training needs and provided technical assistance to the same medical centers. If the two teams didn't work collaboratively, customers would see them as disjointed and could lose confidence in the company and its products.

Whereas the old team model would have looked like this:

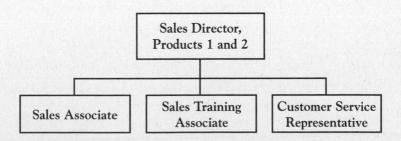

The new team model looks like this:

	Product 1	Product 2	Product 3	Product 4
Kevin	X	X		
Ellen			X	X
Sales Associate 1	X	X		
Sales Associate 2			X	X
Sales Training Associate 1	X	X	X	X
Sales Training Associate 2	X	X	X	X
Customer Service Representative 1	X	X	X	X
Customer Service Representative 2	X	X	X	X

Clearly, the two teams had to learn how to share services, coordinate efforts, and learn about each other's products if they were to successfully compete with other companies. They had to provide what's known as *seamless service*. When I met individually with Kevin and Ellen, it became apparent that both were operating according to the old rules of teams—*they* were in charge, others were expected to follow their directives, and they would be rewarded and recognized based on individual achievement. Nothing could be farther from the truth with a matrixed team. Two of the three people on Kevin's team received instructions from Ellen based on her unique expertise, and vice versa—two of the three people on Ellen's team had to respond to Kevin's requests. Additionally, their success could not be measured individually, but rather as a result of their joint efforts.

The absence of a hierarchical management approach combined with overlapping responsibilities makes the following elements essential for success on a matrixed team:

- Clear and frequent communication between team leaders and team members.
- Clearly defined individual roles and responsibilities.
- Jointly established goals.
- Strong influence skills.
- Regular meetings of all members of the matrixed team to share information and resolve common problems.
- A methodology for prioritizing competing assignments given by the team leaders.
- A means for tracking progress.
- A commitment to mutual success.
- A system of rewards and recognition for successfully achieving joint goals.

Using these factors as an outline for moving forward, Kevin and Ellen learned that they were no longer individually responsible for the direction, supervision, and success of their respective teams. Success could come only through a collaborative team effort where their staffs viewed them as having an equal say in their assignments, development, reviews, and rewards.

TEAM MEMBER GOALS AND ROLES

Whether it's a sports team or a business team, players are assigned roles based on their areas of technical competence. You rarely see the quarterback playing a defensive position, and vice versa. Similarly, it's unusual for an accountant to be transferred into an engineering position. Players who can fill multiple roles due to a wide array of skills are called *utility players*. Although utility players add value in terms of versatility, they often don't possess the depth of ability seen in specialists. For this reason, it's good if you can pinch-hit now and then—but don't forgo the education or training needed to become an expert in your field.

Many people play their *technical* roles well, but fail to understand that teams are much more complex than that. Look at Terrell Owens. He's a good individual contributor but has a track record of being an awful team member. I've said it before, I'll say it again (and you may hear it again before you're finished with this book): *Doing your job and doing it well isn't enough for sustained success.* Most groups work on two fundamental levels: the task level and the process level. The *task* level consists of what players are supposed to do to accomplish team goals and fulfill the expectations of management or stakeholders. The *process* level involves how the group achieves those goals—something harder to measure but equally important. Groups or people that focus exclusively on the task get the job done, but at a great personal cost to team members. Groups that focus exclusively on process assure that team members' personal needs are attended to, but often at the expense of achieving their goals.

THE TASK AND PROCESS FUNCTIONS OF TEAMS

T
E
A
M

T
A
S
K

High Focus on Task / Low Focus on Process	High Focus on Process and Task
Can be appropriate in emergency situations such as after September 11 or Hurricane Katrina. It's about getting the task accomplished safely and efficiently. Too many people who focus *exclusively* on getting their jobs done wonder why they can't get the cooperation of others when they need it the next time.	Successful professionals keep both these factors on the forefront *most* of the time. It entails getting your job done and doing it in a way that lets others know you value them and are equally concerned with their success and the success of the team. Doing so creates the kind of goodwill and support needed to succeed over the long haul.
Low Focus on Task and Process	Low Focus on Task / High Focus on Process
If you don't care about what you're doing or about the people you're doing it with, you can't sustain long-term career success. This phenomenon is often seen among people in tenured or union positions that make it almost impossible for management to terminate them. They are clearly in it for the paycheck, prestige, or security—and their colleagues, customers, and constituents suffer.	People who over-engage in these behaviors usually have an inordinate need to be liked. They want everyone to be happy and play nicely together but miss opportunities to add real value to the team's goals by allowing natural conflict to arise and be worked through. Shifting to a high process focus can be an effective strategy when trying to heal a damaged relationship or a demoralized team.

TEAM PROCESS

In addition to capitalizing on the gifts brought to the team by individuals, team members must fill certain roles if the task and the process are to be addressed. These roles are commonly divided into two categories, which parallel the task and process of a group: task roles and group-building and maintenance roles. Whereas task roles help the group achieve its goals, process roles are designed to maintain the emotional health of the team so that it can function effectively over the long term. Both roles are equally important, but group-building and maintenance roles are frequently ignored in favor of task accomplishment.

Task Roles (Assure Goal Achievement)	Process Roles (Maintain the Life of the Group)
Timekeeper	Gatekeeper (making sure everyone is heard)
Scribe	
Facilitator or leader	Encourager
Seeking information	Consensus builder
Giving information	Jokester (to relieve tension)
Synthesizing information	
Asking probing questions	Commenting on the mood of the group
Coordinating efforts	Mediator

Task roles assure that information is shared, analyzed and assessed, discussed, and acted on so that the team can achieve its goals and objectives. Most people are fairly good at playing task roles. Teams begin to encounter problems, however, when members become so focused on the task at hand that they fail to see the ramifications of their behavior on teammates. They ignore the importance of maintaining relationships in group settings. Put a really good relationship builder into a group setting, and the skills he or she is comfortably able to use one-on-one will go out the window. Suddenly, you'll see counterproductive behaviors such as competitiveness, jockeying for position, talking over people, ignoring the opinions of others, and even mentally checking out when it appears the group is going in a direction different from the one desired. Depending on your childhood family, it may look very much like what happened at the dinner table.

One man was sent to an interpersonal skills training program because he was disruptive at team meetings, always creating more turmoil than necessary and interfering with the team's ability to reach consensus. After a videotaped exercise where he received feedback about the specific behaviors that were troubling to management and peers alike, he explained why he acted as he did. Both of his parents were professors, he told us, and dinner table debate was thought of as sport. His brothers and sisters, in an effort to get parental approval, would routinely take contrary positions and shout over one another in order to "win" the argument. To an outsider, he said, it would look quite bizarre. He considered chaotic team meetings the norm and actually fun. If there wasn't controversy to begin with, he created it—and in turn gained a reputation as something of a loose cannon.

Here's where process or team-building and maintenance roles come in. Such roles include behaviors like gatekeeping (making certain everyone is heard before the decision is made), encouraging the team to work through difficult issues, mediating differences of opinion, and relieving tension through jokes or attempts at levity. High-functioning teams assure that equal attention is paid to the team's process and its product. Failure to do so results in hard feelings among team members, outcomes being delayed, sabotage of the ultimate decision (especially when it's made by just a few group members), and the eventual dropping out of team members with valuable input.

Team-building and maintenance roles, so called because they are designed to maintain the life of the group, are more subtle and somewhat harder to measure, but nonetheless critical for long-term effective team functioning. If a group of people were to come together to make only one decision or complete one task and then disband, never to have to work together again, the group's dynamics would be irrelevant. Exclusive focus on the task might even be appropriate. In the workplace, however, individuals move from team to team and project to project, thereby necessitating assurance that each time a group meets it will successfully carry out its explicit and implicit agenda, unhampered by past or present inappropriate individual and group behavior.

During team-building sessions, I've watched as certain members become increasingly uninvolved with the team. They look out the window, get up and leave the room (always for a good reason, of course), start playing with their BlackBerries, or engage in pseudo-listening. When asked why they mentally checked out, they frequently respond that they didn't have anything to add or that they didn't know enough about the subject to make a contribution. This is all well and good, except that people notice when members drop out, even if they don't say anything at the moment, and the team is no longer a team. Managers, too, observe when you drop out of the process, often making mental notes of who furthers goal attainment and who hinders it via lack of participation. These observations are later used as a basis for making decisions about assignments, promotions, and training opportunities.

To be perceived as an effective team player, you must decide which role you can fill to help the team move forward. Think of yourself as a facilitator, not simply an individual contributor. Even when team meetings have a designated leader, you can help the team meet its goals by observing the process and filling in missing roles. For example, if it seems the team is becoming increasingly frustrated with its inability to overcome an impasse, you can make an observation about the current climate of the group with a comment such as, "It looks as though we've reached an impasse. Let's take a minute to make sure everyone's point has been heard and understood." On the other hand, if team members are so concerned with hurting one another's feelings that decisions are being avoided, you can say something like, "It seems as though we're being very careful with one another. I'm wondering how we can make it safe enough to speak our minds without damaging any relationships."

The roles of facilitator, timekeeper, and scribe are especially good ones to play if you don't have the technical expertise required to add value to a team project or help solve a team problem. Don't wait for the formal leader of the team to take that role; he or she may not always be particularly adept at facilitating, and your intervention will be welcomed. If you're not quite comfortable with what may appear to be usurping authority, you can say, "Since this isn't my area of expertise, I'd like to volunteer to facilitate the discussion so that those of you with the knowledge can fully participate." Playing a group-building and maintenance role keeps you connected with the team's process, clarifies your involvement to anyone who may be observing your behavior, and allows you to help your team accomplish its goals.

People who successfully remain on their career tracks don't check out of meetings. They know they can always fill group-building and maintenance roles if the subject area isn't of interest to them or isn't their forte. For example, if you become lost in the technical aspects of some discussion, look around the room and watch what is happening with the team's dynamics. Become an observer of the event itself. Check to see whether anyone else appears confused as well. If so, you can always help the team by saying something like, "It seems to me that a number of us need more explanation before we can get on board." If an argument is taking place, act as mediator by interjecting, "Clearly, there's a difference of opinion. Let's see if we can reach a mutual agreement before our time is up."

Being able to build one-on-one relationships and working as part of a team are two of the most important things that you will do to assure career longevity. They'll never take the place of hard work and technical competence, but they will complement these two performance givens. If you tend to work independently, find ways to collaborate on team projects and make contributions to team meetings. Although the ability to work independently can be viewed as a strength, it must be balanced with adding value to your team and teammates.

Coaching Tips to Enhance Your Effectiveness as a Team Player

Put a check mark in the box of two or three coaching tips you commit to doing.

❑ **Stay involved in team meetings by consciously choosing the role you'll play.** If you're not a technical expert, offer to be the facilitator or the scribe. If you sense tension in the group, shift to being a mediator. Regardless of the role you choose, stay involved, be an active participant, and contribute to the outcome of team decisions.

❑ **Pay as close attention to the team's process as you do to achieving the task.** Periodically ask yourself, *What's going on in the room?* This will enable you to stay tuned in to the process. Are some people checking out because one person has hijacked the conversation? Do people appear fearful to speak up? Is there frustration over not moving forward at a faster pace? Commenting on what you observe allows the team to overcome unspoken barriers to success.

❑ **Notice and invite quieter or more reluctant members of the team to speak up.** This role is known as gatekeeping. It ensures that everyone's voice is heard before final decisions are made and the gate closes—which, in turn, can lead to getting new information on the table that might change perspectives or opinions. It demonstrates that you care about the opinions of *all* your colleagues, not just the more verbal ones.

❑ **Before team meetings adjourn, assure buy-in by asking whether everyone agrees with whatever decisions have been made.** Don't assume that silence equals consent or commitment. Many decisions have been sabotaged by team members who think they don't have to support an outcome because they didn't agree with it. If time runs out and no decision has been made, suggest that the issues be re-calendared for discussion at a future meeting.

❑ **Suggest that the last fifteen minutes of team meetings be used to talk about the team's process.** Routinely ask the group what could be done differently at the next meeting to make it more productive. Even if people don't respond the first time the question is asked, don't stop asking it. Eventually, team members will come to realize that this is an important ingredient for high-functioning teams.

❑ **When the meeting topic isn't immediately applicable to your present work, look for the opportunity to learn something new that may be useful to you later.** Fast-trackers aren't experts in solely their own fields; they also exhibit a natural curiosity about other areas that can help develop utility-player capabilities. Team meetings present the ideal opportunity to develop a broad business perspective, so ask questions and connect the dots.

❑ **Volunteer for projects that require you to work with at least two other people.** This is especially helpful if you spend the majority of your time running your own department or project. An entirely different skill set is required to be a valuable team member than to be a successful team leader, and you want management to see that you excel at *both*.

❑ **Be willing to acquiesce on the small stuff if it means the team will benefit.** It's easy for talented people to get stuck in the NIH (Not Invented Here) Syndrome. We come to truly believe our way of doing things is the right way. Even if the outcome isn't exactly what you had envisioned, allowing others to have control of the process increases their commitment to the product and buys you valuable goodwill that can be used later for something that's more important to you.

❑ **Exhibit patience with the brainstorming process.** Rather than seeing differences of opinion as obstacles, use them to reach well-rounded solutions to team problems. Encourage what one CEO describes as "noisy debate." If you tend to be conflict-averse or prefer to work in a linear fashion, this one will be hard, but building your muscle in this area will come in handy time and again throughout your career.

❑ **Circulate articles that you think may be of interest to teammates.** You can demonstrate your team consciousness by including others in your own learning process. If you've gone to a conference, summarize key takeaways or share handouts. At team meetings, mention books that made an impact on your work life or distribute articles of common interest. Even if they never read them, teammates and management will know that you've got the best interests of the team at heart.

❑ **Showcase the accomplishments of teammates as well as your own.** If you know that a colleague has achieved a particular milestone on a project, congratulate him or her in front of others. Similarly, when describing your own accomplishments, include the names of people who were particularly helpful to the outcome.

❑ **Share information freely without considering whether there is the need to know.** It's better to err on the side of sharing too much information than not enough. Let others decide what's valuable to them versus what might be just nice to know.

❑ **Celebrate team accomplishments with a small party, public recognition, time off, token gifts, et cetera.** They don't have to be elaborate or expensive—it's the recognition that counts. Read Bob Nelson's book *1001 Ways to Reward Employees* for ideas on how to do this.

❑ **Take a class in group dynamics.** NTL (National Training Laboratories) offers great courses to help you better understand how teams function and ways to maximize team efforts. Check out their Web site at http://ntl.org for more information and a listing of their workshops.

❑ **View other people's strengths as learning opportunities, not threats.** Ask a colleague who's good in an area that's a development one for you to help you identify resources that will allow you to grow. Also ask if he or she would be willing to review your work, act as a sounding board, or mentor you in this particular area.

SUCCESS STRATEGY 3

Capitalize on the Power of Perception

May you have a wonderful idea and
not be able to convince anyone of it.
Ancient Chinese curse

During the 2004 presidential election campaign, incumbent George W. Bush and hopeful John Kerry went toe-to-toe in a series of debates. The opinion of most people who watched the debates was that Bush lost the first one to Kerry. Bush seemed impatient, uncomfortable, and prone to undignified smirking and scowling. Kerry, on the other hand, stood ramrod-straight, controlled his body language, and gave clear and concise answers to the questions. In short, Kerry *looked and sounded* presidential. Winning the debate really had little to do with the *content* of either man's message—it had everything to do with *how* those messages were delivered. After some coaching, Bush returned for subsequent debates with a very different demeanor. He exhibited greater control over his nonverbal messages—the nervous smile, chewing on his lip, and impatient finger tapping were gone. His verbal messages were delivered with less hesitation and with more emphasis on the most important points. And as we all know, he went on to win the election.

Herein lies yet another factor that differentiates otherwise equally qualified people: *the power of perception.* There is a look and sound to success that is often difficult to define, but you know it when you see it. What you wear, how you sit in a meeting, how you stride into a room, the length of your sentences, how loudly you speak, and the gestures you use all contribute to others' assessments of you as a competent and confident professional. These differences demonstrate the significant part that image and communication play for actors on the corporate stage. Tom Henschel, president of Essential Communications, a Sherman Oaks, California, firm devoted to helping professionals develop powerful verbal and nonverbal communication skills, has found that in day-to-day communications the impression we make on others is based largely on how we *look and sound.* The chart on the opposite page reveals that, in fact, a full 90 percent of that impression is based on factors related to other than what we actually say.

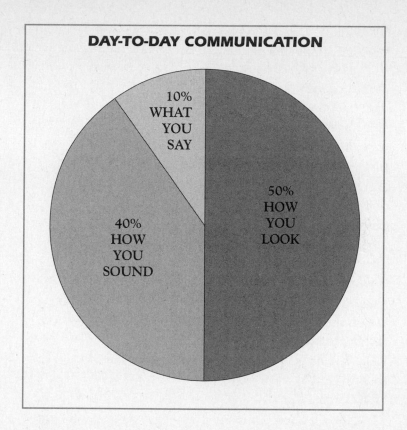

DAY-TO-DAY COMMUNICATION

10%
WHAT
YOU
SAY

50%
HOW
YOU
LOOK

40%
HOW
YOU
SOUND

Before reading farther, check off the items on page 110 with which you agree. This list will help you assess the degree to which you are aware of the importance of the image that you present and the manner in which you communicate.

IMAGE

Studies show that attractive people earn 5 to 10 percent more than average-looking people; attractive students get more attention and higher evaluations from their teachers;

_____ I know that image is important, so I take special care to dress in a manner consistent with my position.

_____ I think before I speak, taking care to express my message succinctly and effectively.

_____ I pay special attention to grooming: hair, nails, skin, makeup (women), facial hair (men), hands, teeth, and so on.

_____ My shoes are always shined.

_____ My body language suggests confidence and poise.

_____ I am no more than fifteen pounds over- or underweight.

_____ My clothes are always freshly pressed when I begin the day.

_____ I know what colors look best on me, and I use that to my advantage.

_____ I am practiced at making presentations in front of a group.

_____ I typically maintain my composure under pressure.

_____ My breath and body are free from unpleasant or offensive odors.

_____ I have no heavy regional accent that might detract from my message.

and good-looking patients get more personalized care from their doctors. But don't worry if you're not movie-star-handsome or model-beautiful. Attractiveness goes beyond just physical appearance, and many of us can do more with what we've been given than we currently are. Although our image does include physical attributes, some of which we can do nothing about, it also encompasses how we carry ourselves, what we wear, how we're groomed, the outward expression of our attitude, and our body language. The good news is, those are things you can develop and hone to work for you—beginning with how you dress.

A rule of thumb in business is that you should dress not for the job you *have*, but rather for the one you *want*. Look around your organization and make a mental note of what people the next level up from you are wearing. If you're in a manufacturing environment, you may need to look up several levels. Here is where you'll find your greatest insight into how you should look when you go to work. As much as you may not like it, your credibility is, in part, determined by the degree to which you look neat, crisp, professionally attired, and well groomed.

I can recall my mother preaching during my teens that I should always iron my clothes and look in the mirror twice before I went out. After all, she would warn, you never know who you're going to run into (and heaven forbid that I should be a bad reflection on my upbringing!). Arguments always ensued about what was more important—what's on the inside or the outside? Like many teenagers, I wanted my identity to be based on who I was, not what I was wearing. Many adults today continue to cling to that teenage opinion. They think that what's inside will supersede what's outside. All these years later I realize Mom was right. We are judged on our appearance first, and on who we are second—if, that is, we're fortunate enough to have a second chance. Many times we never have that opportunity because we're written off with just a first glance.

With the advent of what's known as workplace-casual, it has become increasingly difficult to know what's appropriate and what's not. This is particularly true for women. Whereas men have fairly well-defined formal (suit and tie) and informal (Dockers and a three-button Polo shirt) corporate "uniforms," the same can't be said for women. As hard as it may be for some younger workers to imagine, it's only been about a decade or so since pants became commonplace for women in the workplace. Keeping in mind that I coach people how to distinguish themselves from others so that they can achieve their career goals, my advice to you is to *always dress just a little better than everyone around you.* It's a small price to pay, and it doesn't mean you come in wearing a three-piece suit or a designer dress when the norm in your organization is jeans and a T-shirt. It does mean that you may forgo those jeans for a better pair of slacks or that T-shirt for a casual cashmere sweater. Similarly, if you want to dress to impress, sneakers, sandals, belly shirts, tight clothing, visible body piercing (with the exception of an earring or two), and anything with holes won't do it.

This topic arose during a casual conversation with a friend who is the director of nursing at a hospital in the Los Angeles area. I commented that the professionalism of nursing seems to have declined since the requirement that staff members wear uniforms was dropped. Her response, and one with which I agree, is that it's tough to get this generation of employees to conform to established standards of dress; moreover, she'd rather have a qualified and competent employee than one who is simply willing to wear a white uniform. But the answer isn't that simple. We are always affected by others' perceptions of us. As I so often tell my clients, *perception is reality.*

People will make assumptions about our competence based on how we look. When a nurse wearing a pair of jeans and a wrinkled blouse appears at my bedside, I will most likely make the initial judgment that she is less competent than someone wearing a starched white uniform. Is this perception true? Is one nurse really more competent than the other? Of course not. Your image only gets you in the door. As with all of the coaching hints contained in this book, being concerned about your image is meaningless unless you back it up with the goods—capable performance. It makes a lot more sense, however, to start the interaction, whether it's one between a nurse and a patient, an interviewer and a candidate, or a salesclerk and a customer, with a leg up. Remember the old adage: *You sell the sizzle, not the steak.*

Let me give you a real-time example here. George was an accounting manager in a small division of a major apparel manufacturer. He grew up in a Pennsylvania coal-mining town. He was a son of working-class parents, and the oldest of eight children. His father was the union steward of his mine. Always small for his age, George grew up knowing how to take care of himself with both his fists and his tongue. He could be described as scrappy. He put himself through college at night while working days in a coal mine and, at the same time, raising his own family.

George used to go to work casually dressed in slacks and a short-sleeved shirt—certainly a step up from his mining days. His favorite shoes were a pair of worn black soft-sole loafers—the kind that you can't polish (which he obviously didn't care to try). His gray hair was wiry and often unkempt. On the intellectual side, the guy was brilliant. He was, without a doubt, the most technically competent manager in his division, but a bit of a rebel. He didn't seem to care how others dressed, he didn't need to be like them, and he didn't care about what they thought of him. He knew that he knew his stuff.

When the brass from corporate visited the plant, however, they often ignored George's remarks at meetings and overlooked his valuable suggestions for how to improve bottom-line profits. No matter what he said or how he said it, he couldn't get them to take him seriously. He became increasingly frustrated, belligerent, and intolerant of others. He knew that what he was saying made sense, but he couldn't get anyone to listen to him.

One day, after a trip to the corporate offices, George appeared at the office in a navy-blue suit, red power tie, well-shined black leather shoes, and neatly styled hair. He looked ten years younger and every bit the executive that he was. It was interesting to watch his staff interact with him. Although George had not fundamentally changed who he was, others treated him with more respect and deference. After a while, George actually started to act differently. Always a bit brash and too quick to speak in the past, he now weighed his words carefully and took care not to step on too many toes. He gave new meaning to the saying *Clothes make the man.* Within two years, George had been promoted out of his small division and into the corporate accounting office. Within five years, he was named vice president of one of the company's up-and-coming divisions.

George is a terrific example of someone who stopped sabotaging his career by over-relying on two of his greatest strengths: technical expertise and staunch independence. No one knows who or what persuaded George to change his dress, and ultimately his behavior, but doing so helped him remain on his successful career path. Just as co-workers judged George, people judge us every day by how we look. Before we even open our mouths, people have made a mental judgment about us based on how we are dressed, how we carry ourselves, and the demeanor with which we present ourselves. Within thirty seconds, a first impression is formed, so you'd better make that the best impression possible—it can make the difference in someone giving you the edge or simply dismissing you.

Exceptions to the Dress-for-Success Rule

There's a well-known, highly respected company—which prefers not to see its name in print—that I've done consulting with for nearly twenty years. During that time, I've established my credibility, and people typically take to heart whatever advice or counsel I provide to them. But when it came to advice about how to dress for success in their culture (essentially the same advice I provided above), I always got push-back. People would point to one woman, whom I'll call Liz, who didn't fit the pattern. Because she was director of human resources, many people knew her and interacted with her on a regular basis. In fact, I communicated with Liz regularly myself—she was the person who typically referred employees to me for coaching. So I knew that Liz's dress did not conform to the company's conservative dress code. She liked to wear very tight clothes and short skirts that, combined with open-toed shoes and heavy makeup, made her look—it has to be said—like a hooker. Despite this, her technical capability and institutional memory caused her to be very well respected by management, and she wielded quite a bit of influence. When anyone mentioned Liz as I was offering tips for dressing to impress, I'd always note that she was an exception to the rule; most people would not get away with that kind of appearance in this company or any other one.

After about fifteen years working with this company, and with Liz, she called and said, "Lois, I've got another referral for you. This time it's me." I listened as she described some feedback she'd received about her appearance—which in fact was why she wasn't being considered for a promotion that she'd thought was in the bag. It took many years for her dress to catch up with her, but it did catch up. Who knows how much sooner she could have achieved her career goals if someone had given her the same feedback earlier in her career?

If you think this isn't right, or that's not how you judge others, think again. We are all guilty of doing the same thing. Have you walked up to a particularly well-dressed person in a department store and asked for help, only to be told that he didn't work there? Or have you made an assumption about someone's intelligence based on her appearance, only to find you were totally off base? Who among us, if we saw scientist and author Stephen Hawking—who is disfigured and wheelchair-bound because of his disabilities—would think that he is one of the most brilliant individuals on the face of the earth? This is the same difficult phenomenon that so many people with visible disabilities encounter. Hawking's phenomenal intellectual ability, however, is enough to eclipse his looks. Most of us don't possess such extraordinary talent, and assumptions are made based on very little information. This is why it's so important to leverage image so that the first impression is at worst a neutral one and at best a positive one.

When Less Is More

Is it possible to pay too much attention to your looks and look too good? *Yes!* On a continuum from one to ten, with one being slovenly and ten being glamorous, your appearance should probably be around a seven or eight. Going to work is not going out on a date. Women tend to have more difficulty with this particular problem than men, although I've seen extraordinarily handsome men encounter similar problems.

There is a fine line between well dressed and provocative. Cologne or perfume should be kept to a minimum. Jewelry is meant to complement an outfit. Even though Madison Avenue may dictate pant styles, skirt lengths, or garish colors, it's better to be safe than sorry in most businesses (the fashion and entertainment industries may be the exceptions). Take a moderate approach. One woman executive says that after she's finished dressing in the morning, she stands with her back to the mirror, then quickly swings around. If any one thing stands out, she removes it.

Both men and women who are blessed with outstanding looks can be thought of as dumb blonds. One businessman whom I coached, Jeff, could be described as drop-dead gorgeous. He had a George Hamilton tan, was blond, trim, and impeccably groomed. He could easily pass for a model. During the course of our coaching, Jeff revealed that as a teenager he was the classic ninety-pound weakling. Years of working out and special attention to his looks had transformed this fellow into an Adonis. He admitted that he was obsessed with his looks and never left the house without being the picture of perfection.

Jeff's good looks, combined with native intelligence,

landed him in his career as a sales representative for a pharmaceutical firm. His problem was that people didn't take him seriously. They couldn't get past his looks. His colleagues tended to feel somewhat inferior in his presence and sabotaged his efforts by withholding essential information and upstaging him at sales conferences. His defense mechanism for overcoming childhood trauma was getting in his way. My coaching efforts thus focused extensively on getting Jeff to grow into his adult role and not act out of childhood pain. At the same time, I gave him several suggestions for downplaying his looks in ways that would immediately change how others perceived him: trade in his colored contacts for a pair of glasses; wear plain, inexpensive ties instead of bold ones that demanded attention; let his hair grow slightly longer and out of its precision cut; and exchange manicures for doing his nails himself.

It wasn't easy for him, but Jeff's desire to remain professionally competitive gave him the courage to look different. A secondary gain for Jeff from the change in physical appearance was that he no longer needed to be a perfectionist in other ways. He tended to be less cautious in his choice of words and acted more like one of the guys. Within several months, Jeff found people responding to his messages rather than to him as the messenger, and his relationships with his peers began to improve. More important, Jeff felt better about himself.

Like many people who are coached, Jeff was fearful that he would lose his entire identity if he did anything different. In reality, however, coaching, or self-coaching, is about moving from out of bounds back onto the playing field. It is not about terminating behavior, but rather about turning down the volume on those behaviors that are putting you out of bounds. It is about building complementary skills or behaviors.

And a Few Tips for Petite and Youthful-Looking Women

I am often approached by petite women and asked how they can be taken more seriously or not treated like little girls. This is particularly a problem for Asian women who, as a group, tend to be smaller than the average American woman. Of course it can be a problem for men of smaller stature as well, but I've never had a man come up and ask me how he can compensate for it. So guys, if you get some helpful ideas from this section—we'll just keep it between us.

Being small doesn't have to be an impediment to success. Civil rights activist Rosa Parks, television anchor Katie Couric, and former Secretary of State Madeleine Albright are all wonderful examples of small women with big personalities. I was at an event honoring Barbara Walters and found myself standing next to her in the hotel lobby. It struck me how petite she was. Another good example of a small woman creating a larger-than-life image.

If you're a small or youthful-looking woman who wants to craft a large personality, here are some tips to consider:

- Wear makeup. Not wearing makeup tends to make you look more youthful.
- Wear dark-colored, tailored clothing. Avoid long skirts, flowing blouses, and pastels. They will only contribute further to the appearance of "small."
- Wear heels, not flats. You don't have to wear uncomfortable spike heels, but a little height coming from your shoe won't hurt you.

- Wear glasses. They tend to add a few years to your age.
- Avoid inappropriate smiling. Many small and youthful-looking women unconsciously use a smile to disarm or charm others. It backfires when you're trying to establish yourself as an expert or a professional to be taken seriously.
- If you tend to be soft-spoken, speak more loudly. It will result in getting and keeping people's attention.
- When appropriate, stand to make your point while others are seated. You can do this naturally by stepping up to a whiteboard or flip chart to write down a key point.
- Don't touch or flip your hair, put on lipstick in public, or keep food on your desk. They all unnecessarily emphasize your femininity and youthfulness.

WHAT DOES YOUR BODY LANGUAGE SAY ABOUT YOU?

Another aspect of image is body language. Australians Barbara Pease and Allan Pease wrote a book I highly recommend, *The Definitive Book of Body Language*. What I like so much about this book is how it helps you not only read the nonverbal messages of others but also use your own body language to communicate more effectively. Because the authors do such a thorough job of exploring the subject, I'm not even going to try to reinvent the wheel by going into great detail. Instead, I want to focus on the three most important areas of which you should be aware: face, hands, and posture. Combined, these can shout that you are fearful and insecure—or that you're comfortable and confident.

Former Secretary of State Colin Powell provides an outstanding example of someone who puts these three factors together effectively. When I watch him in interviews, I'm always impressed with how comfortable he seems with himself, the interviewer, and the world in general. When I analyze what gives me this impression, it comes down to how he looks and sounds (the latter I'll save for a bit later in this chapter). These factors all boil down further to face, hands, and posture. When seated, Powell typically has his hands loosely interlocked in his lap, moves them to gesture, then casually returns them to the original position. If you watch him during an interview, he does this countless times, and it gives the impression of comfortable professionalism. Contrast this with someone who fidgets with a pen, tightly clings to the sides of a chair, or is nervously drumming fingers. The message somehow just isn't the same.

When Powell listens to an interviewer's questions, his eyes stay on the reporter, his head nods with understanding, and he sits upright, but not rigid, in his chair. With the toughest of questions, Powell remains the same, never shifting in discomfort or wincing at the deep probes. He smiles when appropriate and doesn't when he wants to convey a more serious message. Whether he's been trained to do all this or it comes naturally to him doesn't really matter. The effect is that Powell provides a model of confidence and ease with himself and others.

Smiling presents a unique problem for women and people of certain cultures. In my workshop Leadership Skills for Women, a petite woman engineer working for a major airline proclaimed that no one ever took her seriously, and she said it with a big smile on her face. Everyone in the room laughed because they could immediately see the problem.

Smiles should be used to communicate happiness, levity, or joking, not serious messages. The smile totally diminished the serious nature of the woman's message. Unfortunately, women frequently use smiling as a means of softening their messages to avoid appearing too strong. Most women could smile less, choose the times when they smile more carefully, and avoid using a smile to ward off criticism.

Expressing emotions, in general, tends to be easier for women than for men. By nature and nurture, women have a broad repertoire of emotions from which to draw, and they use these fluidly—sometimes too fluidly, which can detract from their professional image. Men, on the other hand, tend to be more stoic and limit their range of emotional expression.

Paradoxically, smiling can be used as a valuable tool for both men and women. It increases your likability quotient and makes you more approachable. If you lean toward smiling when you're uncomfortable or nervous, remember that in fact it has just the opposite effect—so be careful. Not too long ago, I coached a man who received feedback that the intensity with which he delivered his messages frequently overwhelmed his colleagues. He was tall, assertive, smart, and always on target, but people were intimidated by him and wouldn't respond when he asked for their opinions. I knew that he'd recently become a father, so I used this to get across an important coaching point.

When I asked him how he talked to his child, a big smile came to his face with a softness that warmed my heart. When I suggested that he think about the child when speaking with his colleagues, he looked at me incredulously. Certainly I couldn't be serious. He thought that people would perceive him as being too soft, but nothing could be farther from the truth. His other characteristics overshadowed this slight change in facial expression. This is another example of how adding to your repertoire of skills, rather than taking something away, can create just the right balance. With this change, and some other coaching hints that he practiced, he began to be seen as more approachable and easier to talk to.

Posture is yet another means by which we reveal our self-esteem. How many times have you seen someone in a meeting slouched down in a chair or hunched over the table, leaning on one elbow? Or statuesque women who walk a bit hunched over so as not to appear too tall? Although rigidity is not the order of the day, good posture conveys the message *I am someone to be contended with.* Your posture increases the perception of credibility and confidence before you ever open your mouth.

One last suggestion about how you look. When standing in front of a room making a presentation or being introduced, people often appear uncomfortable largely because they don't know what to do with their hands. They put them in their pockets, fold them in front like a fig leaf, or clasp them behind their backs—all the while looking none too comfortable. Next time you're in this situation, try interlacing your fingers loosely at about the same height you would hold a glass while standing at a cocktail party. Similarly, when gesturing in front of groups, hands should be kept at about the same height and moved no wider apart than if you were holding a basketball. The exception is speaking before large groups, where more pronounced gestures are required and would not likely detract from the message.

COMMUNICATION

There's a relatively new phrase that's entered the business lexicon: *He drank the Kool-Aid*. It refers to someone who hook, line, and sinker bought into the latest management guru's or senior executive's philosophy. It stems from the macabre events in Jonestown, Guyana, where more than nine hundred members of the People's Temple followed leader Jim Jones to their deaths by drinking Flavor Aid laced with poison. Have you ever wondered how despicable people like Jones, Adolf Hitler, Slobodan Milošević, and Saddam Hussein got people to commit such heinous acts at their urging? At first thought, you may say they used their positions of power to coerce others to perform these atrocities, but that doesn't quite answer the question. There are many people with power positions who fail to influence their followers. Influential people share the ability to communicate their messages with confidence, clarity, and credibility. Their delivery of the message shapes the impression of the listener—perhaps more so than the message itself.

Communication is made up of a number of components: accent or dialect, thought patterns as expressed in speech, and the actual sound of the speech itself. Each contributes to the overall impression of knowledge and credibility. Remember the pie chart at the beginning of this chapter: 50 percent of the impressions others have of you is based on how you look, and 40 percent on how you sound. Only 10 percent is based on what you actually say.

Accents and Dialects

The issue of accents and dialects is a sensitive one that needs to be considered in light of our rich heritage as a melting pot, welcoming of people from all nations and backgrounds. Although some may find it offensive or inappropriate for discussion here, a good coach has the courage to speak the unspoken. Therefore, I would find it an unconscionable error of omission on my part to avoid a discussion about accents and dialects just because some readers might find it uncomfortable. My job is to point out the reality—yours is to decide what to do about it.

As the complexion of society changes, both literally and figuratively, so do impressions about expecting others to look and sound the same in the microcosm called work. If the stereotypes of fifty years ago prevailed, the workforce would still be predominantly white and male. Similarly, if we continue to perpetuate the stereotype of how people should *sound* in the workplace, everyone would be accentless—sounding somewhat like newscasters who are hired partly for their ability to speak without an accent. The goal of this discussion is not to encourage homogeneity, but rather to illuminate the ways in which strong accents and dialects can subtly sabotage a career.

As a Jewish woman, I am all too aware of the fact that what appear to be legitimate workplace expectations can be guises for prejudice and discrimination. Likewise, I know that I must constantly be vigilant about crossing the line between expressing my individuality and being heard and seen in the most favorable light possible so that I can achieve my professional goals. Just as I wouldn't wear blue jeans to a meeting with a client, in that same meeting I wouldn't use the Yiddish jargon that I learned growing up. On the other hand, even if it might in some way damage my career, I wouldn't hesitate to decline an invitation to a private club from which women or people of color are excluded. The ultimate goal is to increase your likelihood of success by playing the corporate game within commonly accepted bounds but *without compromising your principles or ethical standards*. I don't believe a discussion of the impact of accents in the workplace falls into this category.

There are numerous examples of successful people who have strong accents. As the United States continues to establish multinational firms, those numbers will increase and bring with them greater tolerance for other-than-newscaster accents. I simply ask you to consider how your accent or dialect might be perceived by others. Can you be clearly understood? Do you use phrases or jargon that are acceptable in your neighborhood but not commonly used by your workplace peers? Does your accent diminish your self-confidence when speaking before groups or at meetings? Do you feel as if your vocabulary is not sufficient for fluid conversation?

If you answer yes to any of these questions, or if you believe that your manner of speaking has impeded your progress, then you may want to consider doing something about it. Accent-reduction schools and elocution classes are available in most major cities. Conversely, if you believe it is too great a compromise to refrain from using certain jargon or to reduce your accent, don't do it. Like all of the other suggestions contained in this book, it's one more factor to consider in your effort to remain on your career path.

Henry was on the verge of veering off his career path but didn't have a clue why. Neither did his boss. She asked me to coach him, saying his career was stalled despite the fact that he was a good, solid performer. Higher-ups in the European shipping company where he worked began asking that Henry be excluded from certain meetings, particularly those at which clients were present. No matter how hard she tried to find out what the problem was, people were never forthcoming with an answer.

My first meeting with Henry took place in his office in Miami Beach. When his secretary ushered me in, Henry stood and extended his hand to greet me. He was well dressed, neatly groomed, and had an engaging smile. So far, so good. When he began to speak, however, the problem became readily apparent: Henry spoke with a very thick Cuban accent. He also spoke quickly and in long rambling sentences so that it was difficult to understand him and follow his train of thought. Several times during the conversation, I had to ask him to slow down or repeat himself.

We then proceeded to a nearby upscale restaurant for lunch. People appeared to know Henry and greeted him with friendly waves. Another point in his favor, I noted. He knew how to build relationships. Over lunch I listened to Henry talk about his career, how he got to where he was, what he thought might be the problem, and how he was now working harder than ever in the hope of turning the situation around. As I observed his behavior while he ate, I had to call strike two. He began by tucking the linen napkin into his collar, then breaking and buttering a crusty roll before the bread plates were on the table, making an awful mess in the process. During the meal, he talked with his mouth full of food, unaware of how it might appear to others. At one point, he even pulled out a pen and drew a diagram on the linen tablecloth to illustrate a point he was making.

Over the course of several coaching sessions, I learned more about Henry. He was from a poor family who emigrated from Cuba in the 1950s. His parents believed in education and worked hard to make certain that their son could go to college. He was the superstar of the family, the only one to have a blossoming career. In turn, he worked long, hard hours to get where he was and to feel worthy of the efforts his parents had made on his behalf. He truly believed that working harder, turning up the volume on what he did best, was the answer to his problems.

Between sessions, I spoke with Henry's boss to determine whether my assessment that productivity was not the problem was in fact true. She confirmed my hunch that he was always willing to go the extra mile—producing what was expected of him and more. Why, I wondered, was no one willing to tell him that his accent, rambling monologues, and table manners were problematic in his organization's culture? Speaking with his boss a bit longer, I found out that Henry had worked for her at her previous job as well. In total, they had worked together for nearly twenty years. She was so accustomed to him and his habits that she'd never noticed he had reached a stage in his career where they were no longer acceptable. She was too close to the situation. As for the higher-ups, they probably were too embarrassed or fearful of being called elitist to help Henry to get into the boundaries of the playing field.

It is one of the tougher jobs of a coach to talk about personal behaviors such as accents, table manners, and body odors. Believe me, it's a lot easier to suggest you build more relationships than to go into these touchy areas. Nevertheless, I did coach Henry in the areas that were contributing to his career plateauing, and he responded immediately. He enrolled in an accent-reduction class, followed my instructions for table manners, and took care to speak in shorter, better-defined sentences. Unfortunately, his unenlightened senior management wouldn't give him a second chance and directed his boss to fire Henry, which she did with great personal anguish. The coaching was not wasted, however. When individuals are *freed up to find new opportunities* (fired), they often go on to find positions better suited for them. Such was the case for Henry. He is now back on his career track in an organization that highly values his abilities and appreciates his efforts. Without the coaching, he might have found himself in the same situation over and over again until he overcame his perceived weaknesses.

Thought Patterns

As in Henry's case, the ability to speak cogently and concisely contributes to others' perception of us as professional, confident, and competent. Except in unusual circumstances when the speaker or material being conveyed is extraordinarily compelling, people can listen to and comprehend only relatively brief, clearly ordered messages. Countless great ideas are lost entirely when the speaker rambles on long after his or her point has been made. In a recent episode of the HBO series *The Sopranos*, mob boss Tony looks at one of his "family" members and implores him to get to the point already. In videotaping workplace interactions, I see the exact same thing. The speaker makes a point, then explains it, makes the point again using slightly different words, and explains it once more. As the camera pans the room, it reveals undeniably bored, uninterested faces straining to listen politely until the speaker has finished.

The person who rambles loses his or her audience. Although both men and women suffer from this career malady, women tend to use more words and be more indirect in their responses than men. It's as if they're given a quota of words to use at the beginning of the day, and they're not going to stop talking until they've used it up. The result? They appear unsure of themselves and fail to convey complete messages because others tune out before they're finished. Returning to Colin Powell for a moment, it's clear that his credibility is in part due to his speech patterns. Each time he is asked a direct question, he directly answers it using clear, succinct sentences. If he doesn't have an answer, he doesn't fake it. He simply says he doesn't know.

Here is an example of how disorganized thought patterns ineffectively convey the message, lose the listener's interest, and diminish the speaker's credibility in the process:

Boss: *Do you think we should change our marketing strategy next year?*

Employee: *Well, that's a good question. I guess there are a number of different ways of looking at it. If we were to continue along the same path we're on, that is if we were to not make any changes that might upset the apple cart, it's possible, maybe we might—that is, some people think that we're going along the right path now and with a few minor variations could, well, there's a chance that the numbers might increase a bit over last year's sales, but I'm not really sure myself. It seems to me that we've changed the strategy a number of times in the past year or two, well, actually maybe five years, and in most cases, with a few exceptions, the results were average, so you could say they were effective, but nothing really spectacular happened. On the other hand, take a look at what our competitors have done for the past few years and looks like they're marginally edging us out. Of course, there's ABC Company, which did a lot worse than we did, but that's only because* *they sold off one of their cash cows. So I guess it might be worth a try to.*

Even writing this script was painful, let alone listening to it! Yet it's not so far from how people answer questions every day in corporate America. The major mistakes made by the speaker include:

- Failure to express a point of view.
- Soft word choices—*maybe, I guess, we might.*
- Rambling thought process.
- Incomplete sentences and ideas.
- Too much playing devil's advocate.

Let's replay the same scenario, this time using a more Powell-esque approach:

Boss: *Do you think we should change our marketing strategy next year?*

Employee: [Pause to think] *Definitely not. Our current strategy has been in place for less than a year and is already yielding very promising results. There's been a ten percent increase in sales despite a sluggish market, which forecasts well for next year when the market is expected to pick up.*

Who seems more credible to you—the first or second employee? In fewer than fifty words, the second employee clearly communicated an opinion as well as provided a rationale for it. Henry was coached to do the same thing with four **Pretty Darn Simple Steps:**

- **Pause a moment to collect your thoughts.** Don't answer immediately. A second or two may seem like an eternity, but it conveys thoughtfulness, not hesitance, when combined with the next three steps.
- **Directly answer the question asked.** Avoid the tendency to give background data at this point—it only precludes you from getting to the point soon enough for the listener.
- **Support your answer with two to three pieces of data** or facts. Most people can only take in this much data, so don't feel as if you have to tell the listener everything you know.
- **Stop.** If you have difficulty putting a period on the end of your sentence or aren't getting signals that your point was understood, ask, "Do you have any questions?" or "Did I answer your question?"

Getting and Keeping Audience Attention

According to Shakespeare, all the world's a stage, and we humans are merely players. The workplace can be considered just another set and scene. You already wear the costume; now you need to learn how to deliver your lines so the audience responds the way you hope. For most people, the anticipation of making a presentation, be it to a group of five people or fifty, engenders a sense of fear second only to that of dying. Yet we present ourselves and our ideas all the time. The next time you have to give a public speech, think of it the way actors do—as an opportunity to create a special way of sending a message and make a lasting, and positive, impression.

The following are a few simple coaching hints to help you become an influential player on the corporate stage.

• **Never give a presentation you haven't prepared—and remember, every time you open your mouth, it's a presentation.** The saying *Chance favors the prepared mind* is never more true than when you're trying to influence an individual or group. Unless you are one of the few gifted people who can speak effectively extemporaneously, you've got to think about what you're going to say before you say it. If you're responding to a casual question, that thought process may take only a few seconds. If you're speaking before an audience of any size, you can't afford to wait until the day of your presentation to prepare. Even if you only jot down a few notes on index cards, you're more likely to remember the key points and avoid aimless rambling. When planning on speaking to a few people, mentally rehearse what you plan to say, picture people listening attentively to you, and know when to stop.

• **Use the Headline Model to script your presentation.** The Headline Model—which I'll discuss in a moment—will help you avoid long monologues, focus on your most important point, and remember just two to three pieces of supporting information.

• **Use breathing and pace to alter pitch.** If your voice unnaturally goes up several octaves the moment you open your mouth in front of a room full of people or the spotlight shifts to you during a meeting, try taking a deep breath and speaking a bit more slowly. As you slow your speech, your voice tends to drop as well.

• **Use short words.** You don't want to be in the same category as Norm Crosby, the master of malapropisms. Giving a presentation is not the time to impress others with your command of the English language by using long, obscure words. Not only is your audience likely to think it pretentious, but you're more likely to forget or mispronounce them as well. Don't feel compelled to use a dollar word when a quarter one will do. It's easier for the listeners to process the message, it doesn't challenge them, and you tend to enunciate shorter words clearly.

• **Use body English.** Don't forget the importance of body language. Good posture, direct eye contact, eyebrows up or down, and other subtle gestures combine to give the impression of confidence and credibility.

• **Use a camcorder to practice important presentations.** Here's a place to make good use of the family video camera. Videotape yourself practicing a presentation. Critically assess what you can do to be more effective, and don't be afraid to ask the family for feedback. Sometimes they'll give you better coaching hints than anyone else!

Like it or not, the image that we portray and the communication style that we use are the first two things that others notice about us—and they contribute significantly to the impression we make. Fortunately, they are also two of the simpler factors to address when considering how to develop a game plan that help you get noticed for all the right reasons. Think of them as tools that you can use to your advantage. Develop your own unique style, but fine-tune that style so that it works for you rather than against you.

Tom Henschel uses a model he calls Headline Communication. Not only do I use it myself, but I think it's so valuable that I regularly include it in my coaching with most clients. The premise is simple: *The first thing that comes out of your mouth has to be the key message you want people to take away.* The following diagram shows you how to mentally script your message in advance.

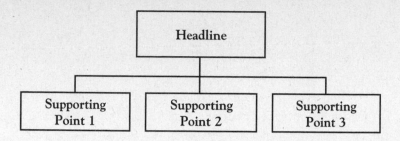

Whether it's a question you're asked or an opinion you want to offer, you'll be considered more credible if you format your communication using this model. Here's how it works. Let's say you're in a meeting where the question is posed, "What's the most important thing we need to do in the next sixty days to overcome the obstacles we're currently facing in the area of product delivery?" This may be the opening you were looking for to get some of your ideas on the table, so the answer could be on the tip of your tongue. Nonetheless, before you open your mouth, think about the first headline you want others to hear, and then two to three reasons why you believe this. Once you get used to using the model, it will take you only seconds to formulate your thoughts. Then you can respond with something like this:

Headline		
The most important thing we can do is decrease delivery time while increasing product quality. There are three ways to do this:		

Supporting Point 1	Supporting Point 2	Supporting Point 3
First, we should analyze returns and address those problems that appear repeatedly.	Next, we need to consider outsourcing deliveries to locations more than a hundred miles from our manufacturing plant. Given our current staff, we can't guarantee timely delivery.	Finally, we should consider an incentive program that rewards employees for simultaneously reducing errors and delivery time.

Putting your thoughts into this format does something else—it lets *you* know when you've completed your message and gives you the cue to stop talking. If you're not sure you've gotten your point across, don't continue to talk. Instead, ask something like, "Have I answered your question?" or "What do you think?" This allows others to ask you for further explanation if needed. If so, go back to the model to answer any resulting questions.

Communicating in headlines isn't as difficult as it might initially seem, but it does require forethought. To be influential regardless of the arena, be certain *before* you begin speaking that you've identified the most important thing you want people to take away from your message.

SEX AND CULTURAL DIFFERENCES IN COMMUNICATION

Most of us would agree that there are well-defined differences between how men and women communicate, but not too long ago I received a call that made me expand my thinking on this. It was from the Asian affinity group of a major US corporation asking me to address its national conference. In case you're not familiar with the term, *corporate affinity groups* have become increasingly popular in our country as a means of providing support to women and people of color. These groups hold seminars and educational activities designed to put members on an even footing with their Caucasian or male corporate counterparts. Someone in the group had read my book *Nice Girls Don't Get the Corner Office* and felt many of the tips it contained pertaining to communication were equally applicable to Asian Americans.

Having spent so much time in Asia conducting training and coaching for multinational corporations, I knew it was true that as a cultural group, Asians tend to communicate in ways we in the United States would consider stereotypically feminine—less direct, less assertive, and less transparent. As such, they often find themselves at a disadvantage when it comes to influencing with authority in *our* culture. When working with women and certain other cultures, I often use the chart opposite to illuminate communication differences.

At yet another keynote presentation, where there happened to be a large group of attendees from China and the Philippines, I was discussing these differences. At the end, an American man came up to me and said, "You know, it's not just women and people from other cultures who make the mistakes you talked about. I'm just not an aggressive kind of guy, and I often find my opinions being overlooked in favor of those from the alpha males." And that's the point. Effective communication in American business requires more than subtle innuendo and veiled expressions— whether you're a woman, Asian, or just a nice guy.

Here are five fatal errors and tips for avoiding them if you want to communicate with more impact.

Error 1. Asking Permission

Although this may appear on the surface to be fairly benign, it in fact puts you in a subservient position. In our society, we expect children to ask permission, not adults. When you ask permission, you set yourself up to hear "no."

Ineffective: *Would it be all right if I took next Wednesday off for my son's graduation?*

More effective: *Just wanted to tell you that I'll be out next Wednesday. If there's anything that needs to be done before then, let me know.*

(Stereotypical of Men and Western Cultures) High Self-Expression + Low Concern for Others = *Aggressive* *Appropriate in emergency situations.*	(The Best of Both Sexes and Cultures) High Self-Expression + High Concern for Others = *Assertive* *Appropriate in most situations.*
(A Small Percentage of People from All Cultures Are Guilty of This) Low Self-Expression + Low Concern for Others = *Passive-Aggressive* *Never appropriate.*	(Stereotypical of Women and Eastern Cultures) Low Self-Expression + High Concern for Others = *Passive* *Appropriate in high-risk situations.*

SELF-EXPRESSION (MASCULINE/WESTERN)

CONCERN FOR OTHERS
(FEMININE/EASTERN)

In the latter example, the speaker shows respect for the boss by informing him or her of what's going to happen, offering to make sure the work gets done, and assuming that if there is a problem the boss will say so. This very situation arose during a team building I conducted in the Midwest several years ago. The women in the group complained that they were expected to ask permission to exceed their monthly budgets while their male colleagues simply informed the boss of such an occurrence. To the boss's credit, he admitted that he did subconsciously expect women to ask permission and changed his expectations.

Error 2. Using Preambles

Using more words *always* softens a message; it does not strengthen it. Similarly, the longer you talk, the more you dilute an effective message and risk losing the attention of the listener. Regardless of why you use preambles, you must focus on communicating in more precise and "pithy" ways.

Less effective: *Would this be a good time to talk to you about something? Thanks. Well, I've been going over our accounts payable system. Did you know that this system was devised over fifteen years ago? That's an awfully long time to be using the same system. A friend of mine over at XYZ Company tells me that in the same time span they've revised their system four or five times. Ours is really antiquated. Well, maybe not antiquated, but certainly in need of looking at. Anyway, where was I? Oh, yeah, improving the accounts payable system. It would appear*

to me that one of the problems lies in how pay-
ables are logged when they arrive. We get so
many dunning notices and even wind up pay-
ing a lot in late fees because of it. Last month
alone we must have paid nearly five percent of
the total payables in late fees. I'm not really
sure why this happens, since we've got plenty
of people in the department working on it . . .

At this point the boss wants to scream, "What's your point?"—and rightly so. Far too many words were used before ever getting to the main point and, more important, the causes of and solutions to the problem. Managers want their staff members to solve problems, not create more. This speaker suffers from a serious case of the preambles.

More effective: *I need about five minutes of your time to discuss something important. There's clearly a problem in our accounts payable system. Bills are long overdue, and we're unnecessarily paying excessive late fees. I just wanted you to know that I'm working on a system to revise the current process, so if you have any ideas on shortening the payment cycle based on your experience, you might want to join our brainstorming session next Friday.*

Crisp. Clear. To the point. Within thirty seconds, the boss knows what the problem is, that it's going to be fixed, and that he or she is invited to be part of the process of solving the problem.

Error 3. Asking Questions Instead of Making Statements

This technique was invented (and probably by a woman) as a means of getting in your two cents without appearing too aggressive. In business, however, you leave yourself open to a critique of the idea rather than a discussion of its value when you couch your opinions in the form of questions.

Less effective: *What would you think about moving toward a smorgasbord approach to employee benefits?*

The savvy listener knows that this really is not a question but may nonetheless exploit the opportunity to engage in debate or even just disagree. It's clear that the speaker has an idea but doesn't feel confident enough to put it out as a statement.

More effective: *It seems to me it's time to move in a new direction with regard to employee benefits. I think the smorgasbord approach merits examination for the following three reasons . . .*

The second example states the case, provides backup data, and expects a discussion based on merit rather than on the whim or goodwill of the boss.

Error 4. Apologizing

Have you ever noticed that most Western men don't apologize? On rare occasions, they may admit they're wrong, but they don't accompany this with an apology. Your self-image is increasingly eroded with each apology.

Let's say a boss gives one of his direct reports a large

graphics project with very clear directions. She follows those directions to a T and presents him with the results before the deadline. He looks at the project and says it's not how he wants it. He proceeds to change the instructions and asks that it be redone.

Less effective: *I'm sorry, I didn't realize that's what you wanted. I'll redo it.*

Don't get me wrong. There's a time and a place for apologies. That time and place, however, is when a large, costly, or high-profile mistake is made. Even then, macho men are hard pressed to get the apology through their lips. Apologies are frequently inappropriate and demeaning.

More effective: *Let's nail down your requirements so I can complete the project to your satisfaction.*

This second statement recognizes the need to get it right, but it also puts the onus of making sure that happens on the person delegating the assignment.

Error 5. Explaining Ad Nauseam

This is the other end of the preamble. You've asked permission, couched your opinion in the form of a question, used a lot of words to get to the point (and perhaps apologized in the process)—and yet you feel the need to explain some more! Now, I must admit that this is not always your fault. Many times others will fail to use body language, such as head nods or verbal remarks, indicating that they've heard what's been said. This results in talking even more, because you assume you haven't been understood. You may explain your point two or three times, waiting for some acknowledgment of the message. A better approach, however, is to use the Headline Model to make your point only once. Let silence be a powerful tool in prodding the other person into responding; you are not responsible for the entire communication.

With very subtle modifications, you can shape others' impressions of your self-confidence and professionalism. Here are some more tips for putting more power behind your messages:

- **Make certain your handshake is firm.** The handshake can be the very first thing you use to convey the message, *I'm someone to be contended with.* Women have asked me if it's appropriate for them to extend their hand first. Absolutely! Being the first to extend your hand in greeting, combined with a firm handshake, communicates control and confidence. Use them to your advantage.
- **Dress appropriately.** *Dress for the job you want, not the job you have* remains your best guide for being taken seriously. It's better to err on the side of overdressing than underdressing in most situations.
- **Use *I* statements.** Don't be afraid to begin your sentences with *I*. Many of us learned in grade school to never start a sentence with *I* (because it sounds too egotistical), but that doesn't hold true in business. If you are giving your own opinion, then own it with statements such as *I believe, I contend, I would expect,* or *I feel strongly.*
- **Make direct eye contact.** Although you don't want to stare people down and make them uncomfortable by never averting your eyes from theirs, looking someone directly

in the eye when you're giving your opinion does add a certain amount of credibility to your message. When someone looks us in the eye, we typically believe he or she is speaking the truth.

- **Know your subject.** You've already heard it several times in this book: *Nothing takes the place of technical competence.* When you know your subject, you speak with a certainty that is impossible to convey when you're unsure. You can build a base of technical knowledge that adds to your confidence by getting a college degree, taking classes or workshops, reading technical journals, or networking with other professionals in your field.

- **Pepper your conversation with the other person's name.** When you want to get children to listen to you, you use their names when speaking to them. A similar tactic works equally well in business conversations. You don't want to sound like a used-car salesperson, but you do want to keep the other person's attention.

- **Make affirmative statements.** Instead of couching your comments in the form of questions, turn them into affirmative statements, beginning with an *I* message. Change *What would you think if we* to *I think that we should.* The latter conveys much more certainty and influence.

■

Coaching Tips to Improve Your Image and Communication Skills

Put a check mark in the box of two or three coaching tips you commit to doing.

❑ **Don't scrimp when it comes to spending money on work clothes.** Your rule of thumb should be dress for the job you want, not the job you have. Consider it an investment in your future. You don't have to wear Armani or Versace, but people do notice the difference between cheap and more expensive or fashionable clothing. Not only that, but you also feel better and act more confidently when wearing clothing that you're proud to be seen in. If budget is an issue, check out the many department stores or outlet malls that carry designer labels at a discount.

❑ **Never leave the house before looking in the mirror twice.** Make it a habit to scrutinize how you look from head to toe before walking out the door. If necessary, go back and change the one thing that looks out of place. And if you're color-blind or suffer from an absence of fashion sense, ask for help in purchasing and organizing clothes that will make you look and feel good.

❑ **Manicure your nails once a week.** Whether you do it yourself or have others do it for you, it's another one of those things people notice. Make sure your hands are as well groomed as the rest of you—and this holds true for men as well as women.

❑ **Get a good barber or hairdresser.** Too many people, both men and women, invest in their clothing but don't invest in ensuring that their hair—often the first thing others notice—looks its best. A skilled hairdresser can help you with color, length, and styles that will complement, not detract from, those expensive clothes.

❑ **Check the shine, heels, and soles of your shoes, especially before an important meeting.** Again, they're part of the overall package, so don't ignore the importance of wearing shoes that look fresh.

❑ **Use appropriate pacing and gestures to strengthen messages.** Simply speaking more loudly usually causes you to increase use of your hands and facial expressions. Don't be afraid to show some emotion when you're talking—it can have the effect of making your message more believable and easier to receive.

❑ **Read *Business Class: Etiquette Essentials for Success at Work* by Jacqueline Whitmore.** This book covers everything from what to do when dining out with colleagues or clients to how to mingle comfortably at a cocktail party.

❑ **Fix what you can.** If there's something in your appearance that you're so self-conscious about, it negatively affects your self-confidence, then have it colored, cut, plugged, removed, lifted, tucked, or otherwise surgically altered! I don't say this so that you'll run out and change everything about your appearance. Still, a little attention to cosmetics can go a long way toward shaping the impressions others have of you. Remember, the emphasis here is on changing those things that diminish your self-confidence.

❑ **Exercise regularly—it improves your physical health, stamina, self-image, and outlook.** Many executives will tell you that their daily workout contributes to their business success. Whether you do it to keep your weight in check or just to feel better, it's a habit that—along with following many of the other tips here—will make a difference in how you see yourself and how others perceive you.

❑ **Absent intervening medical factors, try to stay within ten to fifteen pounds of your ideal body weight.** As someone who has struggled with her weight for her entire life, I know how hard this is, and I can't say I always do it successfully. But when I'm feeling my most fit and at a weight that works for me, I know that I carry myself in a way that exudes self-confidence and credibility. Similarly, studies have shown that given a choice, employers will select candidates and give promotions to those who appear more physically fit.

❑ **Read *The Definitive Book of Body Language* by Barbara Pease and Allan Pease.** This book was an international best seller before being released in the United States. It provides practical advice for how you can communicate with confidence and control in any encounter.

❑ **Join Toastmasters International** (http://toastmasters .org). This is a group of businesspeople who meet regularly to discuss and practice issues related to presentation skills. There are chapters located throughout the world, most typically in downtown business districts. If there isn't one close to you, you can also start a chapter within your own company or organization. People who belong to Toastmasters report a significant increase in their comfort level and skill in speaking before groups— and I've seen it make a difference in the lives of many of my own clients. Even if you don't have occasion to do a lot of public speaking, participation can help you improve your verbal communication.

❑ **Take an acting or improvisation class to increase fluidity of expression.** I find these classes useful for those who have a rigidly defined style of communication and need a nontraditional way of breaking old habits. Don't toss this idea out too quickly—it will take you outside your comfort zone, but perhaps that's exactly where you need to be.

❑ **Use a firm, *I'm someone to be contended with* handshake.** Although men tend to do this more than women, there are people of both sexes who suffer from limp handshakes. And guys, don't assume your handshake should be any less firm with women than with men. Your handshake doesn't have to be bone crushing, but it should convey the message you're a person to be taken seriously.

❑ **Never give a presentation you haven't prepared for—and every time you open your mouth, it's a presentation.** With few exceptions, all your verbal communications should sound polished, clear, and concise. You can ensure that this will happen by mentally planning for what you're going to say before you say it using the Headline Model described in this chapter.

❑ **When using notes during a presentation, use index cards instead of sheets of paper.** First, the cards will be less conspicuous in the event that your hands begin to shake from nervousness. Second, the size of the cards will force you to summarize your thoughts and not be tempted to write out your entire presentation.

❑ **Use simple, easy-to-understand words.** People who use multisyllabic words to impress others often find that this has just the opposite effect: They wind up sounding pompous. If you're trying to show people you know your stuff, you'll be more successful if you keep your messages concise and easy to understand but filled with two to three critical data points.

❑ **Review voice-mail messages after you've recorded them.** Objectively assess how you would characterize the voice on the other end. If it's too long, if the volume is too low, or if the message in other ways doesn't reflect how you want to be received, erase it and start again. It's a great way to practice and get immediate feedback about how you sound to others.

❑ **Read the book *Speak Like a CEO: Secrets for Commanding Attention and Getting Results* by Suzanne Bates.** This is one of the most practical, useful, and reader-friendly books available on the topic of business communication. Bates provides tools and tips for everything from making PowerPoint presentations to making memorable points.

SUCCESS STRATEGY 4

Develop Your Emotional Intelligence and Likability Quotients

You can make more friends in two months by becoming interested in other people than you can in two years by trying to get other people interested in you.

Dale Carnegie

Q: What do three such diverse personalities as former Speaker of the House Newt Gingrich, business mogul Martha Stewart, and basketball coach Bobby Knight have in common?

A: Their careers misfired due to insufficient emotional intelligence.

Their stories provide a wealth of insight into the phenomenon we call the emotional intelligence quotient, or EQ:

• Gingrich not only served as Speaker of the House from 1995 through 1999, but is also considered largely responsible for ending forty straight years of a Democratic majority in the House of Representatives through his "Contract with America." His accomplishments were eclipsed, however, by what many considered arrogant and childish behavior. His illustrious career took a serious downward turn when he urged a Republican Congress to veto a budget, essentially causing parts of the government to shut down. He later admitted that he did so because he felt "snubbed" when President Clinton's staff asked him to leave *Air Force One* by a back door when the plane returned from Yitzhak Rabin's funeral. After later being accused of unethical behavior by Democrats and of being a polarizing force in his own party, Gingrich stepped down as Speaker and left the House entirely after the 1998 elections that left the Republican party in shambles.

• Martha Stewart worked hard, studied hard, honed her business skills, and eventually achieved the American Dream. Why, then, did the government so vigorously pursue her for allegedly selling ImClone stock on insider information, saving herself only forty-five thousand dollars? In the end, she wasn't even convicted of insider trading; she was convicted of conspiracy, obstruction of justice, and making false statements. I believe her ultimate undoing was not the sale of her stock, but rather the impression many had of her of being imperious, controlling, and condescending. Had she admitted from the outset that she "may have unwittingly made a mistake," it's likely she never would have seen the inside of prison. But instead, true to form, she was rigid in her denial of *any* wrongdoing and gave the impression of being recalcitrant. Whether or not she is any of the things people think she is really doesn't matter, because *perception is reality*.

• For twenty-nine years, basketball coach Bobby Knight was a fixture at Indiana University. He was indisputably a coach who knew how to win games, and was rewarded for his efforts by securing a place in the National

Basketball Hall of Fame in 1991, the very first year he was eligible. But he was equally known for volatile and boorish behavior, including kicking his own son during a game (for which he received a one-game suspension), verbally abusing players, and commenting to Connie Chung during an interview, "If rape is inevitable, relax and enjoy it." Many people believe this behavior was tolerated because he did win games. Others wondered how Indiana University could have condoned it for so long. Finally in April 2000, after nearly three decades, the university board of trustees conducted an investigation into Knight's inappropriate behavior, which resulted in a zero-tolerance policy toward him. Unable to control his emotions and outbursts, Knight was terminated in September of the same year.

It is abundantly clear that all three of these people are tremendously talented. Their ascents in their respective fields were nothing less than remarkable. But their careers became tarnished because they each lacked a fundamental level of *emotional intelligence*. If you're a student and observer of emotional intelligence, as I am, you could have predicted what was going to happen to each of them sooner or later. Most people simply cannot act in self-serving, arrogant, cavalier, volatile, or condescending ways and not have it eventually catch up with them.

I often use former Presidents Richard Nixon and Bill Clinton to contrast differences in the areas of emotional intelligence and likability. Nixon's historic fall from power was not due just to his political mistakes; it was due also to the fact that he lacked emotional intelligence and likability—qualities that Clinton possessed. Despite the fact that Clinton lied to the American people, allowed his wife to be embarrassed in her defense of him, and was impeached, he remained a revered political figure—at least among those who were supporters to begin with. In fact, if third terms of office were a possibility, he most likely would have been re-elected. For all his personal and political failings, Clinton not only was likable but also possessed enough emotional intelligence to be contrite.

A conversation I had with the managing director of an internationally recognized consulting firm underscores the importance of emotional intelligence in business. As we shared a drink in a bar in Aberdeen, Scotland, he mentioned that his highly competent, well-educated staff would soon need coaching and training on how to be less "technocratic." This firm has an impeccable reputation and has always prided itself on choosing the cream of the crop from the most prestigious business schools worldwide, so his remark came as somewhat of a surprise. When I probed into his sudden concern, he explained that his clients had begun complaining about the condescending and arrogant attitudes that his staff brought to their interactions. They were even in jeopardy of losing their biggest client because of it. Despite having some of the best analytical minds available, the customer didn't want to work with them.

If you are eccentric (but smart), difficult (but gifted), or an oddball (but a whiz), you've got some work to do if you want to remain on your forward-moving career path. You can't be competitive if you don't possess and exhibit emotional intelligence. Whereas IQ (intelligence quotient) defines the intelligence with which you were born, EQ (emotional intelligence quotient) defines what you do with it. It's considered the sine qua non for success. Although it's difficult to measure and describe, emotional intelligence is noticed and judged in nearly every interaction you will ever have with colleagues, customers, or management. You know when people have it and when they don't, but it may be hard for you to pinpoint.

DEFINING EMOTIONAL INTELLIGENCE AND LIKABILITY

Although Daniel Goleman is largely thought of as the father of emotional intelligence, many others have written about the topic. Dr. Jean Greaves and Dr. Travis Bradberry are the authors of a book I highly recommend, *The Emotional Intelligence Quick Book: Everything You Need to Know to Put Your EQ to Work*. One reason why I like their book so much is that it includes a password that allows you to go online and take an emotional intelligence test. The authors believe there are four key components to emotional intelligence:

- Self-awareness
- Social awareness
- Self-management
- Relationship management

These are then divided into two behaviors: personal competence and social competence. The following chart will help you to better understand the concept:

Self-Awareness The ability to accurately perceive your own emotions and stay aware of them as they happen. This includes keeping on top of how you tend to respond to specific situations and people.	**Self-Management** Your ability to use awareness of your emotions to stay flexible and positively direct your behavior. This means managing your emotional reactions to all situations and people.	**Personal Competence**
Social Awareness Your ability to accurately pick up on emotions in other people and understand what is really going on. This often means understanding what other people are thinking and feeling even if you don't feel the same way.	**Relationship Management** Your ability to use awareness of your own emotions and the emotions of others to manage interactions successfully. This ensures clear communication and effective handling of conflict.	**Social Competence**

Emotionally intelligent professionals exhibit self-confidence and insight into how they affect others—they relate to all kinds of people and make them feel easy being around them. They know that they don't have to control everyone and everything, strive to act with integrity at all times, treat others the way they would want to be treated, and act graciously even in the most difficult situations. The checklist on page 158 will help you assess your emotional intelligence quotient, or EQ.

Likability and emotional intelligence seem to go hand in hand. It's unusual to see someone with high emotional intelligence who isn't likable. But the converse isn't necessarily true. There are many highly likable people who don't possess high emotional intelligence. By all accounts, mass murderers Ted Bundy and Jeffrey Dahmer were pretty likable fellows when people initially encountered them—but they don't fit the definition of people who are also emotionally intelligent. Likability is a characteristic associated with many sociopaths and others with certain personality disorders, but it doesn't translate into emotional intelligence.

People with high likability quotients and high emotional intelligence include television hosts Katie Couric and Oprah Winfrey, movie moguls Ron Howard and Steven Spielberg, Ogilvy & Mather CEO Shelly Lazarus, former Paramount head Sherry Lansing, and British prime minister Tony Blair. They all pass the very scientific test we use in our office to determine likability called the *beer test*: people you might like to sit down and have a beer or a cup of coffee with. Although it's difficult to know how public figures act in private, these examples appear to share the common traits of a strong sense of self, commitment to a cause greater than themselves, and a fundamental respect for all those whom they encounter on life's path. It makes up what is frequently called *character*. Legendary basketball coach John Wooden once said, "Be more concerned with your character than with your reputation. Your character is what you really are, while your reputation is merely what others think you are."

_____ I am aware of how others perceive me.

_____ I keep my personal moods out of the office.

_____ Others would describe me as even-tempered.

_____ It's more important to me that the project gets completed than for me to get credit for its completion.

_____ I generally tell people where I stand on various issues so that they're not left guessing.

_____ People have told me that they enjoy working with me.

_____ I am generally aware of other people's moods and respond accordingly.

_____ I can laugh at my mistakes when the situation calls for it.

_____ I know the difference between being assertive and being aggressive, and typically opt for the former.

_____ It's hard to recall a time when I've embarrassed someone by one of my remarks.

_____ I look waiters and waitresses in the eye when I speak to them.

_____ I give others feedback as objectively as possible and always in private.

_____ I leave my bad moods outside the office.

Conversely, when you think about successful people who are talented and intelligent, but neither likable nor particularly emotionally intelligent, folks who come to mind include radio hosts Rush Limbaugh and Howard Stern, television personality Judge Judy, hotelier Leona Helmsley, and tennis legend John McEnroe. Their own needs eclipse their deeds and the needs of others. Not too long ago, I was at a fund-raiser where both Lily Tomlin and tennis legend Martina Navratilova were present. As you might imagine, people were thrilled with the opportunity to meet these women (not to mention they had paid a lot of money to do so), and many approached them to ask for autographs. Whereas Tomlin was gracious in every interaction, and my admiration for her increased as the evening wore on, my regard for Navratilova diminished with one act. When she obviously became tired of signing, she rolled her eyes and gave a disgusted look to one of the admirers who'd dared to ask for an autograph. The person walked away looking hurt and embarrassed. It was a reminder that it takes a lifetime to build a positive image, but only a moment to have it tarnished in the eyes of others.

The question that most frequently arises in discussions about emotional intelligence is: Can it be developed or is it something that you're born with? My own position is that not only *can* EQ be developed, but most people *do* develop it and are *not* born with it. Let me tell you a story that underlies this belief.

To Change or Not to Change— That Is the Question

When Fred's boss told him that he had to submit to coaching if he had any hope of keeping his job, Fred specifically requested that I be his coach. I had met him when we both served on the board of a nonprofit agency. When I first got the call, I wasn't too excited about coaching Fred. I had watched him in action, and he could be brutally indifferent to the feelings of others, as well as intellectually snobbish. All in all, he was not a pleasant fellow to be around, and although I thought I could help him, I knew it was going to be a challenge—and not a particularly pleasant one.

During our first coaching session, Fred started as he frequently did, by intellectualizing everything going on at the government agency in which he worked. He shared with me his analyses of this person's behavior and that person's motives until I finally asked him to stop. I looked at him and said, "I already know you're a really smart guy. You don't have to prove it to me, but I'm wondering why you have the need to prove it to yourself and everyone around you." He stopped dead in his tracks. After a split second of shock, a boyish grin came across his face. It was as if he'd been caught doing something wrong. "Is it that obvious?" he asked.

Like so many smart people, Fred used his intelligence as a weapon rather than a gift. Growing up smart isn't always easy. In fact, in many public schools, it's more socially acceptable to be developmentally slow than smart. Bright children are often the targets of ridicule and derision by their classmates. Fred's defense mechanism for childhood survival was to keep people at a distance with his carefully chosen but cutting words and indifferent attitude. He knew he could survive using his intelligence, so he didn't consider how he affected those around him—until his personality caught up with him. He made the mistake one day of embarrassing his boss's boss with an offhand remark in a meeting, and his intelligence was suddenly no longer the shield that protected him. His worst nightmare had come to life.

Fortunately (for both Fred and me), he turned out to be ripe for coaching. His wife had recently been complaining about the same qualities I was making him look at. His job and his marriage would clearly be in jeopardy soon if he didn't learn to act differently, win back the people he had offended, and avoid making the same mistakes in the future. Fred's coaching plan involved a few simple but specific steps, which he followed religiously.

To begin with, he was coached *never* to be the first one to speak in meetings. His quick and often cutting responses precluded other people from making their points and gave the impression that he was grandstanding. Instead, he was to use the techniques of active listening (described in this book's first chapter) to ensure that he actually heard what other people were saying.

The next step was to always tie his ideas together with the ideas expressed by others. In other words, he had to seek similarities between his ideas and others'—something that would be impossible if he weren't really listening. By seeing similarities, he could assure that everyone walked away from a problem-solving session feeling like a winner.

The third coaching suggestion was to count slowly to three before answering any questions directed to him. This would diminish the appearance of being flip or rash in his comments, give him more time to prepare a thoughtful response, and reduce the inclination toward sarcasm that often accompanied his quicker responses. In the end, his responses might contain the same content, but the moment of hesitation changed the perception of his being a loose cannon.

Within a few months, Fred changed noticeably. When I

called his boss for input about Fred's progress, he said that Fred was like a new man and that the people working with him could see the difference, although they couldn't quite put a finger on what had changed. Fred remained a vital part of his team by adding to his skill set, and—he tells me, tongue-in-cheek—avoided divorce by practicing the same behaviors at home. Fred approached the coaching suggestions in much the same way he approached intellectual challenges—with tenacity and perseverance. He didn't particularly care to know much more about *why* he acted as he did; he knew only that he didn't want to lose career momentum and was willing to do whatever it took to avoid it—and he did.

Not all people are as successful as Fred, however, when it comes to matters of emotional intelligence. In contrast, another fellow I'll call Adam was advised to get coaching after being sued for sexual harassment by one of his direct reports. Adam claimed that all he did was make some innocent jokes at which everyone laughed. He was the proverbial bull in a china shop. Adam was forever offending someone with his jokes or casual remarks, but he never seemed to notice that people didn't like it. Sure, they might have laughed, perhaps uncomfortably at the moment, but people tended to avoid him so they didn't fall victim to his thoughtlessness.

When I asked Adam why he thought his boss referred him for coaching, his reply was that people in his department were overly sensitive and he supposed he should be more careful. When asked what the value of being more careful might be, he said that it would get his boss off his back. Wrong answer. It appeared from the outset that Adam was not a particularly good candidate for coaching. His inability to see how his behavior affected others, and the lack of desire to correct it for that same reason, made it virtually impossible for him to change. The way he saw it, the rest of the world was up against poor, innocent Adam—a perception he just couldn't, or wouldn't, overcome. Adam will spend his life feeling persecuted, never realizing that he and the world interact; it's not just the world acting on Adam. Within a year he was "made redundant" during a corporate downsizing.

Adam and Fred are representative of the differences between people who respond favorably to coaching and those who don't—people who have the insight to see how they may be sabotaging their own best efforts and people who can't (or won't) admit that their own behaviors play any part in their career difficulties. From my own experience, it appears that 75 to 80 percent of people who are coached are able to make significant changes in their work and their lives as the result of doing the introspection and hard work associated with coaching. It's likely that if you're still reading this book, you fall into the success category.

Successful behavioral change, especially in the area of emotional intelligence, requires a foundation of emotional stability. People who are so damaged by early-childhood experiences that it's impossible for them to see how these experiences affect the present have a difficult time making the leap of faith that coaching requires. It's common to hear people express fear about changing. The major fear is that changing certain aspects of their behavior will cause them to be less effective. After all, for the largest portion of their professional lives they have relied on one or two strengths, and now they're being asked to balance those strengths with complementary skills. The request evokes uncertainty and anxiety. It also brings up fears that even a single change will set off a chain of life disruptions. A strong foundation of emotional stability, however, enables them to have enough faith in the coaching process to at least test out the hints. Absent this foundation, the request for change is just too overwhelming.

Two decades of coaching have taught me that the fundamental ingredients for behavioral change include those in the following chart.

FACTORS CRITICAL FOR BEHAVIORAL CHANGE

FACTOR	DESCRIBED AS
1. Desire	Sees the value in developing skills complementary to existing strengths.
2. Insight	When presented with concrete feedback, can see him- or herself as others do.
3. Candor	Can openly and honestly discuss development areas.
4. Flexibility	Shifts paradigms—does not get stuck in what worked in the past.
5. Risk taking	Is able to engage in new, uncomfortable, and what may be perceived as risky new behavior.
6. A "learning" attitude	Likes to read, experience, or learn for the sake of learning, not because it's immediately practical or utilitarian.
7. Humility	Understands that he or she is human and there's always room to grow.
8. Emotional health	Is free from or in treatment for problems such as alcoholism, drug abuse, obsessive-compulsive behavior, bipolar disease, and so on.

THE FIVE MOST DEADLY CHARACTER TRAITS

Part and parcel of emotional intelligence is an awareness of how your behavior impacts others—and the desire to minimize pain, unnecessary discomfort, or embarrassment to others. People with insufficient emotional intelligence often possess five character traits that lead to losing the competitive edge at work. Of course, there may be others, but these are the ones that seem to trip people up most frequently:

- Condescension
- Abrasiveness
- Belligerence
- Blaming
- Insensitivity

Each one alone is bad enough, but when one person possesses all five traits (and some people do), it's deadly. You may wonder how anyone with all five characteristics could survive for long in an organization. It happens in a number of circumstances. The most common scenario is that the person possesses a unique skill set that's difficult to find or reproduce. The person usually knows this, and it serves only to exacerbate the offensive behaviors. He or she has no reason to change because the behavior gets rewarded along with the valued skills. The obvious problem here is that sooner or later someone with the same skills, but not the offensive behavior, comes along and looks mighty attractive to the organization.

A second scenario is that the organizational culture actually *values* the offensive behavior. I once conducted a management skills program for a group like this. It was the sales department of a well-known manufacturing firm, and out of a group of twenty-five participants, twenty of them possessed each of the five deadly character traits. These twenty people would ignore the ground rules that the group set for itself, come to group sessions late, talk over one another, one-up one another, and, in general, act abrasive, belligerent, condescending, and insensitive. When confronted with their behavior, they blamed the other five for not being enough fun! I'd never seen anything like it. When I spoke with the department manager over the lunch break, he actually seemed proud of his team. He grinned and said that they were on their best behavior. I'd hate to see their worst!

This particular organization isn't alone. There are others where specific, inappropriate behaviors are viewed simply as eccentricities of the company and its employees. You find this in many creative and highly technical fields. Their customers and clients are aware of the behavior, as are candidates applying for jobs and others in their industry, but because of some unusual or special service or product that they provide, they can get away with it. These organizations don't thrive for long, however. The inappropriateness of their actions eventually catches up with them. At some point, another company provides the same services without the offensive behavior.

Here are some examples of how the five deadly character traits play out in real life and people whose careers were negatively impacted because of them.

Condescension

Condescension is characterized by giving others the feeling that you're placating them or doing them a favor. People who are condescending hold themselves above others due to real or perceived status or privilege. Whether or not they really are of a higher status isn't the point. There are people of the highest social standing who aren't condescending, and people of the lowest who are.

A type of social clustering often occurs in the workplace that reflects similar clustering in other circumstances. At work, people who have similar interests will have lunch together or do social things together. However, if common courtesy is not extended to those outside the group due to status, sex, race, ethnicity, or some other subjective variable, clustering becomes condescension. People with long-term career success are the ones who treat the janitor with the same dignity and respect they offer to the company president. These are the folks who really see the service people around them and believe that there are no worthless jobs or people.

Whether or not she actually was, the late Princess Diana gave the impression she was not the least bit condescending, whereas her ex-husband, Prince Charles, was accused of being, not only condescending, but also cold and aloof. It has only been since the passing of Diana that the future king has been forced to face the issue of his public image—and by some accounts he's doing a fairly good job of turning perceptions around.

Abrasiveness

Abrasive behaviors involve acting out against other people. Whereas condescending people are, at times, passive-aggressive (appearing benign on the surface, but subversively acting in their own best interests), abrasive people are just plain aggressive. On the assertive-aggressive chart, they score high in self-expression but low in concern for others. Former House Majority Leader Tom DeLay (known in some circles as "The Hammer") was forced to step down from his position in part because of this fatal flaw. Although criminal indictments and ethical questions surrounded his stepping down, some of these were brought on by opponents who simply didn't like his abrasive style. Newt Gingrich was also a poster child for the term *abrasive*. Regardless of the value or content of both men's messages, these messages were difficult to hear because they were couched in so much negativity about the opposing political party or other people.

Another notable figure with an abrasive personality is hotelier Leona Helmsley. In the midst of legal problems that resulted from her failure to pay sufficient taxes, Helmsley managed to alienate a rather substantial population of would-be guests with her comment that only the "little people" pay taxes. Throughout her trial, similar thoughtless and abrasive remarks (always devoid of remorse) only contributed further to her ultimate incarceration for tax evasion.

Abrasive people care more about the content of their messages and less about the impact that the messages will have on others. They choose "hard" words to get the point across rather than neutral ones. Hard words are those that offend or attack, whereas neutral ones lean toward bridging differences of opinion and problem solving. Hard words are frequently value-laden, whereas neutral ones are more objective. The differences sound something like this:

Hard: *It's obvious that you simply didn't put the time into writing the report that it required. If you had,* *it wouldn't have turned out so ineptly written and blatantly filled with mistakes.*

Neutral: *The report isn't what I had anticipated. It contains numerous errors of fact and grammar. I'm wondering whether the time required to do it was actually devoted to it?*

You will note that the neutral statement did not attack or condemn, but rather presented a simple statement of fact. Additionally, the hard word choices include *you* statements, as opposed to *I* statements—which tend to make others defensive and less likely to want to work through the problem.

Belligerence

As much as I enjoy watching her antics, the behavior of television's Judge Judy can best be described as belligerent. Her comments from the bench are not simply opinions, they're verbally abusive. She's mean-spirited and acts as though she's better than the show's guests. You might say she's just doing her job to secure ratings and further the cause of justice. I don't buy it. I've read enough about her history and watched her during interviews to believe it's not an act—this is who the woman is. Any of us could use the same excuse in our jobs, and it still wouldn't make the behavior acceptable.

In the international political arena, the late Yasir Arafat and Saddam Hussein can't be described as anything but belligerent. Although they verbally professed peaceful intentions, their actions were contentious and designed to inflame the situation, not ameliorate it. Like most belligerent people, they acted not in good faith, but in ways good for them personally. On our own soil, the same holds true for former presidential candidates Ross Perot and Pat Buchanan. Fortunately, the American public recognized their belligerence (and other flaws) and declined to let them near the Oval Office.

Blaming

Most of us have had the great displeasure of working with blaming or Teflon bosses or co-workers. When something goes wrong, watch out, because someone is going to wind up the scapegoat. Their inability to admit their own mistakes goes beyond any single mistake; it's at the very core of their interactions with others. People who are unable to admit mistakes are frequently the very same people who lack insight into their own behavior.

Looking across past decades, we see the phenomenon of blaming occur in late President Richard Nixon's Watergate scandal, Lieutenant Colonel Oliver North's Iran-Contra affair, Bill Clinton casting blame on a "vast right-wing conspiracy" for his own peccadilloes, and former Enron CEOs Jeffrey Skilling and the late Kenneth Lay. In each of these instances, the fingers couldn't point fast enough at someone else.

Insensitivity

Insensitive people tend to disregard others' preferences or desires, embarrass others with thoughtless comments, and make certain that their own needs prevail. They frequently speak before they think, thereby saying things that in retrospect they wish they hadn't—but the damage is already done. Insensitivity isn't always thoughtless—at times, it's an intentionally used tactical weapon.

One woman in a workshop on interpersonal skills spent the first day embarrassing and berating others. To a severely overweight woman, she made the comment, "The food here [at the conference center] is so heavy. I must have gained ten pounds. I feel like a beached whale." During an evening of group singing and dancing, she stood up and mimicked another participant who had a heavy Asian accent and who had just led the group in a song. When I asked to speak with her privately to give her some feedback about how she was affecting the rest of the group members, she proudly admitted that she could find a person's Achilles' heel and go after it. She told me that this was her way of maintaining a competitive edge.

Insensitivity, whether intentional or otherwise, gives the impression that you are a loose cannon. People who are insensitive are frequently excluded from important client or customer meetings for fear of what they're going to say. Insensitive people wind up being avoided in the workplace because their co-workers don't particularly care to set themselves up for hurt or embarrassment. Failing to know how you affect others, being unaware that you may have hurt someone else, and neglecting to ask for feedback about your behavior are other examples of insensitivity, which may also be viewed as lacking insight. People who lack insight have huge blind spots about their own personalities because they are largely oblivious to how people respond to them. They fail to see the reactions of others because they are so absorbed in themselves. Lack of insight probably causes more careers to hit the skids than any other single factor.

The television show *The Apprentice* provides many good

examples of people who have yet to realize that insight and sensitivity are critical career-enhancing skills—with no better example than Omarosa Manigault-Stallworth. Although her behavior was troublesome from the outset of the series, I knew she would never be a finalist at the moment she said something to the effect of "I'm not here to win a popularity contest." People who use this line rarely do. It's just an excuse to rationalize bad behavior. There was, however, one contest that Omarosa did win. In a poll conducted by *TV Guide* and the cable network Bravo, Omarosa won the title Most Hated Reality Star of All Time. And by the way—runner-up *American Idol* contestant Clay Aiken was named Most Loved Reality Star of All Time.

WHEN TOO MUCH OF A GOOD THING IS A GOOD THING

There are five behaviors that counter the deadly character traits: kindness, honesty, humility, genuineness, and self-awareness. Remember, when you're trying to overcome your strengths, it's not particularly helpful to think about *stopping* a behavior. You only focus more on the behavior that you want most to diminish! You must add new skills to your existing repertoire. Add these five, and your personality worries will be over.

Kindness

Many of us grew up with the Golden Rule: *Do unto others as you would have others do unto you*. True kindness takes that motto a step farther. In order to be truly kind, you must now *treat others as they would like to be treated*. I've already described the importance of seeing people for who they are. In order to be kind, you must now respond to who *they* are and what *they* would like, not who *you* are and what *you* would like.

Many of the behaviors inherent to kindness overlap with the relationship-building behaviors described under Success Strategy 1. Kindness goes beyond relationship building, however, because it also encompasses what you do when there is no quid pro quo—when you have nothing to gain from the act. This concept is exemplified in the role played by Kevin Costner in the movie *The War*.

In one scene, Costner's character takes the cotton candy he has just purchased for his wife and daughter at a fair and gives it to some bullies who have been beating up on his kids. When his son looks at him incredulously and asks why, his response is simple: "Because it looks like they haven't been given nothin' in a long time." This type of kindness stems from a sort of generosity—not a generosity of materialism, but a generosity of spirit. You are kind not because someone reminds you to be, or because you know that you will gain something tangible from it, but because you want to make a difference in the lives of those around you—even those you may never see again.

I can remember the exact moment in childhood when I learned my first lesson in kindness. It was on a crowded subway in Manhattan when I was five or six years old. My aunt had taken me to see her office in the city, and we were returning home amid rush-hour commuters packed like sardines into the train. I watched as a young professional woman stood, tapped an elderly woman on the shoulder, and motioned her to the seat she had just vacated. The older woman sat down wearily, and the younger woman remained standing until she exited many stops later. A simple act of kindness that took place nearly fifty years ago had such a profound effect on me that to this day I recall it nearly every time I ride the subway.

Honesty

Honesty can be looked at in a number of ways. Do you tell the truth when asked a question, or do you pass the buck and look for someone else to blame? Do you give people honest feedback, or do you say what you think people want to hear? Are you willing to speak the unspoken—even when not asked—or are you content not to rock the boat? No matter how you slice it, honesty involves having the integrity to say and do the right thing no matter how difficult.

When it comes to speaking your mind, there are different ways of being honest. It is possible to do so without demolishing another person. Honesty should always meet two criteria: It must be direct, and it must be kind. Once, after a lengthy explanation in the ways of being honest, someone in a workshop summarized it beautifully when she pointed out that *honesty is the ability to tell someone to go to hell so that they look forward to the trip!* Let's take a look at how you might successfully meet this challenge.

Quite often, when people are coached to be honest but with kindness, they assume they're being asked to act passively— to care more about the receiver of the message than about making their points. This is far from the case. It's just that people who are brutally honest frequently go out of bounds in terms of their direct, straightforward behavior. It becomes too much of a good thing. By using the **DESC**ript on the opposite page, you will increase the likelihood of getting your message across without damaging the relationship.

DESCript

MODEL	EXAMPLE
Describe to the person why you want to have a conversation.	*I'd like to talk to you about something I observed in a meeting we both attended last week.*
Explain the situation as you see it and Elicit the other person's point of view.	*You may not have been aware of it, but I noticed that each time I made a suggestion about how we could reduce reportable workplace safety incidents, you gave each one a thumbs-down. I was wondering what that was really about?* [Shift to active listening]
Specify alternative appropriate behaviors.	*Now I understand. You had already developed a plan to address the problem. In the future, it would be helpful if you would simply let me know when your mind is already made up.*
Consequences—remember, they can be positive as well as negative.	*Sharing that kind of information would preclude me from taking up valuable meeting time with ideas that aren't currently needed.*

Humility

Humility is embodied in this paraphrase of the great Vince Lombardi's coaching philosophy:

> *When the team loses—it's my fault.*
> *When the team does well—we did it together.*
> *When the team wins—they did it themselves.*

Humility is the absence of arrogance and the presence of modesty. It's the ability to put your own achievements into a perspective that simultaneously recognizes your own limitations and the strengths of others. Humble people do not boast or require extended time in the limelight (we all need a bit). They are so self-assured that they internalize their strengths and use them as stepping-stones for future success.

General Norman Schwarzkopf exemplifies a man of humility. Despite the fact that he was instrumental in the decisive defeat of the Iraqi military during Operation Desert Storm, Schwarzkopf never took the credit himself. He shared the triumph with his colleagues and troops, and, in the process, allowed everyone involved to be a hero. In the world of entertainment, I found one of the highest-paid women in television to exhibit uncommon humility. While I was waiting in the green room to be interviewed on the *Today* show, Katie Couric popped her head in to tell me how much she liked my book *Nice Girls Don't Get the Corner Office*. When she added that she'd learned a few things she could apply in her career, I jokingly said, "When you're Katie Couric, you don't have to worry about these things." Without missing a beat she replied, "That's not true. I have a lot to learn." That kind of humility is one of the things that makes Katie so endearing to so many—*and* so successful.

Ironically, those who are unable to be humble are often raised as children in households so withholding of praise and affirmation that the child must call attention to him- or herself or otherwise fade into oblivion. Once again, the behavior we learned to survive difficult childhoods can later become our Achilles' heel. Self-confident people are able to highlight their accomplishments discreetly for the purpose of furthering their goals; people lacking humility must showcase their strengths as if their lives depended on it—because they do.

It's not as if humble people don't know that they're good—or even great. They do know it, but they lack the need to receive constant praise for it. Humility should not be confused with passivity. They are two entirely different things. Whereas passivity is marked by the unwillingness or inability to be proactive, humility is characterized by the desire to downplay your own position, strengths, or contributions.

Genuineness

Being comfortable with ourselves as imperfect humans—scars, flaws, and all—is the essence of being genuine. It's not quite the same as the expression *What you see is what you get,* because implied in that maxim may be a take-it-or-leave-it attitude. It's more like *I'm not perfect, but I know that I'm not and I don't try to be anyone other than who I am.* Genuine people accept who they are, and are likely to accept others for who *they* are for the same reason. They can laugh at their own foibles and eccentricities without embarrassment or self-consciousness. They have relinquished the need to be perfect.

The opposite of genuineness is pretension—putting on airs or pretending to be who you're not. I knew a man once who repeatedly showered excessive kindness on others that had nothing whatsoever to do with their needs or circumstances. One Christmas, he gave each member of his staff a piece of silver from Tiffany's—a kind and generous gesture on the surface. The only problem was that this same man refused to give performance reviews, say a kind word about anyone, or provide even cost-of-living increases to his employees when they were warranted. His staff would have much preferred to be recognized for their performance throughout the year than rewarded with an extravagant gift once a year. Similarly, he would take them to the most expensive restaurants in Chicago for their birthdays but failed to say good morning to them. It was more important to him that he appear magnanimous than that he be genuine. In turn, he got subversive compliance from his staff. They did what was necessary to keep afloat in their positions, and nothing more.

Self-Awareness

People who are self-aware know their strengths and flaws and act to improve their skills. They're aware of the effect they have on others. Self-awareness is one of the basics of emotional intelligence: combined with genuineness, honesty, and humility, it enables individuals to respond flexibly to different situations.

Self-awareness can be developed in a number of ways:

• **Ask for feedback.** Even if there's no formal mechanism in place for it at your job, ask other people for feedback. Couch it in terms of what they think you could do more of, do less of, or continue. This model provides a nonthreatening way of giving, and receiving, feedback. If you ask for feedback, however, be sure that you're ready to hear it. Once it's given, don't argue with it or try to explain away your behavior. The best way to deal with feedback is to ask for clarification if you don't understand it, thank the giver, and then go off to think about it. Even if it's only one person's opinion, you need to consider the ramifications of the feedback and how many more people may be thinking the exact same thing but not telling you.

• **Use a 360-degree feedback instrument.** This is a performance survey available to all levels of employees—professionals, supervisors, managers, and senior executives. The surveys are completed anonymously by people who know your work and returned to a third party, who then sends them off for computer processing, from which a computer profile of your strengths and needs for development emerges. Because the results can at times be pretty overwhelming, I recommend that you use feedback instruments in conjunction with a business coach. You'll find more information on coaching in the Personal Development Planning chapter at the end of this book.

• **Take self-awareness classes.** These classes focus on behavior in a business context. Unlike EST or Wellspring, they're typically designed for businesspeople who want to examine how their behavior impedes or contributes to career success. The company I consider to be the nation's premier provider of such classes is NTL (National Training Laboratory). This firm has been facilitating self-awareness programs for businesspeople for nearly fifty years. You'll find contact information for NTL, as well as other reputable trainers, in the back of this book.

• **Get a business coach.** Good coaches work with you to build skills that enable you to effectively compete with other fast-trackers. In addition to providing you with coaching suggestions related to your particular situation, they can refer you to other resources in your community that may be helpful for assuring ongoing self-awareness. Many use 360-degree feedback instruments as part of the coaching process; if this is important to you, be sure to ask if it's part of the coach's protocol.

• **Enter into counseling.** At times, behaviors are so ingrained and related to early-childhood experiences that longer-term, in-depth professional help is required to understand and change them. As a licensed psychotherapist myself, I offer this recommendation with somewhat of a bias, but even coaches with no psychological backgrounds report that from 50 to 60 percent of the people they coach are referred to counseling for treatment that goes beyond the scope of coaching.

Empathy

Empathy is a bit like caring. It's pretty tough to teach someone to be empathetic, but this is another important aspect of building relationships. If you can't empathize with people, you can't really understand them. Empathy is the ability to put yourself in other people's shoes and feel what they feel. It differs from sympathy in that sympathy requires only that you be able to intellectually see what another person is experiencing, not necessarily understand how that person feels. Sympathy is a more cognitive process, whereas empathy is a more emotional one.

I am not even sure that I would have thought to include the importance of empathy in relationship building had I not taken the time to have a conversation with a wonderful program administrator named Andrew. As we were both waiting for participants to arrive at a one-week program being held in Prague, we discussed what made certain programs go well and others not so well for him as an administrator. He remarked that it really made a difference when participants could empathize with how difficult it was to respond to their requests in the exact time frame that they wanted. As a program administrator, he is responsible for taking care of all of the little details that participants might require. This includes making flight arrangements, ordering special meals, scheduling ground transportation, sending or receiving faxes, and making dinner reservations. The comment that really got my attention was "When people show a little empathy, I'll go the extra mile. When they treat me as though I have no brains, I act as though I have no brains."

It was one of those *aha!* moments. Part of the quid pro quo involves understanding what it's like to be in another person's position. Not looking simply at the job, but at the person in the job as well—seeing the human being performing the task. It made sense. Treating someone impersonally, like a functionary, does little to secure the relationship and assure longer-term cooperation.

What does it take to be empathetic? It takes surrender, in much the same way as Anne Morrow Lindbergh described it. It takes a suspension of personal need, judgment, or urgency in an effort to connect with the person with whom you are interacting.

Empathy is missing from sociopaths—they cannot relate in any way to the victim. Those criminals who commit brutal murders and feel no remorse lack empathy. People who cry when they see pictures of the atrocities of war have empathy. Empathy in the workplace is exhibited by noticing, and commenting on, changes in mood or behavior, by talking about problems that may be inherent to a particular position, by following up on personal problems that may have been discussed in a passing moment. Empathy is one way of showing that you care *and* you understand.

AVOID GOING FOR THE BAIT

A coaching client of mine once called to tell me about a situation that he thought he'd handled poorly. We had been working on how to overcome the impression that others have of him of being too blunt, undiplomatic, and hurtful in his remarks to others. We discussed many of the coaching suggestions already provided in this chapter, and he was making some headway in winning back the regard of his staff and colleagues. He slid backward, however, when someone did the same thing to him that he was accused of doing to others.

A female co-worker sent him an e-mail message berating him for being rude, slow in responding to requests, and mean-spirited at meetings. She not only sent it to him, but also electronically copied it to all the people reporting to him and to his boss. Furious, he responded in kind with an equally abusive letter in which he let the woman know what he thought of her. In short, he went for the bait. The woman who sent the letter wanted to get a rise out of him, and she did. The situation was now escalating, and both parties looked childish.

One technique to avoid matching the inappropriate intensity level of another person, and thereby avoid going for the bait, is called *fogging*. Although this man and I had discussed it during his coaching sessions, the importance of fogging was underscored by this encounter. Fogging is especially helpful when others catch you unaware or off guard with their intensity or anxiety. When people are angry or abusive, it's human nature to become angry and abusive back. Yet meeting the other person's intensity level typically only escalates a problem.

Fogging involves first putting up a visual fog between you and the other person so that his or her intensity is defused and neither intimidates nor infuriates you. Next, you attempt to de-escalate the situation by remaining calm and using specific phrases designed to permit you to maintain your dignity and allow others to maintain theirs. Comments such as "I can see you're really upset by this. Let me check into it and get back to you," or "I had no idea you felt this way. Tell me more about it," are examples of fogging. This buys you time to gather your composure or investigate the complaint without responding in kind.

When the man asked what he could have done differently, I suggested that he might have responded with a return e-mail message that said: *I had no idea that my behavior is being interpreted in the way that you described. Why don't we schedule a meeting within the next few days to sit down and discuss the problem so that we can remedy it as quickly as possible.* He said that this was all well and good, except that it didn't address the fact that he was embarrassed in front of his staff and boss. *His* response, on the other hand, evened the score, a fact about which he appeared to be proud.

As I explained to him, there are a number of ways to win the battle without losing the war. The preferred response would go a long way toward assuring his ongoing success despite the way his colleague had chosen to act. By smoothing the waters, he would allow others to see that even when provoked, he treats people with dignity and respect. He would wind up looking like a hero, rather than being seen as stooping to his colleague's level. In keeping with Lao-tzu's teaching "Fail to honor people, they fail to honor you," honoring others over the long tenure of your career will always serve you better than acting out of malice or vindictiveness.

Coaching Tips for Enhancing Your Emotional Intelligence and Likability Quotients

Put a check mark in the box of two or three coaching tips you commit to doing.

❑ **Never embarrass anyone—ever.** As hard as I try, I cannot come up with one good reason why you should ever embarrass anyone. If you lean toward aggressiveness, you may say it's appropriate in instances where someone embarrassed you first. Wrong. Didn't your mother ever teach you two wrongs don't make a right? Look for ways to allow others to save face. When something isn't done to your liking or expectations, say something like, "I may not have made myself clear initially. Let me reiterate what I need to make sure we're both on the same page."

❑ **Don't tell jokes at the expense of anyone except yourself** (and think twice before you do that). I've never heard a joke that doesn't in some way put down a particular group or person. Even if you think you're being self-effacing because you're in that group, others may not.

❑ **Read *The Emotional Intelligence Quick Book: Everything You Need to Know to Put Your EQ to Work* by Dr. Travis Bradberry and Dr. Jean Greaves.** It really is just that—a quick guide to learning more about EQ.

It also provides you with the opportunity to assess your own EQ, which is a good place to start identifying your developmental needs in this arena.

❑ **Solicit and act on 360-degree feedback.** There is no better way to have the mirror held up so that you can see yourself as others see you than for you to get written feedback from those familiar with your workplace behavior. Start by asking your human resource department or an outside coach for help. By allowing people to send their comments anonymously to someone other than you, you are more likely to get valuable feedback. You don't even have to use complex or expensive forms. In our office, we ask people providing 360-degree feedback to answer three questions: (1) Describe two or three of this person's greatest strengths, (2) describe two or three things this person can do more of to be even more effective, and (3) describe two or three things this person can do less of to be even more effective. The answers will provide you with a wealth of information you won't get on more conventional, quantitative feedback reports. If you're not sure what to do with the data you receive, hire a coach to help you interpret and act on the feedback. You can find one by going the International Coach Federation Web site: www.coachfederation.org.

❑ **Publicly praise, privately criticize.** This simple maxim will always serve you well.

❑ **Remember to say please and thank you.** It sounds so simple, doesn't it? But I can't tell you how many people neglect to use these words on a regular basis. It costs you nothing, but it pays huge dividends in terms of perceptions of likability.

❏ **Create win–win situations by considering everyone's needs, not just your own.** There are very few situations in which ensuring that all involved walk away feeling as if their needs are important isn't a winning strategy. Even in situations where it's impossible to ultimately design a win–win outcome, you can only enhance a relationship by trying.

❏ **Learn the difference between aggressive and assertive behavior—and with few exceptions, opt for the latter.** I once made this suggeston at a workshop I conducted in Manhattan, and a man raised his hand and said aggressive behavior should be met with aggression back. I had to disagree. It only unnecessarily escalates an already difficult situation and rarely serves to resolve it. People too often use far more muscle than the situation calls for. They think being louder or more belligerent will help them achieve their goals. Although this may be true in the short term, in the long term it will damage a relationship you may later need.

❏ **Be honest, but be careful how you express your honesty.** Being likable doesn't mean you're a doormat. Exhibiting emotional intelligence doesn't mean you don't give tough messages. Use the DESCript explained in this chapter as a tool to help you deliver messages in a way that people can hear and respond to rather than resist and resent.

❏ **Stop what you're doing and pay attention to people when they come into your office.** Mary Kay Ash, founder of Mary Kay Cosmetics, once said the secret to building relationships is treating everyone you come into contact with as if they're wearing a sign that reads MAKE ME FEEL IMPORTANT. One aspect of self-regulation is the ability to shift gears and pay attention to people when they need it most. If you absolutely cannot stop what you're doing for a legitimate business reason (being obsessive-compulsive is not a good enough reason), then be honest with others, letting them know you'd like to schedule a time when you can give them your undivided attention. It's much better to do this than to pretend you're listening when you're actually preoccupied.

❏ **Attend NTL's Human Interaction Laboratory.** Founded in 1947, the NTL Institute offers an array of workshops for those who want to develop their interpersonal skills. Its workshops are experientially oriented and provide participants with the opportunity to explore their own values, attitudes, and actions as well as how others perceive them. They create a positive and supportive environment in which participants are free to explore behavior changes. The Web site is http://.ntl.org.

❏ **Read *The Likeability Factor: How to Boost Your L-Factor and Achieve Your Life's Dreams* by Tim Sanders.** This is one of the few good books available on this important topic, and the premise is pretty simple: Likable people are better equipped to achieve their goals than those who aren't. Sanders breaks likability down into four component parts—friendliness, empathy, relevance (the ability to connect with other people's interests and needs), and realness—and helps you gain insight into how to develop in each of these areas.

❑ **Don't follow the Golden Rule, follow the Platinum Rule: Treat others as *they* want to be treated, not as *you* want to be treated.** Assuming everyone wants to be treated as you would like to be is a setup for failure. True empathy and insight come from seeing individuals for who *they* are and what *they* need. If you're not sure what someone needs from you, ask. You don't have to be a mind reader to show empathy.

SUCCESS STRATEGY 5

Manage Up

I admit it's tempting to wish for the perfect boss—the perfect parent—or the perfect outfit. But maybe the best any of us can do is not quit, play the hand we've been dealt, and accessorize what we've got.

Carrie, on *Sex and the City*

Carly Fiorina was president and chief executive officer of Hewlett-Packard from 1999 to 2005 and served as chairman of the board from 2000 to 2005. In February 2005, however, that same board forced her out. The reason was that the merger between HP and Compaq for which she'd vigorously fought but which was approved by just a slight majority of stockholders wasn't producing the results she'd promised. But that was only part of the story. Many CEOs make business decisions that don't pan out as planned, but they're not forced out of their positions. So why did it happen to Fiorina?

Some people thought it was because she was a high-profile woman, and people love unseating such women from their power positions. But I don't think that was it, either—and I'm typically hypersensitive to these kinds of gender wars. Instead, I believe Fiorina is the perfect example of someone whose career faltered because she didn't manage up effectively—in this case, manage relationships with board members. It was known that she had contentious relationships with the board. One columnist suggested she was seen by many as a "disruptive force, bent on turning two viable companies into an unwieldy monster." Board member Walter Hewlett (son of one of the late founders) even took legal action to block the proposed merger. If she'd had the relationships she needed in place, the board would have been more likely to support her in the face of a decision that turned out to be a financial disaster.

In the days of command-and-control leadership, managing up was pretty simple. The boss said "jump" and you said "how high?" It's not so easy anymore. The latest theories of leadership and followership suggest the workplace is (theoretically at least) more egalitarian, thereby blurring conventional wisdom for how to maximize your relationship management. Don't be lulled into a false sense of security, though. Managers are human beings, and *regardless* of what the latest guru is saying about how you should be treated, they want people reporting to them who make their lives easier—not harder.

Although the labels have become fuzzier and management techniques friendlier, the nature of the employer–employee relationship has not changed significantly. Labor attorneys are as busy as ever representing companies for their decisions to terminate employees as well as employees who believe they have been unjustly treated. The fact remains that you have to satisfy the expectations of the people who supervise you if you are to succeed in the workplace.

The concept of managing up is not to be confused with toadying or apple polishing. I'm not suggesting that you act insincerely or in a way calculated to garner favor from management. *Managing up* means that you are aware of the need to cultivate relationships with management that produce satisfactory results for *both* parties. It also means that you understand the unspoken quid pro quo (something in exchange for something else) between you and your boss and consciously make an effort to keep up your end of the agreement. That quid pro quo can include raises, promotions, or plum assignments in exchange for support, good performance, and loyalty. Although these kinds of trade-offs are rarely discussed, they are potent currency in the marketplace called work.

Whether your organization refers to them as bosses, facilitators, coaches, coordinators, or any other array of nonhierarchical terms in an effort to remove the traditional notion that one position is in any way more important or better than another, a rose is still a rose. If there is a *subordinate,* then there is a *superior.* Modern theories of motivation suggest that to bring out the best in people, managers can no longer rely on the power of their positions but must build relationships of mutual respect. Unlike their predecessors, who saluted authority figures simply for the authority of power they possessed, today's workers expect to actually have a *relationship* with their supervisors, and the new terminologies are reflective of this change.

No matter what you call the boss, the fact remains that most people working in companies and organizations report to someone else who reviews their work and makes determinations about salary, promotion, assignments, and, at times, termination. You can change the term used to describe him or her, you can expect to have an amiable relationship with him or her, but you can't alter the fact that you are ultimately accountable to someone higher in the organization. From an entry-level position right on up to the CEO, everyone is accountable to someone. Successful professionals who remain on their career tracks understand that this relationship, like all other relationships, must be managed effectively.

CONFUSING THE BOSS WITH MOM OR DAD

Managing up is difficult because no other workplace relationship resembles your original family experience as much as the employee–manager relationship. If you're an employee, this relationship may encompass all of the same frustrations, triumphs, challenges, and satisfactions that existed within the relationship with your father, mother, or other primary caretaker. You may unwittingly respond to the boss in much the same way that you responded to the first of life's authority figures.

Because of this association between caretakers and bosses, employees' responses may range between extraordinarily tolerant in the worst of situations and intolerant in the best of situations. This creates a unique dilemma, because being too submissive can be as detrimental to your career as being too argumentative or unwilling to comply with directions. The real trick is to know (1) what the boss expects from you and (2) how to maintain your integrity as you walk the fine line between being a yes-person and being a thorn in the boss's side.

Perhaps this checklist is a place to begin thinking about how well you work with authority figures:

_____ I am able to disagree with the boss when I have strong feelings about something.

_____ I see it as my duty to provide the boss with alternative viewpoints.

_____ I would rate myself high on being able to disagree without being disagreeable.

_____ I know when to disagree with the boss and when not to.

_____ I balance respect for authority with voicing a dissenting viewpoint.

_____ I know what kind of boss will listen to a differing viewpoint and which will not, and act accordingly.

_____ I would never be accused of currying favor with someone in order to advance myself.

_____ I would never be accused of defying authority.

_____ I have worked through whatever issues I may have had with the type of parenting I received (either positive or negative).

_____ I am able to objectively assess my boss's strengths and developmental areas.

_____ I know when someone in authority is being unreasonable with me, and I don't usually take it personally.

An interesting coaching case that portrays the effect of parenting on the boss–employee relationship involved a woman whom I'll call Sheila. She requested coaching as a means of helping her to manage work stress. Sheila was clearly an upwardly mobile career woman who seemed to have all the skills needed to be successful within her current organization—or any other to which she might move. She had a good track record with other companies and was articulate, intelligent, poised, and self-confident. Coincidentally, I knew her boss from some consulting that I had done for their company a number of years before. My recollection of him was that he was a sarcastic, sexist know-it-all. He saw himself as "the boss" and everyone else as merely underlings.

Throughout the first coaching session, I couldn't quite figure out what the real problem was. Sheila never mentioned her boss (an omission I found strange), only that her job was very demanding and creating an abundance of stress for her. Without revealing my own assessment of her boss, I finally asked about her relationship with him. She skirted the issue for several minutes, but each time I gently came back to the topic. Suddenly, Sheila started sobbing. As it turned out, she was feeling inadequate and incompetent. No matter what she did, her boss wasn't satisfied. Sheila was certain that it was all her fault.

After exploring the situation with her a bit more, I turned the topic to her personal life. Was she married? Were her parents still alive? Did she have siblings? With this, she lit up. No, she wasn't married, but she did have a particularly close relationship with her parents. She had grown up an only child, doted on by adoring grandparents and aunts. She thought that she probably wasn't married yet because no man could measure up to her father, whom she described as a loving, considerate, and nurturing man.

Sheila's greatest strengths—her self-confidence and talent—were now being put into question by a boss who was the polar opposite of her father. Sheila came to the job seeing the boss as her loving mother, nurturing father, and doting extended family all rolled into one. Despite all evidence pointing to the contrary, she believed in the boss more than she believed in herself. She was not capable of seeing the boss for who he really was and, therefore, bought into his critical assessment of her. Her perception was that he was the all-knowing, benevolent father figure. There couldn't possibly be anything wrong with him, so it had to be her!

Subsequent coaching sessions with Sheila focused on enabling her to assess her boss's behaviors vis-à-vis her own and to deal with those behaviors more objectively. She was ultimately able to separate the boss from her father in her mind, and when she did, she made the decision to find a boss who was in actuality more like her father. Sheila realized that there were certainly some areas on which she needed to work, but that it would be better for her to leave the company. She is now happily working for a small firm in Indiana that has a familylike feel. She vows never again to let someone take away her self-esteem.

As for Sheila's former boss—he's an example of someone who manages up well. His own boss is a lot like him and, in fact, appreciates and rewards his hard-nosed approach to management. Both former marines, they remain true to the marine motto *Semper fidelis*—always loyal. The man is still with the company, making people's lives miserable, and no one in authority seems to be taking notice.

The opposite phenomenon—total acquiescence to the

boss—can be equally damaging to your career. A manager once asked if I would work with one of his employees. The manager's main complaint was that the employee, Jim, never challenged anything he said. Jim would follow the boss's instructions to the letter, even if it became apparent in the process that there was a better way to do it or a more appropriate path to pursue. The particular behavior that frustrated the manager was just part of a larger problem. Someone who won't challenge authority often won't take the kinds of risks needed to explore, make mistakes, learn from those mistakes, and go on to bigger and better things. As a member of a creative services team, Jim was *expected* to take risks.

Jim's greatest strength was following instructions. He grew up in an Asian culture where respect for authority was demonstrated by close adherence to the directions and desires of the elders. Like Sheila, Jim had to learn to separate his early experience with authority from the business situation with the boss. His coaching sessions involved enabling him to think and act independently of his boss's desires. He was coached first to develop a weekly plan for task accomplishment that included two to three items that he could see were needed in the department but that weren't mentioned by his boss. Next, he was instructed to give his own opinion at least once at every staff meeting. The third thing he was coached to do was to speak more loudly. His quiet, somewhat flat tone gave others the perception that he was someone who could be walked on. The combined coaching hints—to think more broadly, give his own opinions, and do so in a louder voice—were designed to eventually increase his self-confidence. Once this happened, he would be more likely to take more risks. The goal was to get Jim to "walk the walk" and "talk the talk." Fortunately,

Jim had a boss who was very supportive of the process and not only allowed but also encouraged him to overcome his particular strengths.

ADDING VALUE: THE FINE LINE BETWEEN DEFERENCE AND CONFRONTATION

I often tell my clients, "You're not paid to do your job; you're paid to think and add value." Simply doing the job outlined in your job description is not a formula for success. That's just the baseline. As one CEO told me, "I like it when a direct report pushes once. I like it when he pushes twice. Three times is too many." Most bosses want people who complement their own strengths by bringing to the table skills and abilities they themselves don't possess and, when put into play, make them look good. They're human, remember? That means there will inevitably be times when you have to disagree or bring up points that may be uncomfortable. *How you do that* in the context of a boss–follower relationship is yet another determining factor in ultimate career success. Again, I caution you not to be lulled into a false sense of security by bosses who *say* they like to be challenged. We all know there a lot of insecure, passive-aggressive managers who say one thing but do another. A former client, Karen, had just such a boss.

When human resources called me to discuss the possibility of working with Karen, I was given a description of a woman who was technically superior—but her boss was at his wit's end. The two had worked together for many years and in some ways had become like an old, dysfunctional married couple. Karen would nag him, and he would ignore her. She'd step over the line one too many times, and he would bully her into submission. A review of her performance appraisals clarified that he'd he never directly told her that her behavior was less than acceptable. But as the company began to face some financial reversals, both Karen and her boss became increasingly anxious about their own jobs, the direction of the company, and the appropriate strategies for the future. When everything was going well, the boss had the wherewithal to tolerate her, but under stress she became just another thorn in his side. He didn't like it.

When we started the coaching process, Karen was confused about what the problem could really be. After all, *her* behavior hadn't changed. She was doing what she always did—and perhaps more of it in light of the company's situations—but she was now being criticized for it. In meeting with the boss to determine what he wanted the outcomes of the coaching engagement to be, he said he was a proponent of employee involvement and valuing differing opinions, but he also made it clear he had finally grown tired of Karen's interruptions, correcting him in front of others at staff meetings, and not fully listening to—and when appropriate, accepting—his viewpoint on various issues.

The more I worked with Karen, the more I could see exactly what he meant. She had a strong personality and a high energy level. Put these two things together and you often get someone who doesn't read the needs of others too well. From day one working for this man, she behaved inappropriately, but he tolerated it because she was making money for the company and everyone was fat and happy. Once the tide turned, however, he was no longer so accepting of her behavior. And this is actually how so many careers become stalled. An employee's behavior is less than acceptable, a boss doesn't say anything about it, something in the employment arena changes, and the behavior suddenly becomes intolerable. In this case what changed was the company's financial situation, but other changes include new employees coming on board who deliver results but aren't so difficult to work with, new managers taking over who have lower tolerance levels for idiosyncratic behavior, or changes in the corporate culture.

Fortunately, Karen was very open to the feedback and responded well to coaching suggestions. With regard to this particular area of development (and there were others), I urged her to recognize that as much as the boss appeared to be easygoing, tolerant, and open to her style of communication, the fact remained that he was the boss. She needed to stop interacting with him as she might with her husband or best friend. Specifically, I coached her to do to three things:

- Give the boss an array of options from which to choose rather than trying to coerce him to go in one direction. This would have a secondary benefit of enabling him to see that she was thinking broadly and strategically.
- When she presented these options, open the topic for discussion rather than assuming a fait accompli. I did not suggest that she ask permission or couch her ideas in the form of questions, but rather that a dialogue ensue when new ideas were brought to the table.
- Brush up her active listening skills. The boss wanted to feel as if he was heard out. Active listening would help him to feel more satisfaction from their interactions and would help her to truly understand that he had good ideas, too, and could be a partner in the process. I'm pleased to report that they worked together successfully for another

four years after the coaching engagement until he retired from the company.

Going back to the playing field model for a moment may help illuminate how people go out of bounds when it comes to managing up and what it would look like if you were doing it effectively. The chart on the opposite page will help you to better manage your relationship with your boss.

From Enron to WorldCom in the business arena and the My Lai massacre to Abu Ghraib in the military, following orders is no excuse for relinquishing your responsibility to act with integrity. Although it is dated, I find no better example of what happens when you err on the side of compliance than that of Lieutenant William Calley Jr. In 1968, the Vietnam War was raging. Calley was in charge of a platoon that, on March 16 of that year, was instructed to invade and destroy the Vietnamese village of My Lai, an alleged Vietcong stronghold. When they arrived, they found no Vietcong, but Calley and his platoon nevertheless slaughtered hundreds of innocent civilian women and children.

A fellow soldier was so disturbed by the events that he wrote letters to Congress—letters that eventually brought Calley to trial for murder and resulted in his conviction. Calley's only defense throughout the trial was that he was simply following the instructions of his superiors. His remarks at the time were "Personally, I didn't kill any Vietnamese that day. I mean personally. I represented the United States of America. My country." These words underscore what happens when we are blindly loyal to authority.

A glimpse into his childhood gives us a few clues to help understand his actions. Calley is described as an unexcep-

PLAYING FIELD: MANAGING UP

Out of Bounds (Doing Too Little)	In Bounds (Doing About Right)	Out of Bounds (Doing Too Much)
• Asking probing questions.	• Identifying the boss's two or three key objectives and finding ways to help achieve those.	• Blindly following instructions to a T.
• Questioning tried-and-true ways of doing things—challenging the status quo.	• Choosing the right time and place to disagree with or present alternatives to management suggestions or directives.	• Focusing exclusively on the duties in your job description.
• Influencing the organization to go in new and necessary directions.	• Adding value to deliverables by analyzing the data, making recommendations, or illuminating critical pieces of information.	• Turning every discussion into an argument or debate.
• Asking for feedback.		• Challenging the boss's position in the presence of others.
• Supporting decisions once they are made by management.	• Routinely asking management, "What can I do more or less of to be more effective?"	
	• Publicly supporting management decisions.	

tional child and a product of a 1950s upbringing. He was sent to the Florida Military Academy after being caught cheating on a test in the seventh grade. We can only imagine what possessed his family to send him away and what he learned about following instructions once at the academy. One man recalls young Calley being a loyal friend: "His sense of loyalty was wonderful. If you had a problem at three thirty in the morning he would be there for you." After dropping out of junior college, he wandered from job to job until he wound up in the military. The same friend claims that Calley liked the regimentation and needed the discipline that the service afforded.

Calley's strengths apparently lay in these two factors— compliance and loyalty. But they became his greatest liabilities. After his release from prison (most of which, at President Richard Nixon's direction, was spent in his own apartment under house arrest)—he served less than four years of a life sentence—Calley refused to talk about the incident and to this day will not give interviews or discuss the matter. His silence is testament to his loyalty to the service, despite the fact that he was the only person convicted of crimes related to My Lai.

Except for the atrocious scale of his crime, Lieutenant Calley is no different from the scores of businesspeople who salute the boss and fail to add value to their positions due to their inability to confront authority when necessary or appropriate. These men and women are great followers, but the company suffers from their unwillingness to think and act independently of authority. They do as they are told, keep their noses clean, and perpetuate the status quo of their organizations.

PUTTING THE PAST INTO PERSPECTIVE

Beyond the examples above, difficulties with authority affect the lives of employees in all milieus. One illuminating case study comes from psychotherapist and corporate coach Susan Picascia. Susan, formerly with the Employee Assistance Program at Cedars-Sinai Medical Center in Los Angeles, now has her own consulting firm in which she coaches people on how to overcome the effects of childhood experiences in the workplace. She shares with us her experience coaching Alice, the manager of information research at a high-profile Hollywood-based entertainment firm.

As a manager, Alice is a technically proficient relationship builder who shows respect to her peers and staff and receives the same in return. She prides herself on being a compassionate, people-oriented manager with strong technical skills. Although she works independently in relation to others, Alice becomes dependent in relation to her boss, Curtis.

Unfortunately, Curtis reminds Alice of her father, who was a hypocritical perfectionist. In Curtis's case, it isn't so much that he's a perfectionist, but rather that he is so self-absorbed that he never takes time to notice Alice's many achievements or to give her feedback—except for negative comments on rare occasions when something isn't done as he wanted it. At those times, Alice cries in private because she feels like she can never do anything right in his eyes. In front of him, she becomes defensive, to which he reacts by saying, "Don't get your back up." She is beginning to question her ability and competence, despite the fact that she has successfully worked with bosses in other firms.

Although this is the first time in her career that Alice

has experienced a situation like this, it certainly won't be the last. The personal development that Alice must now undertake if she wants her career to remain professionally viable involves developing the ability to put "little Alice" on hold while "adult Alice" takes over. She must learn to judge herself, rather than allowing the opinions of others to eclipse her self-esteem. She can successfully accomplish this with these three specific coaching suggestions:

• **Lower her antennae for tuning in to feelings—both her feelings and Curtis's.** As a result of her experience with her father, Alice is supersensitive to criticism, especially from men. Whereas others would take Curtis's feedback at face value, Alice interprets it as failure. She learned early in life to put extra effort into doing things perfectly in order to ward off potential criticism and has transferred this behavior to the workplace. The obvious problem is that it's impossible to ward off criticism entirely. Inevitably, we all do something differently than the boss wants it done and must make adjustments. Alice's need to be perfect is getting in her way. No one in her present life—not even Curtis—expects her to be perfect. She must let go of this particular childhood defense mechanism and become less sensitive to Curtis's requests for change, as well as the manner in which he delivers these messages.

• **Raise her antennae for message content.** Conversely, Alice should pay more attention to the content of the message, thereby avoiding overreaction to how it is delivered. By focusing on the content, she can remove herself from the role of the child who is responsible for the opinions of her father/boss.

• **Use positive self-talk and visualize success.** When

feelings from the past surface, Alice must say to herself, *I will attend to my feelings later; right now the focus is on content. I will respond to content in an open-minded, nondefensive way.* Self-talk is a powerful tool to tape over the old messages that play in the back of our heads. By using self-talk and by visualizing successful encounters with the boss, Alice can develop new messages and images on which she can rely for support and encouragement when she needs them most.

Alice permits her past to define her present and future. The work of each of us is to be able to objectively see the authority figures in our lives as they really are and not as ghosts from the past. If you find yourself overreacting to your boss or other authority figures, ask yourself these questions:

- Who does he or she remind me of?
- Who or what do I act like when I am around this person?
- Why do I give up so much of my own power to him or her?

The answers to these questions will help you to begin demystifying the boss–employee relationship. And finally, remember these wise words of Eleanor Roosevelt: "No one can make you feel inferior without your consent."

THE SECRETS OF SUCCESSFULLY MANAGING UP

Even in the most enlightened organizations, where the manager's title has been changed to *team leader, coordinator,* or something equally nonhierarchical, there still exist certain expectations for how followers should interact with leaders. Although on the surface there has been a shift toward the appearance of egalitarianism, the Golden Rule of Management still prevails: *He or she who has the gold sets the rules.* The degree to which you are able to work within the boundaries established by the boss, and to adapt to the changing expectations from one boss to another, largely determines your ultimate success in an organization.

Here are the secrets of successfully managing up.

The Boss Is Only Human, with Strengths and Weaknesses Like Everyone Else

Expecting superhuman behavior from the boss, or thinking that you can aid in his or her development, is a little like trying to teach a pig to sing—it frustrates the teacher and annoys the pig. Reminding the boss about his or her weaknesses serves only to rub salt in the wound. Once you see the boss as human, you can overcome your childhood fantasies of having the perfect parent and interact with him or her on an adult-to-adult basis.

The Boss Wants You Not Only to Do Your Job, but to Make His or Her Job Easy as Well

This is not to be confused with threatening the boss by acting as if you want his or her job. Every reasonable request that the boss makes should be met with the implicit or explicit response: *No problem*. On the other hand, if you foresee a problem, let the boss know in a way that encourages problem solving as opposed to presenting obstacles. Bosses don't want to hear that it can't be done; they want to know how it can be done. Seek opportunities to help the boss with his or her workload. Not only is it appreciated, but you get the chance to learn skills that will be helpful to your career.

The Boss Never Wants to Be Embarrassed

If you want to disagree with the boss, do it in private—even if it means calling a time-out during a meeting. If he or she decides to make a course correction given your input, it must ultimately be the boss's decision. If a project fails or loses momentum due to the failure to heed your warning, in no way indicate, "I told you so." Continue to provide relevant information that will help guide the project back on course.

The Boss Doesn't Want to Have to Tell You What to Do

But he or she wants to know what you're doing. You add value by thinking strategically, foreseeing what has to be done, and preempting the boss from having to give you continual instructions. By planning for upcoming events, projects, or special needs, you show that you are capable of more than simply the day-to-day activities. Avoid being a loose cannon, however, by informing your boss of what you're planning and asking for input into the direction (no matter how much more technically capable you think you may be).

The Boss, Whether or Not He or She Admits It, Wants You to Make Him or Her Look Good

In the long term, making your boss look good makes you look good. Rather than always looking for ways to showcase your accomplishments, find opportunities to make the team and your team leader look good. By so doing, you will ultimately look like someone who is politically astute and capable of leading a team yourself.

The Boss Wants to Be Able to Give You Feedback Easily

When given feedback, listen to it, ask for clarification if necessary, think about it, but don't argue with it. No one particularly likes giving feedback in the first place. Don't make it any tougher by arguing your point or trying to negate it in some way. Regardless of the veracity of the feedback, openly listening to it at least gives the impression that you're flexible and open to change. That's half the battle. The other half is making enough changes to meet the boss's expectations without feeling you're compromising your own principles.

The Boss, in Most Cases, Is Not Capable of Helping You with Your Personal Problems

Even the most patient, enlightened, and understanding bosses have trouble with bringing personal issues to the workplace. They may be genuinely empathetic, but the bottom line is that they don't want to play amateur psychologist—nor should you expect them to. The best bosses make special allowances now and then, but as a rule, you shouldn't dwell on personal problems unless they're so severe that you know they will seriously affect your performance. Doing otherwise sets you up for close scrutiny and eventual feedback related to the problem.

The Boss Wants You to Deliver What You Promise

The easiest way to destroy credibility is to renege on your promises—especially those made to the boss. If trust is built on consistency, then lack of trust stems from broken promises. Use the fifty–fifty rule for planning your workload: Once you are given an assignment, you have half the amount of time until the deadline to ask questions and the other half to actually complete the project. If the boss doesn't hear from you within the first half of the time allotted for project completion, he or she assumes it will be done on time.

MANAGING UP WITH A DIFFICULT BOSS

The process of managing up is hard enough when you have a rational, mature boss. It's nearly impossible when you have one who isn't. Some of the worst bosses depicted on film include those from the movies *9 to 5*, *The Devil Wears Prada*, and *Scrooge*. You may not have a boss quite this challenging, but most of us worked with bosses who think employees never do anything right or who act like Scrooges with their compliments. This may be because they didn't give sufficient information, constantly changed their minds about how things should be done, or were so disorganized that the rules constantly changed when new information came to the forefront. Whatever the reason—and there are as many reasons as there are difficult bosses—it is still your responsibility to manage up effectively. Regardless of the difficulty, he or she who has the gold still sets the rules.

One problem inherent with difficult bosses is that they can significantly diminish your confidence and self-esteem. This is yet another situation where early-childhood experiences come into play. If a difficult boss reminds you of one of your parents or some other early authority figure, the likelihood that you will remain with him or her and be demoralized by inappropriate behavior is greater than if this was not your experience. Ray is a good case in point.

A very talented graphic artist working in the animated film industry, Ray consistently produces high-quality results that are admired and valued by his clients. His boss (the company's owner), however, comes from the Neanderthal school of management. Despite the fact that Ray puts in seventy to eighty hours of work a week (with no additional compensation, since he is a salaried employee), he is never given a word of positive reinforcement by his boss. "My boss won't say anything that will make me feel good," says Ray. "It's as if he thinks it will go to my head and I'll ask for a raise. He doesn't want me to have any sense of control. What he doesn't understand is that a compliment now and then would actually make me work even harder and I wouldn't want any more money."

Ray could go anywhere else and write his own ticket. He's that talented. His problem is that his boss is exactly like his father—who never gave him a word of encouragement and kept tight control over Ray during his childhood. When others point out to Ray that he really should be looking elsewhere for a job, he comes up with a litany of excuses. Ray is bound by his history to repeat a familiar situation because it is in some ways comfortable. To leave would mean symbolically breaking the tie with his father.

If Ray's boss weren't the company owner, the situation might be different. The difficulties that such bosses present to their followers typically do not go unnoticed by their superiors. One of two things happens: The bosses are marginalized or even let go because of the behavior, or they are kept in their positions because they do get the job done—even if it's at the expense of others. In their monograph *Coping with an Intolerable Boss*, authors Michael Lombardo and Morgan McCall report their findings of interviews with seventy-three managers who were asked to talk about their experiences working with intolerable bosses. Lombardo and McCall found that patience and waiting the boss out is often the best course of action. Creating an adversarial situation is only counterproductive. Here's what they say:

> *Even an intolerable boss is still the boss. . . . A few of the managers [in the study] tried to change the boss, but in only six situations did a manager report any significant change in his superior's behavior as a result of the subordinate's efforts. The far more productive strategies were to change one's own response or, as a last resort, to get out of the situation.*

In the meantime, the question remains, how do you maintain your sanity and self-respect when working for an intolerable boss? Here are a few ideas for how you can maintain some semblance of control over your life in the face of a difficult situation:

• **See the boss as the boss—not as your mother or father.** As should now be abundantly clear, you must first understand the effect that childhood experiences have on dealing with authority, then separate in your mind your boss from your parents or other authority figures. This is especially true when it comes to dealing with a difficult boss. He or she may unintentionally be pushing the same buttons that Mom or Dad did—and you therefore react the same way as you did when you were a powerless child. When you find yourself angry or frustrated with the boss, first ask yourself whether you feel as you did when you were a child or as you feel around your parents. If so, switch gears and tell yourself that you are now an adult and give yourself permission to respond differently. Such a response may include the realization that you are not bonded by blood to this person and you can leave if you choose.

• **Anticipate and prepare for difficult behavior.** Difficult bosses often exhibit the same behaviors over and over. If you take the time to analyze it, you can predict certain behaviors with quite a bit of accuracy. I once had a boss who, no matter how much time and effort I put into a report, would march into my office and pick it apart. It always made me feel guilty, as if I hadn't done enough work on it to begin with. In order to deal with him and my feelings about his response to my efforts, I made a game of tallying the number of things he claimed that I'd overlooked. I kept my little scorecard underneath the phone in my office; whenever he left, I added chit marks to the score. Anticipating his response, and making light of it without ignoring his comments, enabled me to maintain my self-confidence in the face of ongoing criticism.

• **Weigh the risks versus the benefits of telling the boss what you need.** Consider the possibility that the boss just doesn't have a clue about what he or she is doing that is creating a problem for you. Decide what the worst thing that could happen would be if you told him or her how you felt and what you needed in order to be more effective in your position. This must, of course, be done without affixing blame, but rather by giving an *I* message. For example, if the boss consistently fails to give you enough information to do a project properly, you could say something like, "I think I could be more effective if I had more details at the beginning of a project. Would it be possible to go over the specific requirements and how it fits into the bigger picture?" A riskier, but potentially even more beneficial, strategy would be to give the boss direct feedback as to how his or her behavior is affecting you. Still using the *I* message technique, you could say something such as, "I find it difficult to complete assignments efficiently because of the lack of information I'm given at the start of a project. I'm wondering whether it would be possible for you to be more specific when I begin rather than complete a project." If it doesn't work, you're no worse off than you were before having the conversation.

- **Remember that the best defense is a good offense.** This doesn't mean that you should be defensive with a difficult boss, even though it's easy to fall into that trap. Instead, it means that—knowing what his or her hot buttons are—you should be thoroughly prepared and well organized in those particular areas. If the boss is a stickler for having a document free of typos, make certain that that's what you provide, even if it means having a colleague, or several colleagues, proofread your work for you. If it's tardiness that drives him or her up the wall, then you should be making Herculean efforts to meet deadlines and arrive to work and meetings on time. For whatever reason, what may seem like a small thing to you is a big thing to the boss. Recognize what these things are, and head him or her off at the pass.

• **Evaluate the cost of staying in your position.** There comes a time with a difficult boss when you must ask yourself if it's worth it to stay. If in fact you have tried all of the things suggested above and the situation gets no better, you have only three alternatives: (1) Put up with it, hoping things will change; (2) request a transfer within the company; or (3) quit. I have heard people say that they have to stay in their position because it pays well or because good jobs are hard to find, both of which are true, but there is a psychological cost to doing so. If the benefits of the job outweigh the cost in terms of damage to your self-confidence or self-esteem, then the logical choice is to stay and hope that the situation will eventually change. I have seen people wait it out until the boss eventually quits, is fired, or is promoted to another position. However, when the cost becomes too great, you have no alternative but to request a transfer (if the company is large enough) or seek other employment. Most people with a difficult boss find that life improves significantly once the decision is made to leave, and once they actually begin a new job they wish they had done it sooner.

The ability to manage up is simply another element that successful people include in their skill sets. They know that good followership is as important as good leadership, and they make it easy for others to lead them. However, making it easy for others to lead can be difficult if the parameters of the employee–boss relationship are not clearly understood. Be realistic about the boss's expectations as well as how and to what extent they can be met. Most important, disengage from past personal circumstances and behaviors so that they don't obscure current workplace roles and relationships.

■

COACHING TIPS TO MANAGE UP

Put a check mark in the box of two or three coaching tips you commit to doing.

❑ **Always remember the Golden Rule of Management: *He or she who has the gold sets the rules.*** You can present your ideas and use your best influence skills to try to persuade others of the validity and value of your ideas, but in the end management makes the call. It doesn't mean you didn't have a good idea or even a great one. It only means management holds the trump card.

❑ **Choose your battles carefully.** Not every issue needs to be a battle, and even if you win the battle you could lose the war. Managers often describe employees who are a general nuisance as *high maintenance.* This can mean the employee takes issue with too many management decisions, doesn't understand the politics of the corporate culture, or doesn't know when to back off or let go of an idea the boss is never going to accept. You move from high maintenance to not trustworthy when you go behind the boss's back to further your personal agenda. Decide if an issue is the hill you're willing to die on. Is an outcome favorable to your position so important that you would stake your future with the company on it? If so, then go for it. But if not, leave the door open for ongoing discussion by graciously moving away rather than pushing management into a corner or making managers uncomfortable with endless discussions.

❑ **Make giving feedback to you easy by asking the boss how you can improve.** If you ask the boss, "How am I doing?" you're likely to get the answer "fine" in response. Instead, ask for feedback in these terms: "Can you tell me two or three things I'm doing that you'd like to see me keep doing and two or three things I could do more of to be more effective?" This provides a format where the feedback will be behavioral rather than describe characteristics you can do nothing about.

❑ **Never confront the boss in the presence of a higher authority.** I don't care how inclusive, egalitarian, collaborative, or open-minded bosses are—they don't want to be confronted or surprised in front of the person with whom *they* manage up. If you want to disagree or present a vastly alternative viewpoint, do it in private. On the other hand, you can diplomatically put the issue on the table without being confrontational by saying something like "I have a slightly different take on this. Would this be a good time to share it?"

❑ **Deliver more than you're asked for.** A chief complaint of many managers is employees who do exactly what they're asked but nothing more. When delivering on assignments, consider how you could add value by performing additional analyses, providing related information that wasn't asked for, or making recommendations based on your unique expertise.

❑ **Weigh the risk versus the profit of giving the boss feedback.** If he or she is engaging in behavior that makes it impossible to do your job effectively or borders on unethical or illegal, the potential profit of talking about it far outweighs the risk. On the other hand, if you've got a boss who is known to be punitive or retaliatory, is passive-aggressive, or has more blind spots than a fleet of cars, you'd be better off just waiting him or her out or finding ways to survive her behavior until one of you changes positions.

❑ **View differences of opinion with management as just that.** They're differences to be discussed, not confrontations to be won or lost. Too many employees interact with the boss like belligerent teenagers being told they can't have the keys to the car or can't stay out beyond midnight. They kick their debate behavior into high gear and are more likely to wind up damaging the relationship than winning the argument. When exploring differences of opinion, focus first on points of agreement, then on ways to capitalize on the best of all ideas on the table rather than arguing for your own position.

❑ **Read *Your Boss Is Not Your Mother: Eight Steps to Eliminating Office Drama and Creating Positive Relationships at Work* by Dr. Debra Mandel.** I was asked by the publisher to review this book before it came out and must say I was impressed with the practical advice the author provides, particularly when it comes to identifying and understanding the boss–subordinate relationship.

❑ **Have outside interests that capture your passion so that work issues can be put into perspective.** If you make work your entire life, then even the smallest things can be blown out of proportion. Having a rich and rewarding life outside work enables you to see people and events as they really are—not skewed by the degree to which you're magnifying them.

❑ **Be willing to give the boss your honest opinion and make every effort to influence him or her toward a decision that is in the best interest of the organization, but remember that the decision ultimately may not be yours.** When asked or at the appropriate time, it's perfectly acceptable—even admirable—that you give your honest opinion. Using the best influence skills in your arsenal, make a good case for your position in the most diplomatic way possible, but remember the maxim offered by one CEO: "Push once. Push twice. Three times is too many."

❑ **Once a decision is made, fully support it—even if you disagree with it.** Again, unless the decision is unethical or illegal, management has the right to establish direction and expect that you will help achieve it. If you absolutely can't, then you need to transfer or find another position outside the company. It is simply not acceptable that you sabotage or in other ways diminish the effectiveness of your boss or the company because you don't agree with a decision. If you're accepting the company's money to achieve its goals, then ethically you have the responsibility to further those goals.

❑ **Keep your boss informed about what you're planning to do and ask for input.** Most bosses don't like to micromanage—but neither do they like surprises. They want the people reporting to them to be self-starters who see what needs to be done, then go out and do it. You can increase your value to the company by identifying company, customer, or client needs, developing plans to address those needs, and informing your boss about what you're doing and asking for his or her thoughts on the matter. This is not to be confused with asking permission to take action. In this case, you're just giving the boss a heads-up and showing respect for his or her expertise by asking for input.

❑ **If you are inclined to acquiesce to authority, take small risks standing up for what you believe in.** You don't have to make a federal case out of having an opinion different from your boss's. Look for small, safe opportunities to express contrasting opinions on low-impact topics. This will allow you to work your way up to the more important ones.

❑ **Consider the possibility that you may be better off in a different position or company.** If you are consistently the one out of step with everyone else (particularly the boss), if you can't align behind the goals of your organization or department, or if you feel what you're being asked to do compromises your values, ethics, or morals, then it's time to vote with your feet. And when you do leave, don't slam the door by bad-mouthing the company or its management. They may not have been a good match for you, but it doesn't mean they aren't making a valuable contribution to your business or industry.

SUCCESS STRATEGY 6

Balance Detail Orientation with Strategic Thinking

Strategy without tactics is the slowest route to victory. Tactics without strategy is the noise before defeat.

General Sun Tzu

There may be no better exemplar in modern business of someone whose professional reputation was left in tatters (and in this case *that's* an understatement) because of his inability to balance detail orientation with strategic thinking than the late Kenneth Lay, former CEO of Enron. At least that's what he wanted us to believe before he was convicted of, among other things, willful ignorance. Although he unexpectedly passed away before he was sentenced, Lay was facing up to forty-five years in jail for his criminal convictions. The backstory here is that energy giant Enron filed for bankruptcy in late 2001 after it was found the company had engaged in systematic accounting fraud that made earnings look better and its losses smaller than they actually were. Executives manipulated its numbers, and may have manipulated its employees into believing their retirement savings were safe with the company. Yet

Lay insisted he knew nothing about the fraud being perpetrated and publicly claimed the only thing he was guilty of was being too trusting of his CFO, Andrew Fastow.

Did he know about the complex machinations of the company's finances? At least two former executives, Fastow and Sherron Watkins, testified that they'd told him about the problems. But whether they did or didn't doesn't make much difference legally. The fact of the matter is that as the CEO, Lay *should have known* what was going on. Although there are those—many of them CEOs of major corporations themselves—who would argue that there's no way a CEO can know all the intricate details of what goes on in a company, as Harry Truman said, *The buck stops here.* If Lay didn't know about fraud of *this magnitude*, shame on him. If he *did* know and did nothing to stop it, that's unlawful.

Most of us seem to have a natural inclination to pay attention to either the nitty-gritty details or to the bigger picture. It's what makes us choose professions such as accounting, medical technology, and administration over those in research, social work, or architecture. This isn't to say that there aren't people in accounting who are capable of seeing the bigger picture or people who prefer a detail orientation who become social workers, but rather that such preferences often influence our choice of career and our ultimate success in those professions.

If you refer back to the MBTI Preferences Chart on page 88, you'll see that on the Attending scale (what a person likes to pay attention to), there are two types of people: sensers and intuitors. This gives us our greatest clue to whether we prefer details or the big picture. Whereas sensers prefer to deal with what is concrete, real, and tangible, intuitors are happier operating in the realm of theory and possibility. As you peruse the two lists, think about where you fit in. One source of job dissatisfaction can arise from being in a job that is counter to your natural inclination.

Another way of understanding these preferences comes from research pertaining to the brain's functioning. We know that the left and right hemispheres of the brain each process and handle information in distinctly different ways. Betty Edwards, in her work *Drawing on the Right Side of the Brain*, explains that the left hemisphere "analyzes, abstracts, counts, marks time, plans step-by-step procedures, verbalizes, [and] makes rational statements based on logic," whereas the right hemisphere helps us "understand metaphors, dream, [and] create new combinations of ideas." Her contention, that our culture and educational system tend to focus on and value left-hemisphere activity, explains why so many of us have difficulty bringing our more creative selves to the forefront. It isn't that we don't have creative capability; it's just that this capability is underdeveloped and languishes from lack of use.

It is no wonder, then, that so many corporations suffer from a lack of creativity. The strengths that most of us have in right-brain functioning are not balanced with left-brain activity. Long after we lose our effectiveness, we continue to do the same things in the same way. We fail to draw on our capacity to envision our products or services differently and, instead, perpetuate the status quo. We maintain, but we don't create, thereby losing the competitive edge. This becomes especially problematic when the people who are entrusted to lead organizations are saddled with strength only in right-brain functioning.

People with sustained career success are good at both. They don't sacrifice close attention to detail for broader, more strategic thinking, and vice versa. They successfully

_____ I am equally good at seeing the forest through the trees and the trees through the forest.

_____ Given a project, I first think about how it fits into the overall scheme of things and then become involved in the details of making it happen.

_____ I can take a good idea and turn it into a reality.

_____ I don't get bogged down in analysis paralysis.

_____ I find it as easy to come up with better ways of doing routine tasks as it is to develop processes for implementing these ideas.

_____ I'm patient with projects that require close attention to detail.

_____ I am seldom bored during brainstorming sessions.

_____ If I had the technical ability to do both, it would be as appealing to me to design a house as it would be to actually build it.

_____ I balance my checkbook regularly, but I don't spend an inordinate amount of time trying to find where it may be off by a few cents.

_____ It is fairly easy for me to see and hear nuances in messages and interpersonal communication.

balance detail orientation with a view of the bigger picture. Use the checklist on the opposite page to see how good you are at this balancing act.

STRATEGIC THINKING + ATTENTION TO DETAIL = SUCCESS

Thomas Alva Edison, possibly the most prolific inventor of the nineteenth century, is an example of a historical figure who successfully balanced attention to detail with strategic thinking. Never a particularly good student, Edison was described as "addled" by one teacher; another called him "dreamy, inattentive, with a tendency to drift off during recitations." These comments motivated Edison's mother to take him out of public school and tutor him herself. Even as a child, Edison exhibited the essence of a true visionary: curiosity. In adulthood, that same curiosity and willingness to take risks made him one of the most successful inventors of our time. By the age of twenty-one, Edison had invented a stock ticker-tape machine, and throughout his life he produced more than one thousand invaluable devices, such as the electric lightbulb, steam-driven power stations, the alkaline storage battery, celluloid film, the movie projector, and the phonograph, the invention in which he took the most pride. Edison had vision, but he also had the technical competence and proficiency to make those visions a reality.

On the business front, Elizabeth Claiborne (better known as Liz) provides an inspirational example of someone who had a vision and developed a strategy to turn it into a billion-dollar Fortune 500 company. With a background in art, she worked her way up the ladder of fashion design, ultimately becoming chief designer for Jonathan Logan. Despite her frustration over the fact that she could not sell her fashion vision to her employer, she remained with the company for sixteen years. Like many career women, she deferred her own dream while her husband pursued his and until her children were safely through college. Finally, in 1975, at age forty-six, Claiborne invested her family's life savings of fifty thousand dollars to form the fashion giant that shares her name.

Claiborne intuitively knew what fashions should be designed and marketed to working women and at what price. When she started her business, this was a largely untapped market. Her less visionary colleagues continued producing clothes designed for pencil-thin models, not the average female figure, while Claiborne saw and filled a gap in the clothes market. Her strategy was to design mix-and-match clothes, decide how much women would be willing to pay for each design, and then negotiate to have them produced in Asia at a cost consistent with the sales price.

Within six years of the company start-up, Liz Claiborne clothing generated $117 million in revenues and soon thereafter went public. Within ten years, Claiborne's personal net worth was estimated at two hundred million dollars. Within fifteen years, sales were double those of her established competitors, and the company was named the Fortune 500's most profitable firm. Today the firm dominates the field of women's better sportswear, generating more than four billion annually in revenues.

Edison and Claiborne have markedly different stories, but they're both ordinary human beings who produced extraordinary results. Countless great ideas never become reality because people can't attend to the details required to carry them through. An idea without a plan for execution

THE DETAIL–STRATEGIC THINKING CONTINUUM

Acute Attention to Detail	Balanced Attention to Detail and Strategic Thinking	Overutilized Strategic Thinking
Acute attention is paid to minute detail and to doing the job in a prescribed, routine way, while outside factors that affect the work are neglected, overlooked, or seen as impediments to task accomplishment. Project completion may suffer due to overconcern with detail.	A project is looked at in its entirety with all variables being considered, including the human resources that are required, innovations that would make it more valuable, and a specific plan for carrying it out in the most efficient and cost-effective manner.	Ideas and concepts are of prime importance, while practical implications for executing ideas are overlooked. Projects are stalled due to ongoing changes, revisions, and analyses.

is only a dream. Close adherence to detail conceptualization maintains status quo. The ability to think broadly and act intentionally forms the core of balancing detail orientation with strategic thinking.

With a little practice, we are all capable of functioning on the dual levels of detail orientation and strategic thinking. On the chart on page 227, you can see that there is a continuum running from highly detail-oriented to overly concerned with the big picture.

As you move toward the center of the continuum, there is an increased balance between the two extremes that provides for maximum job effectiveness. People at either extreme are limited in the value that they add to a job or project. Ideally, we would surround ourselves in the work environment with people who complement our strengths, but because this is typically not possible, the job is either done routinely, with little concern for innovation or customer needs, or is stalled entirely due to analysis paralysis.

Jim Harkins, former director of business and strategic planning at AlliedSignal Aerospace, introduced me to the concept of strategic intent, which is another way to approach strategic thinking. He cites numerous examples of companies that had broad visions for what they wanted to accomplish and developed specific plans for how to achieve them—despite seemingly insurmountable odds. One case in point is Canon Business Machines in Costa Mesa, California. Canon's management made the *strategic decision* not to take on the leader in the field, Xerox, but instead to develop inexpensive copiers and provide services ancillary to their use. With this strategic intent, Canon has become better than any of its competitors at building the copier printing engines, and in the process earned the respect of customers and colleagues.

Major corporations such as IBM, GM, and Sears are still reeling from their own failure to do what Canon did—redefine their visions of the future. They were so caught up in their routines and what worked yesterday that they neglected to see the changes in customer needs and what was needed to be successful tomorrow. Strategic intent works for companies and for individuals who want to be seen as adding value to their organizations. Attention to the future helps you focus on what's important, guide your career, and make value-added contributions to your organization.

The business world is full of individuals who have not progressed as far and as fast as they would have liked due to an inordinate focus on either detail orientation or strategic thinking—but not a balance of the two. In his presentations to corporate leaders, Harvard Professor John Kotter routinely mentions two such examples from the airline industry: Frank Borman, former president of Eastern Air Lines, and Donald Burr, founder of the once wildly popular airline People Express. Clearly, both men achieved great things in their careers, but neither really achieved as much as he wanted to because he over-relied on a unique strength.

Frank Borman is remembered by many as the commander of the first human flight around the moon. Fewer people remember that he went on to become president of Eastern Air Lines in 1975—perhaps because he resigned in 1986 under less-than-favorable conditions. As a child, he spent hours engrossed in building model airplanes—a somewhat solitary activity. His schoolmates didn't want much to do with him because they found him bossy, which left him even more isolated. Borman went on to attend West Point, where he is remembered for being staunchly independent. One former classmate recalls that when an upperclassman intentionally stamped on his foot as part of the traditional hazing process (where underclassmen are expected to grin and bear it), Borman instead "called him a son of a bitch and threatened to kill him." When he graduated in 1950, his training as a pilot combined with a scientific education enabled him to become an astronaut in the Gemini program.

Not surprisingly, given his character and background, Borman earned the reputation at Eastern as a command-and-control leader. His goal for the struggling airline was to "restore discipline and profitability." The only problem was that he wanted to accomplish this while at the same time treating his staff like functionaries. He expected them to respond in much the same way as an aircraft would to his deft maneuvering: swiftly and unquestioningly. Borman never understood that his success depended on looking at the bigger picture, seeing how people fit into strategies, and recognizing that creative problem solving would be his only salvation—not command and control. He pounded employees with letters about the problems Eastern was facing and underscored his expectation that everyone would sacrifice for the good of the whole. His training as an engineer precluded him from balancing a strong orientation toward controlling detail with creatively and strategically seeking solutions to his company's problems.

An entrepreneur by the name of Donald Burr, on the other hand, suffered from the opposite limited skill set. From childhood, he did everything with passion. As a youth, he was even a proselytizer for his church, traveling from city to city to recruit other teens into a fellowship program. He approached his work in much the same way. Aviation was more than just a career to him—it was a "romance." In 1981, Burr started his own airline, People

Express, after walking out on former boss Frank Lorenzo at Texas International Airlines. He had a vision for a no-frills airline where passengers benefited from low prices and friendly service and employees from an exciting and rewarding work environment. He made it a contingency of employment that all employees own stock in the company. Burr himself conducted much of the new-employee training, using his proselytizing skill to generate enthusiasm and rally people behind his vision.

At the time, the concept of cheap fares was a radical one: Other airlines would charge $189 to $250 or more for a flight that cost only $79 on People Express. To do this, Burr shifted outside the normal airline paradigm and expanded the scope of each job, limited services offered, and made employees partners in the business. Whereas Eastern had dozens of job categories and a terrible relationship with its unions, People Express had only three categories: the people who fly the plane, the people who fix the plane, and everyone else. A truly creative solution to rising airfares. So why did Burr stumble? He failed to manage the details inherent to his business and listen to his advisers, who tried to talk him out of expanding when there were no systems in place to manage the expansion. His staff, including top management, burned out while Burr continued hammering away at the vision. Burr was great when it came to developing a vision, but short on attention to the kinds of details with which executives are expected to be familiar.

You may be surprised when you read that a person who successfully combined the two skill sets was a woman who worked with cosmetics and had a penchant for pink Cadillacs—the late Mary Kay Ash, founder of Mary Kay Cosmetics. She began her business with a clear strategic intent: to create a company that would enable women to be financially independent while permitting them to focus on God first, family second, and work third. Next, she had the foresight to surround herself with good people who complemented her own natural abilities. Mary Kay thought strategically and planned thoughtfully—a combination of skills that contributed significantly to her success and the success of everyone involved with Mary Kay Cosmetics. When less enlightened leaders attempted to embarrass her about the fact that she rewarded employees with pink Cadillacs, her typical response was "What color Cadillacs do you give to your employees?"

SQUARE PEGS IN ROUND HOLES

People with a natural inclination for either detail orientation or strategic thinking often choose jobs that enable them to rely on one or the other skill. It is no coincidence that those who are happy working for the IRS generally have an ability to pay acute attention to detail, whereas those who find job satisfaction at the Jet Propulsion Laboratory are likely to be strategic thinkers. Both types of people, however, may find themselves in a quandary when they are forced into a job or assignment that requires the complementary behavior. Just one skill or the other isn't enough to assure continued success.

A few years ago, a client company of mine had a significant reduction in its workforce, entirely eliminating its public relations department. One staff member, whom I will call Amanda, had been with the company for nearly twenty years, and her management wanted to reward her loyalty by finding a place for her in another department.

Amanda had been a public relations coordinator and, as such, had significant contact with the media, senior executives, and esteemed guests. She was superb at finessing all of the relationships involved in her job.

Amanda's managers were pleased when they found her a job as a clerk in their benefits department. Now they wouldn't have to lay her off. Amanda was pleased as well—at least in the beginning. After Amanda had been in the new job for several months, I called her to see how she was doing. This normally upbeat and optimistic woman was extremely unhappy in her new job and was thinking about leaving the company. When I probed into what the problem was, she said that she couldn't stand working alone day after day and paying such close attention to the most minute details that her job required.

For twenty years, Amanda saw the big picture, juggled multiple tasks and people, and paid close attention to people problems. When she was put into a job that required close attention to detail and afforded little contact with people, it wasn't so much that she *couldn't* do it, but that she didn't want to do it. And herein lies the mistake that so many companies make: When people fail to succeed in their positions, they send them for training rather than assess their suitability for the job. The fact is, most of us can do whatever we put our minds to—provided, of course, that we have the necessary basic skills. When we're not doing what we're capable of, though, it does no good to get more training. Job satisfaction comes from doing what we're good at and naturally incline toward. When we enjoy our work, we are more likely to be able to balance the big picture with the details required to do it.

A case in point is that of a woman who was sent for coaching because she "wasn't detail-oriented enough and displayed poor judgment." When I asked her boss to be more specific, he gave the example of how she'd chosen the wrong kind of furniture for the executive offices. Instead of choosing conservative, dark wood, she chose to go with a lighter, more contemporary look. Before my first meeting with the woman, I went to the executive floor to take a look at the furniture. It was a lovely choice that complemented the surroundings, but it couldn't be called conservative.

At our first meeting, I asked the woman why she thought coaching had been suggested for her. She said that she supposed it was because she didn't fit in. She had an artistic background and had been hired as an interior decorator for the company based on her knowledge of design. Nevertheless, management always second-guessed her decisions. She brought to our second meeting a portfolio of watercolors that were incredibly beautiful. As she proudly displayed each one, she said that this was what she wanted to be doing—painting. It occurred to me as I looked at the artworks that one has to have an eye for detail to be able to paint on the scale that she was clearly capable of. On the other hand, she had to see the world in a way that was very different from that of her corporate counterparts. It wasn't that she didn't have detail orientation or that she lacked good judgment; she simply wasn't inclined to pay attention to the details required in her job.

Both this woman and Amanda were fortunate to have enough self-confidence not to settle for jobs for which they were ill suited. Once Amanda recognized the true nature of her problem, she asked for a transfer to a different type of work that would more fully use her talents. She's now working happily as the administrative assistant in a busy department where she gets to interact with many different types of people and use her fine administrative skills. And as for the artist—she's now living in Taos, New Mexico, a perfect setting for artists and watercolor painting.

Just because you aren't detail- or big-picture-oriented in one situation doesn't mean you can't be in another. The trick is to find work that allows you to use both skills and to know when to apply each. The more you like your work, the greater the likelihood that you'll be able to call on the full range of your capabilities instead of exclusively relying on just a few strengths. It is this delicate balance that contributes to long-term success.

One last anecdote before providing you with some suggestions for how to find that balance. I received a call from a man whom I had met during a supervisory skills training program. He said that he was going to do an employee's annual performance review and wanted to run by me what he was going to say to make sure he wasn't being too subjective. He faxed me the review, and as I was studying it I noticed that it pretty much revolved around the need to develop more follow-through and attention to detail. When I called him back to discuss it, I mentioned that it seemed as though the employee might not enjoy what he was doing. Generally, when people like their work, they quite naturally pay attention to the details of it and complete it in a timely fashion. In other words, we do well the things we like doing and put off what we don't enjoy. After a moment's pause, the man said that this was indeed true. He had spoken on numerous occasions with the employee about the fact that he seemed mismatched for the job, but that there were no more suitable jobs available in the company at the time.

I don't envy the manager who has to coach people doing work they dislike. When employees try to fit into the wrong job, their energy is diverted by trying to make the work fit, rather than doing the job efficiently and effectively. Your ultimate success depends on doing work that you love and for which you are well suited. You cannot expect to achieve peak performance when you aren't interested in the fundamental nature of your work. Certainly, there are aspects of all jobs that we may not like but need to do nonetheless. We have to learn to do these tasks with enthusiasm and attention equal to that which we bring to the tasks we enjoy. Still, lasting satisfaction comes from our enjoying the nature of our work. Balancing details and the big picture is much easier when you're in the right job than it is when you're doing something simply because it pays well or because someone always expected you would do it.

FACTORS CONTRIBUTING TO A NARROW FOCUS

The tendency to focus on details to the exclusion of the bigger picture is characterized by the need to micromanage people and processes, overattendance to minutiae, and the inability to see the relationships among issues or factors. People with high detail orientation typically do well in jobs that require precision and meticulous singular concentration. It is a wonderful gift to be that precise. It is necessary, but not sufficient. It must be balanced with the opposite—the ability to think strategically.

Although there is evidence that the inclinations toward either detail orientation or strategic thinking are something we are born with, both can become overdeveloped. For example, logical, linear thinking, or detail orientation, is valued in our educational system. Overdevelopment of this particular strength can also stem from the need to function effectively in a chaotic childhood home or from having parents who were not sufficiently attentive to the child's needs. The child, then, learns to compensate for this household deficit by becoming hypervigilant. Fearing that important things will be overlooked or neglected entirely, he or she ensures that nothing is missed by paying close attention to the details of daily life. Paradoxically, however, things *are* overlooked because he or she is not able to view the entire situation.

In the workplace, acute attention to detail is displayed by people who follow instructions religiously and honor tried-and-true ways of doing things. If they're given an assignment with incorrect instructions, instead of realizing that the instructions are wrong, they may continue along the path until someone else points out the problem. For example, when told to "hold all calls and take messages," a person may do as instructed, but fail to realize that when the company president is on the line it might be appropriate to put that particular call through (or at least check with the boss). Or employees may prepare reports with illogical conclusions because they fail to see that there has been a mistake in a formula or procedure used to reach those conclusions. This is why outstanding bookkeepers may not make particularly good financial analysts. The skills required to be accurate are not the same as those needed to assess the broader financial picture. It's easy to see how someone with strong detail orientation adds only limited value to an organization.

In addition to the childhood factors contributing to detail orientation, there are a number of other reasons why people fail to think strategically. They include:

- **Fear.** In an effort to get it "right," some people miss the nuances in a message. They try too hard and wind up listening selectively. Such fear may be generalized to all situations, or may apply only to those that involve people in authority. I recall early in my career giving instructions to an assistant to cancel the arrangements previously made for a visit to a particular city. She asked me for all of the details about the date, flight, and airline and canceled them, but neglected to cancel all concomitant plans—car, hotel, and so on. She was great when given specific instructions, but she could not take the next step to assure that all related aspects of a project were similarly attended to. The woman's fear of making a mistake caused her to miss the bigger picture in favor of focusing on a specific task. The value that she could add was limited by this fear.

- **Rigidity.** People who engage in ritualistic or other narrowly defined behavior frequently can't see new and different ways of doing things. They plod along the same path, every day, in the same way. They would never think of driving a different way to work, eating something different for breakfast, or solving a problem in an unorthodox way. Instead, they do things in prescribed and familiar ways. When asked why they didn't do something more effectively, they often reply that it never occurred to them. Rigidity impedes the ability to think broadly and strategically.

- **The inability to deal with ambiguity.** I've never forgotten a line from a college textbook that said something to the effect of "The sign of the mentally healthy person is the one who can deal best with ambiguity, because that's all life is—ambiguous." Those people who must deal with the known, as opposed to the possible, have tremendous difficulty thinking broadly. By operating within a constant comfort zone of what is known, as opposed to what could be, such people never take the kinds of risks required to successfully balance detail orientation with strategic thinking.

• **High sense of urgency.** Individuals may focus so hard on completing a task they feel is urgent that they miss its how, why, and what. In an effort to get the job done expediently, they fail to see how it may tie in to the bigger picture. Ironically, the opposite end of the spectrum—being involved in the big picture to the exclusion of attention to detail—can also result from a high sense of urgency, for reasons that I'll discuss later.

• **Low sense of urgency.** This factor affects people on both ends of the spectrum as well. People with an overdeveloped detail orientation and a low sense of urgency frequently underestimate the amount of time they actually have to complete a project and spend an inordinate amount of time on the technicalities involved. They spend their time making fail-safe plans, nitpicking, and reviewing the most mundane details as opposed to understanding that a project must be completed both accurately and in a timely fashion.

• **Narrowly defined roles.** One mistake made by many businesses is to define employee roles too narrowly. This was a trend in the 1970s and 1980s, and a generation of specialists emerged. People were asked to do one thing really well. They developed a depth of knowledge in their fields but lacked a breadth of experience that would later be useful to them. When the layoffs of the 1990s hit, they were ill equipped to take on broader responsibilities. Although job descriptions provide an in-depth understanding of a particular role, they can narrow the employee's perspective and expectations. In the past, organizations had plenty of people with each type of preference—detail and big-picture people—to meet their needs. As they have downsized, however, it's expected that the people remaining will be able to function comfortably in both arenas. It's now more critical than ever that people be able to both initiate and implement new ideas—a feat requiring both detail and strategic thinking skills.

WAYS TO DEVELOP STRATEGIC THINKING

The shift from detail orientation to strategic thinking is probably the toughest behavioral change suggested in this book. It requires not only specific behavioral changes, but also changes in how you look at the world. The factors contributing to the former are so strong that they completely eclipse the ability to engage in the latter. Even the term *strategic thinking* is ominous to some who perceive this function to be the exclusive domain of people in think tanks or strategic planning jobs. Instead, it's simply a way of describing the behaviors required to think more broadly. The following suggestions can help you become a strategic thinker:

• **Avoid taking notes when someone is talking to you.** So many people tell me they have to write everything down or else they'll forget what they've been told. Most of those same people never refer back to their notes after the initial conversation, proving you *don't* have to write everything down to remember it. The technique of active listening described under Success Strategy 1 can help to take the place of note taking. To comprehend the entire picture, you can't grasp only one aspect of it. I once coached a woman who tried to write down everything I said (can you guess what she had to work on?). Inevitably, she missed the point of what I was saying by attempting to capture the details. Surrender yourself to the speaker, ask questions, and paraphrase what you've just heard. This will allow you to hear and understand the subtleties of the message.

- **Ask yourself,** *What's the bigger picture here?* Take time from the task to think momentarily about what it means, how it fits in with other projects, and why you are being asked to do it. Avoid the tendency to jump into a project before you've thought it through completely. Learn to become comfortable with negligible delays—especially when those delays are for the purpose of upfront planning. Most assignments aren't as urgent as you might initially think. You may even be imposing your own sense of urgency where there is none.

- **Consciously seek ways to improve processes.** Instead of doing the job in the same old way, think about how you might do it more efficiently or creatively. If necessary, get input from others about how they might approach the same task. Make suggestions for improving processes in ways that might prove to be more cost-effective or in some other way add value to your department or company.

- **Read books and journal articles that expand your understanding of trends in your field of expertise.** All too often we read only materials that address the technical aspects of how we do our jobs. This is important, but equally important are materials that ask you to think about where your field is headed, current challenges that it faces, and concepts that go beyond business as usual. See yourself as someone who anticipates and responds to the requirements of the future, rather than just reacting to them.

- **Broadly define your role.** Whether you're a secretary, first-line supervisor, or division vice president, look for ways in which your role interfaces with those of co-workers, other departments and companies, or customers. Talk to these people about their needs and ways in which you can partner with them in an effort to add value, and envision yourself at the center of a complex network rather than as a lone performer. Consider the possibility that you can create the ideal job for yourself by expanding, not changing, your role.

- **Resist perfectionism.** Perfectionists spend so much time attending to details that they often fail to see the larger issues involved in a project. They wind up missing the clues to success that often lie in the periphery. Rather than spend time perfecting perfection, use that time to think broadly and strategically about critical points of interface, better ways to do the job, and tomorrow's trends.

- **Be creative.** Betty Edwards's *Drawing on the Right Side of the Brain* and Julia Cameron's *The Artist's Way* are places to start. Both books provide exercises that stimulate right-brain thinking. You can also take classes in creative writing, drawing, or acting that will help you express your innate creative talents. Most important, don't worry about being good at it or doing it right; do it for fun.

STRATEGIC THINKING IN THE EXTREME

Even if you work in the most creative of environments where possibilities abound, such as a movie studio, fashion design house, or genetics engineering laboratory, you are still expected to produce well-thought-out and practical results. People who are gifted with the ability to think broadly, creatively, or strategically often suffer from analysis paralysis. They become so caught up in the idea that they overlook the need to turn it into reality. This is one way in which a strength taken to the extreme becomes a liability.

I once worked with a man who was brilliant at conceptualization. He could come up with ideas for any major project on which his company was working. If you wanted to brainstorm, he was the man to go to. The only problem was that he was short on implementation. He often provided solutions so complex that they couldn't possibly be carried out cost-effectively. Unable to work within boundaries, he was forever exceeding his budget without really producing results. When the company went through a downsizing, he was one of the first people tapped because his contribution to the organization was limited. He couldn't make his dreams a reality.

Another form of overutilization of strategic thinking comes with people who are manic. They are often off the scale of the creative continuum. You may know some of these folks. They are energetic, enthusiastic, and innovative—but so much so that they exceed the bounds of acceptable behavior. They tire us mortals out with their continual flow of ideas and concepts. They are frequently successful in entrepreneurial efforts, provided they don't overextend their resources, because they believe in their ability to overcome any obstacle and won't take no for an answer. They are less successful in the corporate arena because they typically can't function within the bounds of expected social and group behavior and are perceived as loose cannons by their management.

The factors contributing to overutilization of strategic thinking are not quite as clear-cut as those contributing to acute attention to detail. Certain types of personalities seem more inclined to be able to think broadly and creatively than others. Certainly being raised in a home or working in an environment where creativity is valued and encouraged is a plus, but there must also be a degree of imagination in the individual to begin with. Whereas innovativeness can be thwarted and not allowed to blossom fully, the opposite is not always true. It may be more difficult for people who have never developed a creative pursuit to develop an ability to innovate later in their lives, no matter how much they are encouraged to do so. Yet we can all stretch the boundaries of thinking that confine us by rejecting strict adherence to outdated norms, self-limiting paradigms, and early-childhood messages that have outlived their usefulness.

If you think too broadly and overlook the importance of producing results, the following suggestions should help you achieve balance with greater attention to detail:

• **Schedule time for both project development and project implementation.** When you're given an assignment, allocate a specific amount of time to be used for brainstorming, research, or development. Resist the tendency to use more time than you have allocated or to cut short the implementation period. On the front end, realistically assess how much time it will actually take to complete the project once it's designed and schedule adequate time to meet that requirement. To avoid being top-heavy with creative types, be certain to include people who complement your strengths on project teams.

• **Solicit input from (and listen to) your more practi-**

cal colleagues. Bounce your ideas off people you can trust who can see the realities of a situation. Ask them for their opinion of the practicality of your ideas, reasonableness of direction, and value to the company or customer. Rather than viewing these people as overly simplistic or obstacles to your brilliant ideas, consider the counterpoint they offer as valuable insight into what the organization might expect or find feasible.

- **Consider your audience.** When making presentations, consider the fact that you will most likely have to influence an array of personality types, most of whom don't share your big-picture orientation. Couch your remarks within a framework that will stretch the imaginations of the most conservative people in the audience without making them roll their eyes in disbelief or think that you're from another planet. Remember to include well-thought-out suggestions for how your idea can be implemented practically, efficiently, and cost-effectively.

- **Find an external outlet for creative endeavors.** If you work in an organization that just doesn't appreciate your creativity or ability to think strategically, ensure that you have outlets in your personal life to exercise those talents. Join clubs, write books, paint pictures, or associate with like-minded people who will validate and encourage you. A very creative woman who worked down the hall from me had a boring, mundane job poring over tables, data runs, and figures all day long. But to her, her work wasn't her life. Her life started when she left at 5:00 PM.

- **Consider the possibility that you are in the wrong job.** As with the artist who is now in Taos painting, it's an awful feeling to think that you have to sublimate your greatest gifts in order to fit into your organization. If you've tried everything suggested above and still can't quite focus on detail and planning to the degree that your management wants you to, then you might do better switching to a job or career that will value and use your unique skill set. There is a caveat here, however: *Wherever you go, you bring you along,* and that means that your developmental areas as well as your strengths follow you from job to job. A more creative environment may not expect such excessive attention to detail, but it will most likely demand *some* attention to it. Changing jobs typically doesn't solve the problem entirely.

Although balance is required in all the suggestions for overcoming your strengths contained so far in this book, it is in the areas of detail orientation and strategic thinking that this is most critical. Good technical skills balance good people skills, but good technical skills don't balance excessive detail orientation or overutilized strategic thinking. They balance each other.

Coaching Tips for Balancing Detail Orientation and Strategic Thinking

Put a check mark in the box of two or three coaching tips you commit to doing.

❑ **Take a stress management class so that you don't succumb to the need to treat everything with the utmost urgency.** Sometimes it's not that people lack ability in the area of strategic thinking; it's just that they don't feel as if they have enough time to devote to it. With so many other things on their to-do lists, they anxiously move to making sure details don't fall between the cracks. A stress management class can help you to keep that critical balance between doing and thinking.

❑ **Learn to play chess.** This is yet another way you can learn to overcome your natural tendency to focus on details. Chess requires you to think ahead, patiently wait out your opponent's moves, and act with strategic intent. Playing regularly can give you the strategic edge in many aspects of your life.

❑ **Take small risks by doing things differently from the way you usually do them.** Sometimes we just need to be jump-started out of our routine ways of seeing the world. Drive to work a different way each morning. Sit somewhere different in the company cafeteria. It doesn't so much matter *what* you do differently as that you do things differently.

❑ **Read *Orbiting the Giant Hairball: A Corporate Fool's Guide to Surviving with Grace* by Gordon MacKenzie.** This business cult classic is a terrific little book that makes you realize how creativity can be stifled by organizational expectations—and what you can do about it.

❑ **Plan projects *before* beginning them so as to allot sufficient time for completion.** When you just jump into a project, you often miss nuances related to how it might best be done, who might be able to help you, or how the ultimate goal could be altered to add even further value. Similarly, if you don't plan the project, you may assume you have plenty of time to get it done, only to realize once you really do start it that it's going to take longer than you anticipated and you're going to have to rush through it to meet the deadline. Neither of these scenarios allows you to be your strategic best—but front-end planning will help.

❑ **Subscribe to a magazine that addresses trends in your field of expertise.** You don't have to reinvent the wheel—but you do need to know it's available. Get in the habit of reading about new directions and products that you could introduce to your business.

❑ **Trust your ability to do things right the first time and then use the remaining time to plan for the future.** If you're someone who makes a habit of going back and checking your work—then checking it again just in case you missed something the first time, you're wasting time that could be put to better use. Engaging in unnecessary (say, when a low-profile error won't matter) fail-safing behavior only gives you an excuse to avoid strategic thinking and planning.

❑ **Question and stretch the rules now and then.** You won't be able to do this if you don't think broadly and articulate a rationale for why a particular rule may not apply in a certain situation.

❑ **Spend time brainstorming a project with more creative colleagues before diving into it.** They will undoubtedly see the project differently from you, and the synergy that is created can yield exponentially better results.

❑ **Take a class in drawing, writing, or sculpture just for fun to open your mind to the possibilities.** The goal isn't to become the next Pablo Picasso; it's to experience the world differently so that you can approach your work more creatively.

❑ **Take a time management class to help you develop methods for working within time constraints.** Some of the most strategic people I know get so caught up in the process that they lose all track of time. That may be all right when you're working on a project in your basement or den, but not in the workplace. Meeting time commitments is just one of the details you've got to master if you want to be effective. Strictly adhere to deadlines—missed deadlines should be the exception rather than the rule.

❑ **Consider the implementation practicalities before suggesting solutions.** Have you ever worked with or sat on a committee with someone who kept coming up with ideas, but none of them was practical? When managers see people like this, they write them off as "dreamers." If you want to be able to sell your strategies, you've also got to be able to show they can be realistically implemented. Be certain that your presentations include concern for conceptual validity and practical implementation.

❑ **Meditate to help improve your focus.** Although this coaching suggestion may seem a little off the wall, it has been shown to help broad thinkers narrow down their ideas to those that are most important or reasonable for the moment.

❑ **Mentally prepare and practice your message before giving your opinion.** In this day of information sound bites, people don't want to hear you thinking out loud (except in brainstorming sessions—and even then I would coach you to prepare your message in advance). The listener wants to be able to glean the key points of your message in sixty seconds or less. If you're an expansive thinker, this means you've got to distill your message to meet the needs of your audience.

❑ **Ask detail-oriented colleagues for input into the logistics of a project.** You may have the greatest idea in the world, but you won't be able to sell it to people with less vision than you unless you can show them how it works in reality. Don't be afraid to ask for help from people better than you at filling in the details.

❑ **Volunteer to chair meetings, and use an agenda to keep the group on track.** Not only is it good practice for winnowing down your tendency to be more expansive than most people can tolerate, but it also gives you more exposure that can help your career.

❑ **If you're a manager, hire staff who complement your own natural ability with their attention to detail.** The late Kenneth Lay probably did this, but he ignored a basic tenet of management: *What you were responsible for before you delegated it, you're responsible for after.* Yes, you want people who will bring complementary skills to the table, but you still need to stay involved with the results of their efforts.

SUCCESS STRATEGY 7

Develop Your Value-Added Brand

*Express yourself and what you stand for to everyone you
meet—clients, colleagues, friends, neighbors, and strangers.
Do this constantly and consistently, and you will create
an effective—and lucrative—personal brand.*
Peter Montoya, personal branding guru

If I were to ask you to list five brand names, which ones
come to mind immediately? Most people pretty quickly
come up with some of the best-known and most respected
names in America: Coca-Cola, Kleenex, Xerox, HP, Lexus,
Kodak, Microsoft, GE, Procter & Gamble, Sony . . . These
are names typically associated with quality and consistency, not to mention top-notch research and marketing.
Some of the brands have even become synonymous with
the product itself; most of us ask for a Xerox copy regardless
of the kind of copier used, a Coke when we want a cola, or
a Kleenex for a tissue.

Although you might not think of yourself as such, *you*
represent a brand in the marketplace known as work, and
your long-term success is contingent upon crafting a brand
synonymous with quality and value-added service. Tiger
Woods, Oprah Winfrey, Debbi Fields, Mary Kay Ash, and

Wally Amos have all done it—and so can you. Personal branding guru Peter Montoya focuses on how to "attract and keep more customers by actively shaping public perception." Although he does this primarily for entrepreneurs interested in building their businesses, the same principles apply to anyone in the workplace. Your customers or constituents include all those people upon whom you depend for success. This means the person who cuts your expense check is every bit as important a constituent as the client you provide service to. Knowing that and treating people accordingly is one of the secrets of success known to savvy professionals.

A value-added brand is typified by the willingness and desire to serve the customer, meet all reasonable requests, go above and beyond the call of duty, and find creative ways to solve seemingly insurmountable problems. It is the opposite of what psychologist and author Dr. Judith Bardwick calls an attitude of *entitlement*. In her book *Danger in the Comfort Zone*, Bardwick describes the phenomenon of entitlement as "an attitude, a way of looking at life. Those who have this attitude believe that they do not have to earn what they get. They come to believe that they get something because they are owed it, because they're *entitled* to it. They get what they want because of *who* they are, not because of what they *do*."

A person who has developed a value-added brand is not to be confused with a yes-person or a sycophant. Whereas such people act to please others in an effort to ward off criticism or garner the favor of others, the person with a value-added brand acts in ways that further the goals of the company or department. He or she knows that adding value is part of the job, not adjunct to it. It's easy to see how you can get caught up doing the basic requirements of your job without realizing that this often is not enough to assure long-term success.

People who are recognized for adding value to an organization do something more than their jobs. This is what distinguishes them from their colleagues. They are viewed by their management as adding value based on a contribution over and above what may be contained in their job descriptions, and they understand what it truly means to be of service.

People with a value-added brand tend to check off most of the items on the list on page 254.

USING YOUR "WALLET" TO DEFINE YOUR BRAND

There are six basic steps to follow in defining a value-added brand. I use the acronym **WALLET** because I believe if you follow these steps your wallet will be widened as a result of having become a brand that others want to "buy."

Write Down What You Want People to Say About You

There's a word on the street about all of us. It's what people say when you leave a meeting or walk out of a room. To begin shaping this message, you first have to define it by writing it down. What distinguishes you from your colleagues? What do you want to be known for? What unique skills do you bring to your role and your workplace? Put the answers to these questions into a statement of about twenty-five words that you can rattle off when someone asks you what you do. For example:

- I add value to my company's bottom line by providing state-of-the-art legal advice that limits our exposure to unwarranted liability.

_____ I look at barriers to goal achievement as challenges, not insurmountable obstacles.

_____ I tend to be overly optimistic about how much I can accomplish in a day.

_____ It is unusual for me to turn down uncommon or special requests.

_____ I view my colleagues, management, and clients as my customers.

_____ I gain a great deal of personal satisfaction from knowing that I went the extra mile for someone.

_____ Although my initial internal reaction to unrealistic requests may be "no way," I rarely voice that to the person making the request.

_____ I have no problem with putting a routine project or task on hold so that I can attend to something more urgent that comes up.

_____ I believe that providing service to others is an integral part of my job.

_____ I typically search for new or better ways of serving my customers.

_____ If it's within my capability, there is no task too inconsequential for me to perform if it will further the goals of my organization.

_____ I promptly answer my phone messages, regardless of who they're from.

_____ I frequently offer to help others with their work when I see that help is needed.

_____ I don't promise what I know I can't deliver, and I try to deliver more than I promise.

- I improve the quality of patient lives by providing competent and compassionate care and partnering with other professionals to create a health care facility known for outstanding service.

- As a member of the quality control team, I ensure customer satisfaction by conducting in-depth product inspections that catch flaws before they ever leave the plant.

- I contribute to executive effectiveness by allowing them to focus on their strengths while I handle administrative details in a professional and efficient manner.

Act on It

It's not enough to simply write it down—that's just the beginning. Next you must turn those words into actions. For example, if I had a video camera taping you before, during, and after you provide "state-of-the-art legal advice that limits exposure to unwarranted liability," what would it see? I'd like to think it would see you attending professional meetings as a means of staying abreast of legal issues, reading professional journals, asking probing questions that seek to fully understand potential liability, and using a wide array of skills to influence your constituents and protect the company's assets. Take your brand statement and complement it with three to five specific, measurable behaviors.

Look to the Edge

In previous chapters, I talked about the workplace playing field. Each corporate culture has its own boundaries, rules, and strategies, so your brand has to at least be on the same field. But don't make the mistake of placing your brand smack-dab in the middle of the corporate playing field.

This isn't where brands win games. It certainly wasn't how Tiger Woods created his legendary brand. After breaking into the professional golf scene in 1996, he was named that year's Sportsman of the Year by *Sport Illustrated* and won the 1997 Masters by a record twelve strokes. But within a very short time, his game started to falter—and so did his brand. He knew that being a champion meant playing consistently week in and week out, and so he focused less on winning tournaments and more on retooling his entire game, from his drive to his putt. Since returning from this effort in 1999, he has achieved what many consider to be the longest sustained success in golf history. When defining your brand, then, be certain to look to the edge—who is winning games there, and what are they doing? What do you have to do to bring your own game up?

Let Others Know About It

It does no good to have the best brand in the world if people don't know about it. Marketing your brand is every bit as important as defining it—but that doesn't mean you have to be egotistical or self-centered. Let me give you an example. When my book *Nice Girls Don't Get the Corner Office* was first released, the publicity department at Warner Books did a phenomenal job of marketing it. The publicity staff got me interviews in some of the biggest media outlets in the country, including the *Today* show, CNN, Fox, *USA Today*, *The Wall Street Journal*, and *People* magazine. One day I was at an author reception, meeting and greeting many of the Warner staff and authors, when someone approached me and said, "I see you were talking to my boss." I ask who that might be, and he pointed out the vice president of publicity—the same woman who moments before had introduced herself to me with "I work in the publicity department." Now, there was a missed marketing opportunity. She had obviously created a wonderful brand by assembling a fine team and empowering them to do their jobs effectively—but she didn't capitalize on it. She could have done so modestly yet impressively by saying something like "I'm the vice president of publicity for Warner Books, and I'm delighted that my team has been so successful in getting your book the media exposure we all felt it deserved." To learn more about how to market your brand, I highly recommend Peggy Klaus's book *Brag! The Art of Tooting Your Own Horn Without Blowing It*.

Elicit Feedback

Most brands get input from customers or potential customers as to what they want, need, or think about the product or service. You can do the same for your personal brand by soliciting 360-degree feedback. It's called *360-degree* because it's collected from people above, lateral to, and below you as well as outside colleagues. How else can you possibly know the strengths and weaknesses of your brand? Of course the caveat here is that you also have to respond to the feedback when you receive it—and as we say in the coaching business, "When three people say you're drunk, lie down." There are hundreds of companies that specialize in collecting and reporting 360-degree feedback, but you can do it simply and inexpensively by asking your human resource department to send out a questionnaire with just these three questions:

• Please describe two or three things this person does that contributes to his or her effectiveness.

- Please describe two or three things this person could do more of to be even more effective.

- Please describe two or three things this person could do less of to be even more effective.

The questions are intentionally worded so as to elicit behaviors that you can address, not characteristics that you may or may not be able to interpret.

Treat Others with Abundance

Many people raise their eyebrows when I get to this last branding ingredient. They wonder what it has to do with developing a personal brand. I firmly believe it is an essential part of every successful brand. Treating others with abundance in the workplace means you are known as someone who does not withhold information, who freely gives help and support, and who isn't hesitant to publicly praise others. It also means giving your constituents not only what they ask for, but more, and doing it consistently. Inconsistent quality or service results in frustration, mistrust, and missed opportunities to be of service in the future. Consistent quality means:

- Regularly delivering error-free work.
- Anticipating needs and addressing them *before* being asked to do so.
- Meeting—and at times beating—deadlines.
- Responding to *all* requests with a positive, upbeat attitude (even if you have to manage expectations about realistic delivery times).
- Proposing solutions to common problems.

- Developing new services or products that enhance efficiencies or profits.
- Sharing information about trends in your field.

GOING THE EXTRA MILE

I was waiting in the lobby of a large and well-known nonprofit agency when the receptionist answered the phone. Although I could hear only her half of the conversation, I got the gist of what must have been said on the other end based on her responses. It went something like this:

Caller: *Can you tell me where you're located?*

Receptionist: *6578 West Main.*

Caller: *What's the cross street?*

Receptionist: *Sixth Street.*

Caller: *What exit is that off the freeway?*

Receptionist: *Belleview.*

Caller: *Are you east or west of the freeway?*

Receptionist: *West.*

Caller: *Are there any landmarks?*

Receptionist: *There's a hospital on the corner.*

Caller: *I'm familiar with that area, but I can't picture your building.*

Receptionist: *We're behind the hospital.*

Caller: *Thanks.*

Receptionist: *[No response, just hangs up.]*

Listening to the conversation, I was struck by the fact that the receptionist did nothing to help this person, who was obviously trying to figure out how to get to the building, find the way. Despite the fact that the building is situated behind the hospital she mentioned and therefore easy to miss for a first-time visitor (I had the problem myself), she simply answered the questions she was asked. She did nothing to offer value-added service.

The situation provides a good example of indifference to customer or client needs and the unwillingness to do anything more than what's minimally required. I am certain that if the receptionist had been asked why she wasn't being more helpful, she would be indignant at the implication. After all, she answered the questions the caller posed to her. Yet how much different an impression the caller (and I) would have had if the conversation went something like this instead:

Caller: *Can you tell me where you're located?*

Receptionist: *Where are you coming from?*

Caller: *The north end of town.*

Receptionist: *You'll take the freeway south to the Belleview exit and turn left. Go about four stoplights to Sixth and turn right. When you reach Main, you'll see a hospital on the right corner. Go another half block and turn right into the first driveway. We're located directly behind the hospital.*

Caller: *Thanks.*

Receptionist: *My pleasure.*

Doing your job is not a strategy for success—it's what you get paid for. People who are known for producing high-quality results or possessing an above-average service mentality understand the fundamentals of creating their brand in the workplace. Many of the behaviors discussed in the previous chapters contribute to what's commonly called a *can-do attitude*. For example, people who have relationships in place that contribute to getting the job done, who see the bigger picture rather than simply the details involved in a project, and who manage up successfully are more likely to view new or potentially complex assignments as interesting challenges rather than as obstacles to getting their routine tasks out of the way. Such people have the tools required to react confidently to nearly any request that may come their way.

A can-do attitude is exemplified by the second scenario described above, as opposed to the first. It means having the outlook, *I'm not sure how I'll do it, but it* will *get done*, as opposed to something more ambivalent like *I'm not sure I can do that*—or even worse, *That's just not possible*. Another way of looking at a can-do attitude is having a customer service orientation, recognizing that *all those people with whom you interact are, in fact, your customers.*

WHY SOME ORGANIZATIONS SURVIVE WHILE OTHERS THRIVE

Not only do individuals derail, but entire organizations can derail as well when they condone poor customer service or fail to anticipate and meet client or customer needs. Case in point: the US Postal Service. The second largest employer in the United States, with nearly eight hundred thousand employees (only Wal-Mart employs more), missed many opportunities to capitalize on Americans' need for speed and simply watched as competitors such as FedEx, UPS, and DHL moved into its market. The monopolistic, bureaucratic nature of the organization continues to result in a slow and at times nonexistent response to customer needs. Americans continue to use the post office because they *have* to, not because they *want* to. Although it claims to operate without taxpayer support, it fails to mention that it does receive more than thirty-six million dollars annually in taxpayer funding for certain services the government requires it to provide free or at a discount.

Large is no excuse for indifference. Wal-Mart, with even more employees and a similarly complex operation, has remained successful because it's responsive and continues to identify opportunities to even better serve its customers. Service is typically friendly (Wal-Mart was among the first to employ greeters to welcome you as you walk through the front door) and consistent. United Parcel Service, the largest package delivery company in the world, can be counted on to deliver what it promises (both literally and figuratively) with no excuses and no subsidy from the US government or its taxpayers.

To Be of Service

A common complaint heard today is that "so-and-so acted as though he was doing me a favor when all he did was his job." And it isn't an ill-founded complaint. Whether in a restaurant or schoolroom, at the post office, in a department store, or in your own office, you see people performing the job to which they're assigned act as though they were being put out by requests from the very people they are there to serve. This was certainly the case with the receptionist described above. We each perform a service that, presumably, is of value to the company or the customer or we wouldn't be paid to do it. Why, then, do so many people resist providing the best service that they possibly can? Perhaps the answer lies, at least partially, in our interpretation of the word *service* and the fact that it is closely aligned with the word *servant*.

Although most of us don't like to think of ourselves as servants, Robert K. Greenleaf, a former AT&T executive and founder of the Indianapolis-based Center for Applied Ethics, illuminates another way to think about it. Greenleaf's book *Servant Leadership: A Journey into the Nature of Legitimate Power and Greatness* significantly changed my view of the role that I play in serving others. His use of the term *leadership* in the title should be looked at broadly in the context of service, as opposed to simply a reference to those in authority. Even with formal leaders in place in organizations, we each play the role of leader from time to time. The example that Greenleaf uses is the character Leo in Hermann Hesse's *Journey to the East*. Leo is the servant, in the traditional sense, to a group of men who are on a mythical journey. He performs menial tasks for them, but he also is an influential spirit within the group. Leo buoys the men through his powerful presence. When he disappears, the men find that they can't continue the journey without him. Greenleaf writes: "to me, this story clearly says that *the great leader is seen as servant first*, and that simple fact is key to his greatness. Leo was actually the leader all of the time, but he was servant first because that was what he was, *deep down inside*."

Unfortunately, we have come to regard service as something done by anyone in a lesser position than ours. Even in organizations that claim to be nonhierarchical, a pecking order still exists. It begins with the company president and continues to entry-level positions. This order dictates whom you can have lunch with, be social with, and offer assistance to. It's somewhat ridiculous when you think about it, because within any organization everyone is there to serve the customer or client. We are all, then, servants in one way or another. Whether or not we have direct contact with customers, our work affects the final outcome. You frequently hear line people describe staff people as "overhead." Staff people (also called "back office" or "corporate") don't directly contribute to developing, producing, or selling a product or service, so they are not thought of as contributing to the bottom line. Staff people, however, provide valuable services to line people—services without which the product or service could not be produced as efficiently or effectively.

This concept was beautifully illustrated at yet another leadership program held at the Ritz-Carlton in Pasadena, California. To make the point about the importance of value-added service, I asked if two of the maintenance men responsible for setting up the room would answer some questions about why they provide such high-quality service. Participants asked these men questions to help them better understand the can-do attitude exhibited by all the staff's employees.

Q: *Why do you think you provide service so superior to that of your counterparts at other hotels?*

A: Because we're treated so well. We're trained that we are ladies and gentlemen serving ladies and gentlemen. When we pass another employee in the hall, it's expected that we will treat that person the same as we would an important guest.

Q: *Do you think that how you set up this room has any effect on the profits of the hotel?*

A: Yes. If we put a tablecloth on that is stained, and you lift your glass and find a stain, then you'll look at that all day and remember it when you're deciding whether or not to come back and stay with us.

Q: *How is it that you deliver even the most obscure requests?*

A: We're each given a budget so that if a guest asks for something that we don't have, we can go out and buy it. All we have to do is present the receipt to the boss and we're paid back by the hotel.

Q: *You mean you can just leave the hotel, get in your car, and go down to Office Depot, and buy what you need?*

A: Yes. After we tell our supervisor that we're going.

If you examine this notion of serving as Greenleaf does, that "the work exists for the person as much as the person

THE CAN-DO ATTITUDE

QUESTION OR REQUEST	NO-CAN-DO RESPONSE	CAN-DO RESPONSE
Do you think that you'll be able to meet the client's deadline?	I'm not sure. There are an awful lot of obstacles that make it look unlikely.	I have a few concerns, but nothing that can't be overcome if we put our heads together.
Can I exchange this pair of pants for a sweater?	There are no returns or exchanges on sale items.	It is not within the scope of my authority to approve the request, but let me see if I can find someone who can.
Because Todd is on vacation, I'd like you to prepare the monthly status report for the president.	Well . . . I've never done it before. I'm not sure I know how.	Sure. I've never done it before but I'm sure I can figure it out. If I have any questions, I'll ask.
Would you take a look at these recommendations for changes to our product delivery system and give me your input?	I don't know what's wrong with our old system. Besides, it will take at least six months to get it up and running and we've got a new product line coming out around the same time.	I'd be happy to. If we're going to make any changes, this is a good time, since it will take six months to get it up and running and we've got a new product line coming out just after that.

Would you mind processing this expense report for me today? I'm leaving town again tomorrow.	We only process expense reports on Fridays. You'll have to wait until you get back to get your money. Besides, this isn't filled in correctly. You'll have to go back and change it.	We normally process those checks on Fridays, but I don't think that there will be a problem making an exception for you. I did notice that it's missing some necessary information. Why don't I show you what's needed.
We need someone to train the new person on Windows. Would you mind doing it?	I'm not a trainer, you know. I'll need an outline of the goals and objectives before I start and someone else to relieve me of my duties for the six hours that it's going to take.	I've never trained anyone on it before, but I'm willing to give it a try if she'll be patient with me.
I've never used your services before. I was wondering whether you could help me understand what's available?	What is it that you need to know?	I'd be happy to. Which services in particular were you interested in, or would you like me to go over all of them?
I need some information for tomorrow's presentation by 4:00 PM today.	You've got to be kidding. Why is everything around here an emergency?	I don't think I'll be of much help— I'm already on a high-priority project. Let's find another way to get it done on time.

exists for the work—the business then becomes a serving institution—serving those who produce and those who use," then being a servant isn't such a bad thing after all. We each serve others in different, but invaluable, ways. People with a can-do attitude understand that their positions exist to serve the customer as well as their colleagues.

I once walked past the employee lounge in a department store and saw a posted sign that read: PEOPLE ARE NOT AN INTERRUPTION OF OUR WORK—THEY ARE OUR WORK. It was a simple sign, but one that I never forgot. It acted as a reminder to employees that their role was to serve others. A can-do attitude is prevalent in those who understand this very basic premise. Can you imagine working in a company where the executives see themselves as servants? Or in a school where the principal sees himself or herself as there to serve the teachers and students? How might it change the environment? Would their constituents think any less of them? On the contrary—it would create an enhanced sense of teamwork and customer-driven behavior.

Here is a list of some of the most common complaints that I hear about people who are not perceived as adding value to their organizations:

• **Works to rule.** Does just enough work to get by—doesn't do anything extra or beyond the scope of his or her job description.

• **Not a self-starter.** Does the work to which he or she is specifically assigned, but doesn't seek additional responsibility or see what else needs to be done unless told, and even then requires an inordinate amount of supervision.

• **Resistant to new ideas.** Prefers doing things in routine ways and is unwilling to consider new methods for improving the quality or quantity of work.

- **Not a team player.** Does only his or her own work—doesn't help out others in a pinch.
- **Lacks enthusiasm.** Does the job, but without excitement or energy.
- **Uncooperative.** Fails to help implement or may sabotage new ideas that others generate for improving products or services.
- **Unmotivated.** Often fails to meet even the basic job requirements and requires constant prodding or coaxing.
- **Bad attitude.** Has a generally negative, critical, or condescending approach to customer service or team efforts.
- **Unpredictable.** Others never know what kind of mood the person will be in and can't count on consistently high-quality deliverables.

If you see yourself in one or more of these terms, then you must seriously consider why this is the case—*and do something about it.*

WHY NO-CAN-DO?

By now, it should be no surprise to you that I do not believe that people are born with a lack of service orientation. They develop it—and for good reasons. Whether it's developed as a childhood defense mechanism in response to unreasonable demands or as a method for dealing with ineffective leadership, it will quickly derail the best of employees before they realize it. An understanding of why and how it develops can help you to move toward creating a brand that you can be proud of and that will serve you well.

- **Poor management.** Although managers are often quick to point the finger at underperforming employees, they fail to realize that they themselves may be the cause. The most common ways in which managers curb enthusiasm and motivation are to be too controlling or overly critical. If you are a manager, remember to delegate the project, not the process. When managers control how someone does something, they eventually succeed in having everything done their way, but their way may not always be the best way. It serves only to thwart creativity and innovation. Similarly, overly critical managers make staff members afraid to show initiative for fear of being unjustly criticized for their efforts. In either case, employees eventually wait to be told what to do and how to do it—and brace themselves for anticipated disapproval.

- **Poor job match.** Countless people are in jobs for which they are ill suited because they were steered into them by well-meaning parents or teachers, or because they can't see the options available to them. High salaries, family expectations, prestige, and other perks and benefits keep people in jobs they hate going to each day. These reasons become what are known as "golden handcuffs." People dislike the work, but remain tied to it for social or financial reasons. As a result, they suffer from lackluster performance and low motivation. It's pretty difficult to enthusiastically perform a job you just don't like.

- **Powerless or powerful parenting.** Either end of the power spectrum can impede a child from developing a healthy sense of initiative. On the one hand, when parents present themselves as all-powerful, it's tough for children to think they know the right thing to do; instead, they look to authority for the answers. The old maxims *Father knows best* and *Children are to be seen and not heard* summarize what's at the root of these behaviors. Employees who won't make a move without being given permission or direction may have had parents who expected them to be compliant and submissive. On the other hand, parents who see themselves as lacking control over their own lives often instill the same in their children. Parents who allow themselves to be controlled by the desires of others may unwittingly impart to their children the message that their lot in life is to follow the instructions given to them and not make waves with their own ideas or methods for doing things. As adults, people who had either powerless or powerful parenting may lack the confidence to take the kind of risks required to extend themselves beyond what's asked.

• **Inordinately high detail orientation.** What strategic thinkers call resistance to new ideas may in actuality be a manifestation of high detail orientation. Such people often see only the complexities of an idea and retort with the many reasons why it can't possibly work, instead of seeking solutions to those barriers that are less obvious to the big-picture person. They become overwhelmed by the morass of details required to make a new idea a reality and are unable to break it into smaller, manageable pieces.

• **Monopoly of products or services.** The absence of competition can lead to a *take-it-or-leave-it* mentality. We see it in the US Postal Service, Department of Motor Vehicles, Internal Revenue Service, and other government agencies. Whether it's the only grocery store in a small town or the only provider of air transportation out of a particular city, a monopoly can serve to diminish the attention paid to and value placed on customer service. People working in a monopolistic organization tend to forget that they are there to serve others and instead take advantage of their position in the market.

• **Depression.** The incidence of depression in the US population is far greater than most people realize. Statistics suggest that women have a 20 to 26 percent lifetime risk for depression; men, an 8 to 12 percent lifetime risk. Symptoms of depression include, among others, the loss of interest in activities you normally find enjoyable and feelings of general fatigue or lethargy. Depression is a significant factor that can contribute to lack of enthusiasm or motivation to perform the job in anything more than a perfunctory manner. In order to address the appropriate cause, it's important to understand that the work can contribute to the depression as well as the depression contributing to failure to perform the work.

No matter how difficult it may be for you, exhibiting a positive, upbeat, can-do attitude is yet another factor critical to long-term career success. It doesn't mean that you have to do everything asked of you, regardless of the reasonableness of the request; it simply means that you take a positive approach to work, serving the customer, and meeting unforeseen challenges. With the exception of an abrasive personality, the absence of a can-do attitude is easier to spot than any of the other potential career busters described heretofore. This is what makes it such a critical ingredient in your repertoire of skills.

TIPS FOR DEVELOPING A VALUE-ADDED BRAND AND CAN-DO ATTITUDE

Certain companies provide outstanding examples of the presence of a can-do attitude. A few that come to mind are Nordstrom, Lexus, JetBlue Airways, the Ritz-Carlton, and Four Seasons Hotels. A number of years ago, I was caught in a snowstorm in Boston that began on a Friday morning. I was staying at the Four Seasons and was hesitant to check out for fear of not getting another room in the city if the storm persisted. The desk clerk assured me that there would be no problem. Knowing that "no problem" can mean anything from just that to "really big problem," I remained worried and skeptical throughout the day. By four o'clock that afternoon, Logan Airport had been closed, and I trudged through the snow back to the hotel. While I waited in line behind irate would-be guests demanding rooms that just weren't available, I noticed that the same woman who had earlier promised that there would be no problem was still there. I dreaded what I was sure I was about to hear. When my turn came and I stepped up to the desk, she smiled and said, "Welcome back, Dr. Frankel. When I heard the airport was closed, I went ahead and checked you in. Here's your key."

I was more than just a little impressed by the woman's service orientation. She delivered exactly what she said she would—and a bit more. She could have made me feel fortunate even to have a room, given the fact that she could have sold it several times over, but she didn't. She made me feel like a welcome guest. In our respective fields, we are all capable of providing this kind of service, but most of us don't, despite the fact that it's what builds successful companies and contributes to successful careers. Instead, we rely on our technical competence and assume that it will get us over the rough spots. Then we scratch our heads with wonder when we are passed over for promotions or developmental opportunities.

A second example of a value-added brand is a company that redefined service in the retail clothing arena: Nordstrom. Despite the fact that the company is a high-end concern, it flourished financially even in down markets in no small part because of the customer service attitude exhibited by its sales associates. When you shop at Nordstrom, you are usually met by friendly, knowledgeable, and helpful staff. Without being particularly pushy or aggressive, they make certain that you find what you are looking for. Long before Nordstrom's competitors were doing it, the company had a full return policy—no questions asked, your money was refunded. Countless times I've heard people say that even though Nordstrom costs a bit more, they continue shopping there because of the service they receive. I wonder how many firms can say that *their* customers exhibit the same loyalty for the products or services they offer.

There are seven specific tips you can follow to add value and assure that you are perceived as someone with a can-do attitude. I preface them by saying that logic and common sense must prevail when responding to any request. There are people who constantly demand unreasonable things of you, and to always have a can-do attitude with these people may be unrealistic or even inappropriate. The customer is *not* always right. You are not expected to be a doormat. On the other hand, you should consider the effect your attitude has on customers, clients, and colleagues and how you can be a better ambassador for the product or services that you provide.

Tip 1. Develop Self-Confidence

Each of the remaining suggestions is predicated on this one: you need a healthy degree of self-confidence. A can-do attitude and brand stem from a belief in yourself and your abilities. It isn't a false sense of confidence, but rather one that comes from the knowledge that even when you're unsure of yourself, you know from past successes and accomplishments that you can do this, too—and if you can't, you'll find someone to help. By exhibiting self-confidence, we often find that we can do more than we originally thought or learn something that will be useful in the future. In essence, we stretch ourselves to the limits of our abilities.

It appears to me that men tend to have more of an edge than women when it comes to exhibiting self-confidence in new or challenging situations. For example, when a job or assignment comes open for which a woman has no direct experience, she'll often decline it or fail to apply for it, because she thinks she can't do it. In the same situation, men tend to jump in wholeheartedly with the confidence that they'll figure it out as they go along.

Regardless of their sex, people who approach assignments and challenges with confidence instill in others a sense of confidence in them. They are perceived as performers who can handle any task, creatively solve problems, and add value to a department or company.

Tip 2. Create Win–Win Situations

Success in creating win–win situations has a lot to do with managing the impressions that others have of you. You want to convey the message that you are ready, willing, and able to help—even when on the inside you're not sure how. When it's clear that you can't do something you've been asked to do, you turn it into a win–win by helping to find an alternative solution.

Tip 3. Deliver What You Promise— And More

It never ceases to amaze me how many people fail to deliver what they say they will. Although there are myriad reasons why people don't come through with what they've promised, not many of them are good ones. You may know people who have a can-do attitude but who don't produce what they've committed to. The natural corollary to meeting or beating deadlines is assuring that you don't promise *more than* you can deliver. Building contractors are notorious for having a can-do attitude, then not delivering. No matter how specifically you explain your requirements and closely supervise them, it seems that they finish the job late and over budget. They underestimate either the time required or the complexity of the task, and then they wind up falling short on delivering what they promise. Once this happens, their credibility is seriously damaged. As a result, you see contractors going out of business at a fairly high rate.

Going the extra mile to meet, or even beat, a deadline pays huge dividends in the long run. If it means that you have to work late, come in early, or skip lunch, then so be it. This is not to say that you should miss some important event such as your child's recital, your spouse's birthday, or a parent's anniversary in order to deliver what you promise. Rather, you must anticipate these events vis-à-vis your commitments and make certain that they are *all* met. It means that you must *realistically* plan your work and work your plan.

A common complaint heard from managers is that employees seem to lack the commitment to get the job done within predetermined deadlines. One client called bemoaning the fact that one of her best staff members comes in late and takes extended lunch hours, despite the fact that a particular project is already past due and her client is awaiting the results. Regardless of the employee's technical competence, his failure to deliver on his promises is tarnishing his reputation and brand. The person with a can-do attitude does whatever it takes to get the job done on time and under budget.

Delivering more than you promise serves to add chips to your account. For example, if you say you'll prepare an outline for an upcoming project, why not include more specifics than typically required, such as costs, a detailed methodology, and ways to overcome anticipated obstacles? If you're known as someone who does more than you promise, then those occasional times when something prevents you from meeting an obligation are overlooked or tolerated (the key word being *occasional*). You have built credibility that fares well for you in the long term.

Tip 4. Anticipate Requirements

It is often difficult for people who are detail-oriented to foresee ancillary requirements or peripheral issues that will affect the completion of a project. They may be great at checking things off their written or mental lists, but if it's not on the list, it doesn't get done. Remember the assistant I mentioned previously who canceled plane reservations as instructed, but neglected to deal with related hotel and car arrangements? The person with a can-do attitude goes above and beyond what is specifically requested by considering all related factors and responding to them in advance.

I once appeared for an all-day training session in a client's office to find the office manager stewing over the fact that the person responsible for scheduling the training room had neglected to order the food for the meeting. When I asked whether she had specifically told the person that she wanted food ordered, she said, "I shouldn't have to. Every time we have an all-day meeting, we have food. She should have known to do it." Although it could be argued that the manager shouldn't expect the person to read her mind, her expectation that this staff member would anticipate her needs, especially in light of the fact that a certain protocol is typically followed, isn't unreasonable.

Unfortunately, the old adage *If I knew better, I'd do better* applies here. Some people simply aren't very good at anticipating requirements. Many of the coaching tips suggested under Success Strategy 6 for developing a better sense of the bigger picture hold true. In particular, before beginning or completing a project or response to a request, take the time to think about it in its entirety. If you're not sure what may be required in addition to the obvious, ask questions—particularly of people who are better than you at seeing the big picture.

Tip 5. Offer Help Freely—Don't Wait to Be Asked

Failure to offer to help doesn't always stem from a withholding or stingy personality, although it certainly can. People who are reticent to offer help are often afraid to be intrusive or overstep their boundaries. It reminds me of the person who watches as someone struggles to get through a door with an armload of packages, whereas someone else hurries to help open the door. It goes back to the need for a generosity of spirit.

A can-do attitude doesn't only mean that you can do your own job; it also means that you have the best interests of the organization in mind and work to achieve its goals as well as yours. You may have worked with people who leave the office when their work is completed, even when they see others in their group or department working late to meet a deadline. It may not occur to them to offer help, or they may think that it isn't their job. Keep in mind that the job is to best serve the customer. This means that your work isn't limited by your specific job description.

Tip 6. Always Offer a Solution or Request Assistance in Finding a Solution

Managers frequently express frustration with people whom they perceive as malcontents or troublemakers. They describe such people as those who complain about their workload, co-workers, or the injustice of a system that overworks and underpays, but make no effort to do anything about it. Their whining and complaints bring down the morale of the entire office or department.

People with a can-do attitude, on the other hand, assume responsibility for making things better by pairing any complaint that they may have with suggested solutions or requests for assistance with finding a solution. They don't complain for the sake of complaining, but rather openly discuss problems with the parties concerned in an effort to make things better. If they can't find a solution to the problem themselves, they ask for help. They know that if things are going to get better, it will be because of their willingness to meet problems head-on.

This tip is particularly pertinent for team building. People will grumble to one another in small groups about problems in the department, but seldom do they see improving the situation as their responsibility. Once it's made a norm for everyone on the team to assume responsibility, rather than only the manager or team leader, then entire departments move forward with a surge of new ideas and solutions to old problems. It won't work, however, if the team leader fails to empower team members and still expects them to resolve team problems. Success, in this regard, is contingent on the collective wisdom and energy that spring from groups of people who work collaboratively toward a common goal.

Tip 7. Do What You Love—Not Only What You're Good At

Doing what you love can contribute not only to the ability to think more broadly, but also to a can-do attitude. When you do what you love, you quite naturally want to be of service and share your enthusiasm with others. No problem is insurmountable when you approach your work with passion.

If you're lucky, what you love and what you're good at are one and the same, but this isn't always true. I know a surgeon who is brilliant in his field. He has a full practice and is trusted by his patients and admired by his colleagues for his skill. He once confided in me that he hates his work—and unfortunately, this is reflected in his attitude toward his patients. It is not uncommon to hear them complain about his curtness and dour attitude. Given a choice, many patients say that they would prefer another physician. He's a good example of someone who remains successful primarily because his skill is so specialized that he has no local competition.

A man with whom I used to work left the company at about the same time that I did to start his own business. Nearly two years after we'd each headed out on our own, we were talking about how quickly the days and weeks fly by now that we're doing what we love. His comment "My worst day on my own is better than my best day working for someone else" frequently resonates in my mind because it's true. Whether you work for someone else or for yourself, you know when you're doing what you love because the challenges are easier to meet and the positive attitude with which you approach your work is obvious to all those with whom you interact.

Some of you may now be thinking, *Doing what you love is easier said than done.* From the surgeon who stays in practice for the money to the engineer who needs the health insurance that the job provides his family, people become stuck in careers for which they no longer have enthusiasm. Social, family, and financial pressures keep people in unsatisfying jobs long after they have stopped enjoying their work and being productive. Feeling stuck contributes to lackluster performance and can also be one cause of depression and physical ailments. The belief that you have no options and are instead constricted by considerations outside of your control is frequently a factor in depression.

You may never have thought of yourself as depressed, but think about these questions:

- Have you given up after-work activities in which you were once interested because you lack energy to engage in them?
- Do you find yourself coming alive on Friday afternoon and becoming more morose on Sunday afternoon with the thought of the next day being a workday?
- Do you pace yourself, in terms of expenditure of energy, so that you can get through the week?
- Do you find yourself frequently daydreaming at work or unable to concentrate on the task at hand?
- Are vacations the highlight of your life?
- Do you catch colds easily and find yourself complaining about a host of aches and pains (either real or imagined)?
- Do you exceed your allowable sick days at work?
- Do you use alcohol or other substances to camouflage your feelings about work?

If you answer yes to any of these questions, it may be that you are in the wrong job and that your situation is making you more depressed than you realize. It's important that you objectively assess your situation and determine ways in which you can balance your obligations with a fulfilling career or outside interests. Talk to friends and family members about your dreams and aspirations and ask for their input. Speak with a career counselor. Interview other people who have successfully moved from an unrewarding job to one they now love. Once you do, you may find that you're not as stuck as you thought you were and that you have more support than you thought for making a career move.

About a year ago, a man named Brett asked me to coach him. At our first meeting, he described what seemed to be a wonderful job that he had as the chief financial officer at a midsize company. He reported that there were no problems with his supervisor he couldn't handle, and announced that his pay and benefits exceeded his expectations. What then, I asked, could I possibly do for him? As it turned out, Brett was bored with his job and didn't feel that he was using the skills he valued most—working with his hands in the building trades. After we explored possible opportunities within his company, it quickly became clear that there were no jobs there that would be any more appealing to him than the one he had. When it appeared that he would have to begin a job search outside the firm, he said that this wasn't possible. His wife was in a low-paying job, and he bore the burden of supporting the family, his in-laws, and two residences. Brett felt like he was stuck.

Our work together focused on getting Brett to open up with his wife about his dreams; to talk to a financial planner about how much the family *needed* to live on, as opposed to what they *were* living on; and to begin investigating the possibilities in the field where he would be most happy. He wasn't expected to make any moves right away; just to plant seeds that might grow to fruition over time. It turned out that his wife was incredibly supportive—more so than he had anticipated. The financial planner gave him good ideas for how he could save money and areas of the country where he might be able to live more economically than where he currently resided. As a result of his legwork, Brett came up with a two-year plan for leaving the company and moving toward a career that would be more rewarding for him and enable him to spend more time with his family. He has another year to go before he actually leaves, but the past months have been a breeze for him at work because he knows he has a plan in place that will soon free him from the golden handcuffs.

The preceding example is intended to illustrate that you may not be as constricted as you think. Existential philosophers say that two of our greatest burdens in life are freedom and responsibility. Even in the most dire circumstances, we have the freedom to choose how we will handle the situation—and the responsibility to deal consciously with that choice. Staying in a job that you no longer like or that positively depresses you is a choice. Before you settle for that choice, be certain that you have explored creative alternatives for living your life differently. Not only is your well-being at stake, but the well-being of your family is up for grabs as well.

The importance of having a value-added brand and can-do attitude should by now be abundantly clear. People with a can-do attitude attract similar people and positive experiences. The world works in synchronicity with the person who has a positive, upbeat attitude. Managers report that when interviewing job candidates, a can-do attitude is often weighted more heavily than technical competence. They know that they can teach the basics of a job to someone, but they can't teach someone to have a positive attitude.

Coaching Tips to Develop a Value-Added Brand

Put a check mark in the box of two or three coaching tips you commit to doing.

❑ **Think about your role in and contribution to your organization broadly instead of limiting yourself to a job description or title.** In leaner organizations, this has become increasingly important—and noticed. Doing your job isn't enough. The expectation in today's workplace is that you will add value to departments and processes other than those for which you have direct responsibility.

❑ **Never miss a deadline—and when it's possible to do so without sacrificing quality, beat it.** To achieve this means you have to plan in advance, negotiate unreasonable deadlines, and avoid analysis paralysis. If, as you delve into a project and get more information, it becomes clear that you're going to need more time, go back to your boss or customer, explain what you've found, and establish a new target date for completion. If you provide a legitimate rationale, most people will respond positively.

❑ **Replace resistance with creative problem solving.** Often our initial response to a challenging assignment or new idea is negative. We see all the reasons why something can't be done and none of the ways in which it can be. If you lean toward being a skeptic, get in the habit of suspending judgment until you have completely thought through new concepts. It doesn't mean you have to wholeheartedly agree when you know there will be challenges, but rather that you not shoot the idea down before you've engaged in creative problem solving.

❑ **Always accompany a complaint with a proposed solution or a request for assistance with finding a solution.** No one likes a complainer, and no one likes complainers less than bosses. If you've got a concern, present it in conjunction with a proposed solution. This transforms the impression of you from a whiner to a problem solver. If you absolutely cannot come up with a solution, then ask for help with finding one rather than just dumping the problem in the lap of someone else.

❑ **Actively search for ways to better serve the customer or client.** In an article titled "The Customer Is Clueless" (*BusinessWeek SmallBiz*, spring 2006), author Doug Hall asks, "When developing new products or services, is the smartest strategy (a) to create ideas based on listening to the voice of the customer or (b) to come up with ideas that customers are not necessarily asking for?" He suggests that the correct answer is b, because it means creating things that customers haven't even imagined yet. Think about it. Are you more impressed when someone comes up with a variation on a theme or a complete paradigm shift? Part of your brand needs to reflect the desire to answer *tomorrow's* problems today. You can do this by being a perpetual learner, exhibiting curiosity about all aspects of your field, and remaining active in your professional associations.

❏ **Volunteer for unusual or nonroutine assignments.**
This can provide a great entrée into meeting people
with whom you might not otherwise come into contact, providing balance to a job where you might feel
as if you're stagnating but there's nowhere to currently
move, and even teaching you some new skills.

❏ **Return all phone calls and e-mails, regardless of whom
they are from, in a timely manner.** If you're one of
those people who are good at managing up but not
necessarily laterally or down, you're laying the ground-
work to be sabotaged (intentionally or otherwise) at
some point in your career by someone you snubbed.
Showing courtesy and respect to folks at all levels almost guarantees you receiving the same in kind when
you need it. It's not just the old *You never know who
you're going to report to someday* maxim that matters.
When you need others to provide you with access, information, or support, it's too late to worry about how
you treated them in the past.

❏ **Respond to requests with a time frame for completion.**
Don't leave people guessing about what you're going to
do and when you plan to do it. You may know you're
going to complete a request within a particular time
frame, but others can't read your mind. If you want to
avoid being micromanaged and give yourself the motivation for getting a task completed on time, then let
people know your plans.

❏ **Realistically assess what you can or can't do, and don't
promise more than you can deliver.** As much as I'm
a firm believer that all requests have to be met with a

can-do response, I also know this sometimes means you have to manage expectations. Women tend to have a harder time with this than men. They spend inordinate amounts of time and energy making "miracles" (getting something done with fewer resources than the task calls for) when they should be negotiating deadlines or outcomes. Here are some phrases you can practice in response to requests that require negotiation:

- I'd be happy to do that. At this point it looks like Wednesday will be the earliest I can get it to you given my other commitments.
- If you want that to go out today, I can see that it's done, but I should tell you that to do the job properly it will take at least two days and two people. Is it more important to you that it simply be done or that it be done properly?
- I'd be happy to do that today. Given the other high-priority assignments I'm working on, I'm wondering which ones are most critical to you so that I get to those first?
- We can get the job done with the staff we currently have, but it will take about two weeks to complete. Realistically, if you want a top-notch product in a reasonable amount of time, we'll need to bring in two contractors—which will increase the cost by about 15 percent. Just let me know which direction you'd like to go.

❏ **Strive to create win–win situations.** It does no good to win the battle only to lose the war. Long-term career success consists of ensuring small wins for *everyone* along the path. This is part of treating others with abundance.

Look for opportunities to provide others with what they need so that they will be more inclined to do the same for you when you most need it.

❑ **Attend a Peter Montoya workshop.** Whether you want to develop a personal brand internal or external to your organization, these workshops focus you on the key elements of branding. No one knows branding like Montoya, so visit his Web site at www.petermontoya.com.

SUCCESS STRATEGY 8

Network for Success

Call it a clan, call it a network, call it a tribe, call it a family:
Whatever you call it, whoever you are, you need one.
Jane Howard, author

Before you decide to skip this chapter because the thought of networking (a) disgusts, (b) scares, or (c) bores you, take a moment to consider the *concept* of networking. In telecommunications, computer technology, transportation, and electronics, a network always implies an interconnection of channels, components, or equipment. It's no different for human networks. They are simply *the means by which professional goals are achieved through connections.* As my good friend and colleague Dr. Bruce Heller says, "Networking is one of those activities that is always important but only urgent when it is too late." Which is a little like what you've heard me say throughout this book: *When you need a relationship, it's too late to build it.*

Far too many people settle into their jobs and drop the people, activities, and organizations that helped get them there. But strong network relationships aren't only about finding your next job; they also play an instrumental role in ensuring success in the one you already have by providing you with things like:

- Access to information
- Contact with like-minded people
- Exposure to people who *should* know about you (executive management, prospective customers, new clients, et cetera)
- Technical assistance
- New ideas
- Friendships
- Support
- Referrals

Given today's proliferation of information technology and the increasing popularity of team-based efforts, individuals are no longer expected to perform their job responsibilities in isolation. The Internet is testimony to this fact. Whereas in the past people worked independently on projects and were by and large rewarded for their individual contributions, today's worker is expected to function interdependently with a large base of information accessible through his or her relationships with others. Harvard Professor John Kotter has conducted extensive research into the factors that contribute to success as a general manager. One of his findings, that a strong network is an essential ingredient of managerial effectiveness, holds true not only for managers but also for people at *all* levels in an organization. Kotter describes a network as the *sum total of the people, both inside and outside your organization, on whom you depend to get your job done.*

Assess your networking acumen with the following checklist:

_____ I belong to professional groups related to my field and am actively involved in them.

_____ I can specifically name the people in my network.

_____ I know what I have to offer others in my network.

_____ I don't view networking as a waste of time, but rather as an invaluable tool for assuring ongoing success.

_____ I spend some portion of each week engaged in at least one networking activity.

_____ I freely share expertise, information, or other commodities with those in my network.

_____ I feel comfortable calling on others in my network and asking for help when I need it.

_____ I can honestly say that my work is made easier because of my network relationships.

_____ I have network relationships at all levels of my organization as well as outside it.

_____ At times, I use informal gatherings as an opportunity to network.

_____ I'm known as someone who helps others connect professionally.

FROM ORGANIZATIONAL
CHARTS TO NETWORKS

In the old scheme of things, we used to refer to organization charts to determine where we fell in the pecking order. Hierarchical by design, they typically looked something like this:

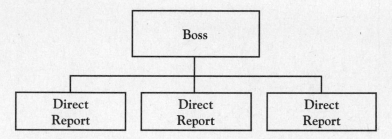

Organizational charts provided order to the workforce but did so in a manner that preserved the ranking system, created vertical fiefdoms, and discouraged interdepartmental dependencies. Today it is more helpful, and appropriate, to think of yourself at the center of a complex web of people, both inside and outside your organization, with whom you interact in an effort to get the job done effectively. Although some facets of the hierarchy remain, the boundaries between organizational levels have become less clear, and crossing them (intentionally and otherwise) is more acceptable while trying to accomplish interrelated tasks.

The following diagram exemplifies how you might now look at your network. It takes Kotter's concept of the manager's network, described in his work *The General Managers*, and expands it to include any position within an organization. As you can see, in this new configuration you are central to the interconnecting web of relationships required to successfully meet the organization's goals. With so many relationships to manage, you can also see why building and maintaining relationships is a time-consuming but essential part of career success.

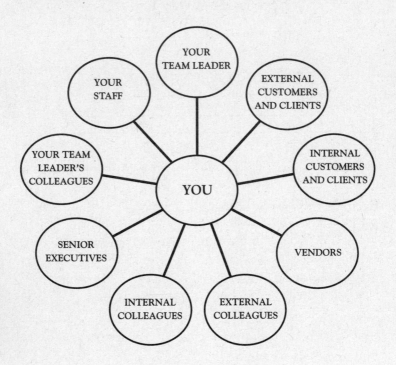

Networking is nothing more than simple recognition of the fact that every person with whom you come into contact is potentially helpful, or harmful, to your success. The moment you enter into a discussion with a colleague about a mutual project, you are networking. When you meet someone at a party whose company uses the same products or services that your firm provides, you are networking. The caveat is, you can't build a network for only selfish purposes. People will see through it. You must approach your network relationships in the same manner as you do other relationships—with a generosity of spirit and genuine desire to help, and be helped by, others. At the moment you build a relationship, you are never certain whether you will help it or be helped by it.

WHO NEEDS TO NETWORK?

Even people who are willing to change their behaviors in significant ways to become more professionally competitive seem to resist networking and come up with a plethora of excuses for avoiding it:

Excuse 1: *I'm not a good networker.*
Response: Not one of us emerged from the womb a good networker. Although some people are better at it than others, most of us have to make a concerted effort to build relationships. As with other relationships, networking requires certain social skills and comfort with being with others. One tactic that makes networking easier is the active listening technique described under Success Strategy 1. Most people love it when others ask them questions and really listen to their responses. If necessary, take the Dale Carnegie course in how to make friends and influence people. The fact is, *the more you network, the easier it becomes.*

Excuse 2: *It's a waste of my company's time and money.*
Response: The knowledge, goodwill, and potential business that you gain from networking are all highly beneficial to your company. Through networking re-

lationships, you increase the pool of resources you may need in the future. Similarly, by acting as a resource for others outside your firm, you indirectly call attention to your company's products or service. Even internal networking pays dividends in terms of the productivity, brainstorming, and cost savings that result from increased cooperation between teams and individuals over time.

Excuse 3: *My workload doesn't permit it.*

Response: Your workload may not permit it because you *don't* network. If your schedule is so heavy that you don't have time to network, it may just be that you aren't effectively pooling resources and building bridges of collaboration with internal and external colleagues. Instead, you wind up reinventing the wheel. You must view networking not as an option, but as a *responsibility*. It is your responsibility to have in place any relationships that can further the attainment of your company's, and your own, goals.

Excuse 4: *I already have plenty of contacts.*

Response: Except in cases where your work suffers because you spend *too* much time networking (in which case you wouldn't be using this excuse), you can never have too many contacts. Go back to the preceding networking illustration and fill in the names of actual people in each category with whom you actively build positive working relationships. If any of the categories have few or no names, then these may be the areas that require your attention. Some people are great at internal networking but neglect their outside contacts. This situation works until downsizing occurs. Others, especially people in sales and marketing, focus their efforts on external networking. The numbers look great, but often at the cost of creating a strong internal network.

Excuse 5: *Networking is manipulative.*
Response: It is only as manipulative as you make it. If you network only for what you can get out of it personally, then it probably is manipulative. On the other hand, if you remember the quid pro quo of relationships— *something in exchange for something else*—then you are more likely to see and acknowledge opportunities for helping others when they arise. Whether you care to admit it, you are networking every time you meet someone. I'm only putting a name to what happens when people enter into mutually beneficial or rewarding relationships. There is no doubt that you gain personally and professionally from networking. It typically isn't an act of altruism, but it also isn't such a bad thing. Everyone walks away a winner when networking is done properly.

HOW NETWORKING WORKS

Every interaction is a networking opportunity. The benefit or quid pro quo may not at first be clear—and indeed it may *never* materialize; nevertheless, networking is important in building positive workplace relationships. It can mean the difference between making and losing a career. A case in point is the brouhaha that arose early in Bill Clinton's presidency when he named his wife, Hillary, as chair of the White House Task Force on National Health Care Reform. The commotion can in part be ascribed to the fact that prior to the appointment, Hillary had few allies in Washington. The Clintons were relative outsiders. There is no doubt that the first lady could capably handle the assignment, but she had no network in place to support the unprecedented decision. It was the same for a previous Southern president, Jimmy Carter. Having a very small Washington network contributed to Carter's inability to influence others to accept his ideas and ultimate one-term presidency.

George W. Bush, on the other hand, ascended to the presidency with a wide network of political colleagues both of his own and from his father. When it came time to fill key positions in the White House, he called on these people, and they were immediately accepted because they were known to one another and Washington insiders. Initially, at least, it's why Bush had such success with passing his agendas. Not only was he blessed with a Republican Congress, but he also had a strong network of relationships surrounding him.

People who fail to network, or see it as superfluous to their primary tasks, miss out on untold opportunities. Networking provides you access to inside information about upcoming trends in your business, client leads, information essential to accomplishing your work, assistance with special projects, and myriad other benefits. Often the networking process isn't obvious, however, and the benefits may not be realized until long after a relationship is established.

Let me give you a very personal example. A woman I'll call Rachael was a client of mine in the late 1990s. We worked together on several projects at her company, so when she called one day asking if I would have lunch with her, I wasn't surprised. Before we scheduled the lunch appointment, though, she said she wanted to make it clear that this wasn't about work, it was personal. Despite the fact I was swamped with work, I did agree to have lunch with her. When we met, she told me she was thinking of quitting her company to venture out on her own and wondered if I would be willing to share with her the realities of starting a consulting business. We talked for nearly two hours and on the phone several times after that. Then one day I called her office to find that Rachael had indeed left the company and moved to the Chicago area. I really didn't give it much thought—we weren't close enough for her to feel the need to inform me, nor did I feel she should.

Now fast-forward about six years. I was working at my desk and my assistant buzzed me to let me know there was a woman on the phone by the name of Rachael who claimed we used to work together. Since I knew of no one else by the name of Rachael with whom I'd worked, I assumed it was her and took the call. She reported that her business was flourishing and she was the president of a national association of women professionals looking for a keynote speaker; she wondered if I'd be interested. She had read my books and thought I'd be perfect. As it happens, I did fly to Chicago to do that keynote, and in introducing me, Rachael told the story of how I'd taken time out of my busy schedule to meet with her to discuss her career goals. Quite honestly, I had completely forgotten the scenario. But the result of maintaining network relationships wasn't just one keynote—it was a series of them as other chapters of this particular association began calling and scheduling me to speak.

Even if you never plan on having your own business or rely on others for your income, you never know when you might be in the position of looking for a better job, trying to gain access to difficult-to-find information, or requiring assistance with a project. In the end, it always pays to offer help when needed and to build positive professional relationships. Here are a few other networking success stories:

- Larry decided to take a voluntary separation package from his company. He knew that with the money he received, he would have six months to find other, more satisfying work. Within six weeks, colleagues from professional associations he belonged to called to let him know about opportunities in their respective companies. He is now considering several offers—all of which came through his network contacts.

- Armando was working on a salary study for his department that entailed getting information from competitors about their salary structures. The project was made easier because of his membership in a professional organization of compensation specialists. In exchange for the information others provided, Armando offered to share his findings and final report with his network colleagues.

- Melissa works for a large corporation and was unhappy in her job but didn't want to leave the company entirely. She spoke with several people from other divisions with whom she had kept in contact and asked them to let her know whether any jobs became available that might provide new challenges for her. She was contacted by the vice president of one division and asked to apply for a job for which he thought she was qualified. Her network relationships enabled her to move into an assignment that is more rewarding—both financially and personally.

- Jacob had an idea that could substantially benefit his

manufacturing firm. He explained his idea to his boss, who didn't seem interested. So Jacob casually mentioned the idea to one of the company president's direct reports while they were flying home from an out-of-town conference. She thought it warranted attention and arranged for him to make a presentation to her boss. Jacob received a bonus, and public recognition, for his contribution to the company—a contribution made possible through a network relationship.

- Shirley was the administrator for a large commercial property management firm. As such, she had significant contact with building contractors, plumbers, electricians, and so forth, and always took care to treat these people with the respect they deserved—something that many of her colleagues neglected. When she left the company to start her own property management firm, her clients were impressed with her ability to get vendors to respond to her requests promptly. Although Shirley's own company is nowhere near the size of her former employer, she is given the same service afforded a large company. She is successful where many of her competitors fail because of the network she built during her career.

Clearly, these and other similar experiences validate the importance and benefit of networking. You don't build network relationships with the intention of benefiting from them, but networking does pay dividends.

CHARACTERISTICS OF
EFFECTIVE NETWORKERS

Certain characteristics form the basis for effective networking. People who network well typically possess a combination of the following:

- **Genuine interest in others.** Having a genuine interest in others is at the core of every good relationship—networking or otherwise. A genuine interest in others is manifested by asking people about themselves (and listening to the response), exhibiting a desire to be of help to them, recognizing their needs without them necessarily telling you, and the willingness to go out of your way to help meet those needs. You can't fake genuine interest in others. If you try, others will perceive you as manipulative or exploitative.

- **Ability to put others at ease.** If you're uncomfortable in networking situations, you can overcome this by focusing attention on making others comfortable. It gives you a role to play that provides something valuable while assuaging your own anxiety in new or unfamiliar situations. One way you can put others at ease is to show genuine interest in them. Another is to introduce them to others whom you may know in the group. When you're the one new to a group, consider finding someone who may be sitting or standing alone and beginning a conversation with him or her.

- **Commitment to a cause greater than themselves.** Kiwanis and Lions Clubs and chambers of commerce are good examples of groups committed to causes greater than simply promoting the well-being of the members. The boards of directors and operating committees of nonprofit

organizations are often committed to the cau
they volunteer their time. Networking throug
activities is a wonderful way to meet new peo
tribute something to your community at the
Such causes bring people together in a positive and meaningful way without focusing exclusively on the benefits of
membership.

- **Willingness to give more than they anticipate receiving in return.** You don't network because of what you expect to get from it. You network because you believe in the need to work collaboratively and cooperatively with others. This often means that you find yourself giving more to others in your network than you yourself may be receiving at any given time. As described under Success Strategy 1, you want to have an inexhaustible supply of chips in your account, earned by extending yourself to others without concern for what you might get in return. One of the best networkers I know is a Cleveland woman who is well respected in the community for her commitment to various charitable causes. Despite her busy schedule, she spends considerable time sharing her resources with others who ask for advice and information. She gives generously of her time and freely shares with others the knowledge gained through her networking activities.

- **Ability to ask for what they need.** This one seems to be particularly tough for women. I love to tell the story of a woman I know who is the daughter of someone quite well known in his field. She went into the same field and eventually wrote a book on a related topic but was having difficulty getting it published. Because her last name was different from that of her father, I asked if she let potential publishers know who she was related to. She responded with obvious distaste for the suggestion. She told me she

.dn't want to capitalize on her father's name. It's not capitalizing if you have a high-quality product or service to offer that someone else legitimately wants or needs. If you're always doing for others but not willing to ask for what you need, eventually the relationship suffers because of its lopsided nature.

- **Ability to act as a conduit between others.** Good networkers help others connect with the resources they require. They don't simply build relationships for their own personal use; they also help others succeed by acting as a referral source. For example, when you run into the woman from Cleveland whom I mentioned earlier, she never fails to introduce you to the many people she knows. When she does so, she comments on something flattering about you both: "Lynn Smith, let me introduce you to Steve Wilson. Steve single-handedly prevented my computer system from crashing last April right at tax time. Steve, Lynn knows more about investment strategies than anyone I know." Such generosity of spirit displays not only the ability to connect people, but the desire to showcase their talents at the same time.

- **Ability to remember people, information, and events.** It does no good to network unless you remember the people you meet and their unique circumstances or story. It's one thing to listen as someone tells you what a difficult year it's been because his or her child was diagnosed with cancer. It requires something entirely different to remember this piece of information and ask how the person and the child are doing the next time you meet (or to call that person). Remembering what people tell you is the sign of a good listener and of someone who networks not only for personal gain but because of a genuine interest in people as well.

WORKPLACE POLITICS AND NETWORKING

A unique aspect of networking involves the dreaded P-word: *politics*. If you avoid workplace politics like the plague, you're missing out on opportunities to do your job with maximum efficiency and minimum muscle. When it comes right down to it, politics is simply another form of reciprocal relationships. Author Kathleen Kelley Reardon has her finger on the pulse of workplace politics and writes extensively about it. Her work in this arena is so thorough and on-target that I urge you to read her two books *The Secret Handshake: Mastering the Politics of the Business Inner Circle* and *It's All Politics: Winning in a World Where Hard Work and Talent Aren't Enough.* Both are great reads filled with practical advice, including the following suggestions for how you can build "relationships the politically savvy way."

Know What Others Need and Want—and Let Them Know When You Provide It

Knowing and delivering value-added services isn't where it ends. Don't assume that others will notice when you've gone out of your way to get a job done or done it with particular precision and skill. "People are far too busy to follow or be aware of your accomplishments," says Reardon. "You have to let them know. The key here is to be strategic in telling them. Choose the right method and the right time." One way you can do this is to factually inform management of your achievements. For example, rather than simply say a particular project was completed, you might note, "I'm proud to report my team completed the Crenshaw project two weeks ahead of schedule and fifteen percent under budget." As a friend of mine says, "If you don't blow your own horn, no one will know you're in the band."

Manage Reciprocity

I frequently talk about the quid pro quo inherent to every relationship: the constant exchange of favors, assistance, information, friendship, and so on. If you're not mentally keeping track of it, you're making a mistake, but not because you may not be getting your fair share of the bargain—you may not be *giving* enough in the exchange to begin with. In Reardon's words, "Asking someone you've never bothered to establish a relationship with for a favor . . . is a form of political fumbling. She doesn't know whether you'll ever return the favor since she doesn't know your track record. She doesn't owe you anything and hasn't the foggiest idea what you'll ever be able to do for her." If you've read any of my other books or heard me speak, you know this is a point with which I could not agree more. In *my* words, *When you need a relationship, it's too late to build it.*

Develop Your Favor Bank

You may ask yourself what you have to offer as a favor. Believe me, there are plenty of favors being exchanged all the time—some more obvious than others. From providing information that may not be commonly known to covering people's responsibilities when they're out on sick leave, you probably do more favors than you realize. Each time you provide a favor, you collect a favor chip—and you always want more chips in your account than you could possibly use.

Surprise People with Unexpected Favors

Reardon points out that unexpected favors aren't always obvious. "If a person did you a favor by meeting with you, an immediate thank-you note is effective. If, however, the person has only spoken with you in passing, the impact of a personal note recalling something he said might be greater if you send it a month after you met. That you remember his interests so long after parting company indicates that you were really listening to him and that he's remained on your mind."

Show Gratitude Consistent with What You Received

When it comes to favors, I do them willingly for others and rarely expect anything in return. I know that the universe will reward me appropriately when I least expect and most need it. That's why I'm surprised that I remember an incident from many years ago that bugs me to this day—but it does speak to the importance of proper gratitude. A corporate client of mine wanted to add a component of workplace communication to a training program we conducted quarterly in countries around the world. Not only was this a lucrative piece of business, but it was also fun because we stayed at the best accommodations in exotic locations, paid for by a client that treated its outside consultants quite well. I recommended a colleague of mine for the work; he landed the contract for this project as well as several others in the company over a period of years. He sent me a "chocolate pizza" with no personal note as his thanks. As much as I appreciated his thoughtfulness, it just didn't match the magnitude of the favor. A personal note indicating appreciation for the confidence

I'd placed in him through the referral would have meant so much more. A referral to one of his clients would have been even better!

Give Credit Even When It Isn't Due

I'm sure your mother, like mine, had a little saying for nearly every life lesson. Remember the one, *You catch more flies with honey than with vinegar?* Well, that's what this suggestion is all about. Letting people save face and reinforcing even small points of agreement goes a long way toward building politically effective relationships— and it doesn't cost you a dime. Rather than looking for the point of *disagreement* in what someone else is saying, look for the point with which you can specifically and genuinely *agree* as a means of giving credit. Here are some examples:

- I like what you're saying about the need to investigate other options. I was focusing on the way we've always done it. Let's see how we can take the best of both.
- Thank you for collecting all of this information in advance. It's helped me to see what we still need, so let me give you a little more direction for how to fill in the blanks.
- Your attention to detail is so much better than mine. Now let's take a look at how we can connect the dots to reach the right conclusion.

Make Connections

Unlike actually building relationships, making connections means simply getting on the other person's radar screen. It isn't that you don't enjoy or aren't cordial to everyone you come into contact with, but when you meet certain people, you know they have certain things in common with you. That's when you want to be sure to get their contact information and ask if you might call them in the future. This is making a connection. Sometimes those connections do turn into relationships, but most don't. "The more sophisticated organizational politicians don't haphazardly fling their cards at complete strangers. They seem to have a kind of radar that tells them whom they should seek out. This radar comes from having done their homework. A true mover and shaker works the room—any room—intelligently," explains Reardon.

Play Close to the Vest

In the name of fairness, you may think you need to share everything you know about a subject or every piece of information that may have been given to you about a project. Nothing could be farther from the truth. Knowledge is power, and there are times when keeping all or some of it to yourself is the best course of action. "You have to know whom to trust with information. Friendship complicates things because it brings with it certain obligations to share information. So the fewer intimate relationships you have at work, the less you'll feel pressured to spill the beans when you should be keeping information to yourself," says Reardon. You need information coming to you at all times, but you need to manage the reciprocal aspect of it. One suggestion Reardon makes for dealing with people who try to provoke you to disclose information is to use apparent self-disclosure: sharing information that may be new to the person but actually isn't risky for you and is usually discoverable with a little digging.

TIPS FOR SHY TYPES

Although most people would never guess it when they meet me, in social situations I am painfully shy. On Myers-Briggs, I score at the top of the Introversion scale. Put me in front of an audience of five hundred people where I have a role to play and I'm okay, but don't put me at a cocktail party with fifteen people. When I actually took the self-assessment at the beginning of this book after designing it, my own development area was networking! That's why when I came across these tips by Michelle Tullier, vice president of career management consulting with Right Management Consultants in Atlanta, I knew they would be perfect for readers who may be shy types:

- **Take baby steps.** Don't try to become a master networker overnight. A common mistake introverts make is to wake up one day and announce, "Today I'm going to become an active networker!" That proclamation is, unfortunately, about as likely to succeed as the announcement that you're going to lose weight or quit smoking once and for all.
- **Don't assume you're being a pest.** Introverts tend to assume they'll be bothering the people they contact. They may be projecting their own feelings onto others. Introverts often prefer to be left alone—to do their work without interruptions or having their own little world invaded. Before you assume you're going to be a pest if you try to make contact with someone, think twice. Most people will be glad to hear from you. Keep in mind that 75 percent of the US population is extroverted.
- **Rely on your supporters.** People you know well and who are accessible can provide emotional support when

the going gets tough, encouragement on the way up, and a kick in the pants when you're slacking off. Networking invariably brings challenges that result in less-than-positive feelings. Supporters can offer encouragement and empathy along the way.

- **Get the competitive juices flowing.** Try to remember that lots of people who aren't half as capable, qualified, talented, or nice as you are advancing simply because they connect with others and make themselves visible. Even people who aren't competitive by nature usually can muster some competitive drive when they see how unfair it is that less qualified colleagues are getting ahead.

- **Rest on your laurels.** Remember the times you've been successful in group endeavors or one-on-one interactions with others. These recollections will give you courage to face the next networking situation.

- **Be a leader.** An advantage of any type of leadership position is it gives you a built-in excuse for connecting with people. Introverts often don't seek leadership roles because these positions inevitably require such dreaded tasks as committee meetings and team projects. More behind-the-scenes leadership roles such as being a newsletter editor or secretary for a professional organization can play to your strengths without forcing you to be too outgoing or political.

- **Enlist a spokesperson.** If you're hesitant to contact someone you don't know, consider having another person act as a go-between for you. If someone in your network has given you the name of a colleague, ask your contact to call the person first for you to give a heads-up that you'll be calling. Most people are willing to do this.

- **Don't underestimate the power of listening.** Those who don't have the gift of gab shouldn't despair. Listening is just as important as talking when it comes to establishing good relationships with others. There's nothing extroverts like better than having someone listen to them talk.

- **Don't sweat the small talk.** Small talk is just what it sounds like: small. A sense of humor or some profound insight is nice, but there's nothing wrong with a mundane comment to break the ice like, "Large turnout, isn't it?" or "This is great dip." Asking a question is often a great way to initiate a conversation.

- **Like birds of a feather, flock together.** If you find group interaction difficult, look for other people who seem uncomfortable and approach them. It's easier to start with other introverts than with the intimidating woman in red who's surrounded by a phalanx of fans in the center of the room. But don't get stuck with the introverts. At some point, you have to leave the nest.

- **Make the most of what you know.** What you know is just as important as who you know when it comes to networking. Unlike extroverts, introverts are likely to be the ones who take the time to read the industry newsletters cover-to-cover. Let people know that you're the one they can call for the latest information on whatever's relevant to your field. Take the initiative to pick up the phone and share your findings with others.

- **Rehearse, rehearse, rehearse.** It's likely you'll find yourself having the same sort of conversations repeatedly. If you tend to get tongue-tied when meeting someone new, try practicing what you're going to say. If you freeze up or babble incoherently when leaving messages, get in the habit of taking time before picking up the phone to plan what you'll say if the person doesn't answer.

- **Don't keep it to yourself.** Introverts worry they'll bother people, so they tend to reach out to others only when they're really worried or excited about something. Instead, try to get in the habit of connecting with people over small things—not just the big ones. Doing so enables you to develop ongoing relationships and ensures that contacts are there for you when you need to share the big stuff.

- **Attend events that have a purpose.** If you're uncomfortable or nervous at events that are solely networking opportunities, try to attend gatherings that have a purpose, such as educational or cultural seminars. Interactive classes and workshops are good bets because they have a built-in agenda that involves structured networking.

- **Write often.** If you can't get yourself to pick up the phone and make a cold call, or even a cool one, then consider writing. A letter of introduction can make the follow-up phone call less nerve-racking.

- **Get out among them.** Do you tend to hole up in your office or other workplace? Just getting out of the house or office to be among people helps. Although walking isn't direct networking, it propels you out of your own little world and brings about a powerful mind-set change that can lead you into networking.

- **Be positive.** Before you declare that it's not going to be worth your time to talk to Joe Shmoe or to attend a particular event, stop and think. Do you have rational proof that your prospects are dim, or are you just afraid? Almost all encounters are worthwhile, if for no other reason than for the practice.

- **Consider seeking professional help.** If you think your shyness or introversion is more than just a mild nuisance, you might need to consult a psychologist, therapist, or other mental health counselor. Shyness that seriously hinders social interactions can keep you from doing what you need to do, and you may benefit from professional treatment.

- **Be comfortable in your own skin.** Sometimes reluctance to network results from insecurity about your appearance. While physical attractiveness is by no means a prerequisite for being a successful networker, the package you present to others is important. If something about your outward image is undermining your confidence, consider fixing what's fixable and learn to make the most of what's not.

- **Just do it.** You never know where a job, lead, or some good advice is going to turn up. Sure, networking can be difficult, anxiety provoking, and a pain in the neck, but at some point you have to abandon all the excuses, take a deep breath, and just do it.

NETWORKING OPPORTUNITIES

Even though nearly every interaction is a networking opportunity, it's also important to seek specific experiences that promote networking. Finding organizations or opportunities that blend with your own particular interests makes networking more natural and less burdensome. Ideally, you want to be able to spend time with people you enjoy and engage in activities that are of value to you—not only with people or causes who need you (or vice versa). Once you give it some thought, you will be able to come up with your own outlets for networking, but for now here are some ideas that may be of help.

Professional Associations

Nearly every profession has an association of members devoted to furthering knowledge in the field, developing expertise in its membership, and providing a forum for members to exchange ideas and information. Typically, if the association is large enough, it has local chapters in addition to a national body and provides members with benefits such as newsletters, magazines, and bulletin boards. Everyone should belong to at least one professional association and actively participate in its events by attending meetings, volunteering for committees, and taking part in its conferences and special events.

Nonprofit Organization Boards or Committees

These groups are frequently in search of committed people to join their boards of directors or serve as members of functional committees. They typically look for businesspeople with skill in one or more specific areas such as fund-raising, finance, human resources, or a related technical field. By becoming involved with a nonprofit organization, you can make a valuable contribution to your community while gaining access to influential people in the community, learning more about the community itself, and developing skills in networking.

There are a number of ways to find out where opportunities for nonprofit involvement lie. Depending on your interests, try making these contacts for starters:

- Your company's foundation or human resource department
- The YWCA or YMCA

- Your church's pastor or synagogue's rabbi
- The Red Cross
- The board of education or schools in your community
- Friends who are involved with nonprofit organizations
- Political campaign offices
- The police department
- The chamber of commerce
- Hospices
- The Heart Association
- The human interest section of the newspaper
- Big Brothers or Big Sisters of America

Special-Interest Clubs

Networking doesn't have to be all work and no play. There are numerous clubs that cater to nearly every interest imaginable. Whether you like computers, chess, ballroom dancing, hiking, tennis, stamp collecting, or antique cars, there's a club out there waiting for you to join. Choose one that relates to something in which you have an avid interest, and network for fun. The Internet has made it easy to find groups of like-minded people.

Discussion Groups

Many cities have informal groups that gather to discuss recent books, movies, or topics of community interest. They provide a unique opportunity to network while discussing a subject of interest to you. If you can't find one in your town, why not consider starting one? This allows you to play a role instead of just mingling, and is especially helpful for those who are uncomfortable meeting strangers.

Informal Gatherings

Have you gotten into a rut where you only go to work and come home, rarely socializing anymore with friends? Why not invite a group of people with whom you share similar interests to join you for a Sunday brunch or dinner? Or organize a trip to a local museum. Networking can be casual and informal as well as professional and organized. The group may decide to have regular monthly events (hopefully not always at your house) or other weekend activities.

Doorway Conversations

Don't forget something as simple and obvious as making a point of dropping by people's offices for a few minutes of casual conversation. If you're uncomfortable with not having a specific purpose or issue to discuss, bring by an article that you think may be of interest to a person, or ask for advice in an area in which the individual has particular expertise. Again, it doesn't have to be work-related. You can ask for a referral to a good pediatrician from someone who has children, or for a recommendation for a Friday-night movie.

Spiritual or Religious Groups

Aside from recommending volunteer work, your church, synagogue, or other spiritual meeting place might have groups that you can join. Frequently, these organizations have groups tailored for various segments of the community—for single parents, singles in search of friendship, and the like—and typically welcome all prospective members.

* * *

You may want to view networking the same way you view physical exercise: It's difficult (and sometimes painful), but you know it's good for you. Just as you wouldn't begin a running regimen with a twenty-six-mile marathon, don't choose the hardest opportunity you can think of as your first networking activity. It will only turn you off and make you reluctant to continue over the long term. How you network, or what groups you choose to join, isn't nearly as important as just getting out there, meeting people, and having a good time while you do it.

Coaching Tips for Networking

Put a check mark in the box of two or three coaching tips you commit to doing.

❑ **Organize group outings.** (Just take care not to be viewed as a camp counselor!) From holiday parties to company barbecues, there are opportunities to bring people together. Being the one who sometimes organizes these events allows you to be seen as someone who understands the value of relationships and is capable of orchestrating the details these affairs entail. Don't fall into the role of the person who always does so, however. This will cause people to think you have nothing more important to do.

❑ **Introduce people to one another.** This is one of the easiest, but most overlooked, opportunities to build your network. It entails making connections between people who have common interests. You can do it as simply as passing along contact information or arranging a breakfast or lunch where all parties are present. As a courtesy to the people involved, you should first ask permission to make the connection. Although most people will readily agree, they must trust your judgment about knowing whom they might want to be contacted by.

❏ **Remember names and personal information.** Unless you have a superior memory, you're unlikely to remember data points about everyone with whom you come into contact. That's what databases are for. Get in the habit of entering into your database the information on the business cards of those you meet. I keep mine on my PDA so that it's always handy. Whenever possible, make personal notations as to birthdays, the names of wives or children, or hobbies these folks may have mentioned. Then, when you know you're going to be in a situation where they might be in attendance, review the information.

❏ **Circulate articles to others who have similar interests or needs.** Many people use this tip to keep their networks alive, but few do it well. Sending out a mass mailing of information *you* think is interesting doesn't cut it. The people in my network whom I most value are those who know what my interests are and limit what they send me to just that. And while I'm on the subject, think twice about circulating jokes or cartoons. Again, unless you know someone is going to appreciate them, don't expend the effort.

❑ **Be a mentor.** There are many ways available to mentor others—both inside and outside your own organization. You can volunteer for a formal mentoring program within your company or alma mater, or through a professional association. Women can also check out mentoring opportunities through the Web site www.menttium .com. Expanding your network by mentoring those with less experience or who are new to your organization exposes you to different people and ideas than you normally come in contact with.

❑ **Invite colleagues and their families to your home for a barbecue or potluck.** Let people get to know you as a human being, not just a human doing, by allowing them to see you in your own environment outside work. These events don't have to be frequent or elaborate; they should simply allow for casual conversations and the kinds of interactions that offer a slightly more intimate experience of you.

❑ **Read *Networking for Job Search and Career Success* by Michelle Tullier.** If you liked the tips she provides for shy types, you'll love the book. It's filled with equally practical suggestions for jump-starting your career through network relationships.

❑ **Volunteer for a nonprofit board.** Not only will you meet people who share your interest in a particular cause, but you'll also learn how to be part of a team, sharpen the technical skills you bring to the group, and have the satisfaction of doing something good for your community.

❑ **Be an active member of a professional association or a community service organization.** Good examples include the Rotary, Kiwanis, Lions, and chambers of commerce. Many people join these groups to beef up their résumés, but the real benefit of professional associations is the exchange of ideas and information that comes when a group of like-minded people assembles. If you're the shy type, volunteer to be on the membership committee—this gives you a role to play and puts you in contact with people who need you to help them learn about the organization.

❑ **Take up a sport that requires at least one other person.** Not only is the exercise good for you, but you'll also enjoy an opportunity to be social in a healthy way that isn't limited to eating and drinking.

❑ **Be active in your college or university's alumni association.** These groups can be a great source for filling vacancies in your company, identifying career opportunities for yourself, and meeting people who can connect you with the networks you need to be part of. Don't wait until you need it to join and become active.

❑ **Conduct pro bono workshops in your area of expertise for nonprofit organizations.** Okay, so maybe you're not a joiner. You can still get out there and meet people by offering to share your experience with a group that can benefit from it. Many corporations keep a list of organizations that need professional advice; check with your human resource department if you're not sure how to do this.

❑ **Write articles for professional journals.** Long before I wrote books, I wrote articles as a means of becoming known in my professional circles. They provided a kind of calling card to offer to be a guest speaker or lead a discussion group. Of course, they also look good on your résumé and force you to delve deeply into a subject so that you become an expert.

❑ **Check out online networking sites.** Friendster.com and spoke.com can get both men and women started. For women, WorldWIT.org has networking groups in major cities around the globe and is a great resource; I highly recommend it.

Personal Development Planning

Now that you understand how and why smart people sabotage their careers, and ways in which you may be sabotaging your own best efforts, it's time to make a commitment to do something to prevent it. The following quotation from Johann Wolfgang von Goethe, one of the greatest and most versatile European writers and thinkers of modern times, sums up the need to take affirmative action on behalf of your career success:

> *Until one is committed, there is hesitancy, the chance to draw back, always ineffectiveness. Concerning all acts of initiative (and creation), there is one elementary truth, the ignorance of which kills countless ideas and splendid plans: that the moment one definitely commits oneself, then providence moves too. All sorts of things occur to help one that would never otherwise have occurred. A whole stream of events issues from the decision, raising in one's favor all manner of unforeseen incidents and meetings and material assistance, which no one could have dreamed would have come their way. Whatever you do; or dream you can, begin it. Boldness has genius, power and magic in it. Begin it now.*

FINDING A COACH

Although each of the previous chapters is filled with suggestions for what you can do to take charge of your career, there are just a few more resources I want to provide to you, beginning with the answer to one of the questions I am most frequently asked: *How do I find a coach?* The past two decades have seen an exponential increase in the number of people calling themselves business coaches. Sometimes these people are highly qualified, but all too often they're just out to make a quick buck. One organization in particular, International Coach Federation, has done a superb job of bringing standards and a code of ethics to the field. For this reason, I often suggest people go to its Web site, www.coachfederation.org, as a place to begin their search. You can search their database by geographic location, coach gender, area of expertise, and fees. Because there's so much variation in the expertise, philosophies, styles, and fees of coaches, it's in your best interest to carefully screen anyone you entrust to become your coach. The most important things to do before selecting any coach are to:

- **Assess the coach's credentials.** What is his or her educational background, work history, and expertise in the area in which you require assistance—presentation skills, interpersonal skills, career development, or the like?
- **Assure that there is a match between your personality and the coach's personality.** I know from experience that a good fit is essential to achieving your career goals. Whether you're paying for it or your company is, when you're interviewing people to be your coach, don't just focus on qualifications; also look at how you will feel

working with this person. As we used to say in graduate school, *It's the relationship that heals.*

• **Locate a coach whose fee fits within your budget.** Whether you pay for it out of your pocket or your company pays, coaching can be an expensive investment. Many companies today will pay for employee coaching in much the same way as they pay for other training programs, so check with your human resource department before dipping into your own pocket. If your employer doesn't pay, let the coach know that you will be footing the bill. Coaches often have different fee arrangements or coaching programs for private clients than for corporate clients.

When it comes to selecting a coach, be a smart consumer. If your company is paying for it, you may get only one chance to be coached, so don't settle for someone with whom you have never spoken or who doesn't have the specific expertise needed to assist with your development areas. Much of successful coaching depends on the coach–client relationship, so ask to speak with the coach in advance, either by phone or in a personal meeting, and ask questions such as:

• What is your coaching philosophy?
• What companies have sent clients to you for coaching? What are some of the companies your clients work for?
• Are there any kinds of clients you don't like working with?
• How much time will be spent in face-to-face contact versus phone contact?
• What kind of information will you share with my employer (if the employer is paying)?

- How long will the coaching process last?
- What kind of follow-up with you can I expect?
- Will you provide me with a written action plan?
- Do you make referrals to other professionals when needed?

Whether the coach you select is across the street from your office or across the country, you can anticipate that the coaching process will more or less follow certain steps.

Phase 1. Determining Fit

With anyone you identify as a potential coach, there will be an initial discussion that allows you to determine mutual suitability of fit. You are assessing whether or not this is a person you believe can help you, and the coach should be assessing whether his or her areas of expertise are a good match for you. If you live at a significant distance from the coach's office, this initial discussion may take place by phone. Most reputable coaching firms *do not charge* for this initial consultation.

Phase 2. The Coaching Plan

Once you select a coach, this person will meet with you (either in person or by phone) to discuss your goals, the coaching process, matters related to confidentiality, and other logistics. If your company is paying for the coach, you should anticipate that he or she will also want to speak with your boss and perhaps the human resource department to elicit their suggestions for development areas.

Phase 3. Data Collection

This can include giving you aptitude or personality tests to assess your work style, an in-depth personal interview, and feedback about your performance from colleagues, management, and, when applicable, staff reporting to you. Feedback may be collected through interviews, the use of a feedback instrument, or both. The purpose of the data is to give both you and the coach a clear idea of how others see your strengths and areas for development.

Phase 4. Coaching

Once the data is collected, and sometimes even before, the coaching begins. This is where the coaching process varies most from one coach to another. Some coaches will charge you an hourly fee and contract with you for a set number of sessions. A different approach, used by firms such as my own, involves contracting with your employer for a fixed term of coaching, typically from four to nine months. During that time, several coaches will meet with you, each with expertise in the development areas identified through the data collection. The actual coaching sessions consist of in-depth discussions related to your goals, workplace behaviors, and areas for development. Don't be surprised if it feels a little like the coaches are digging deep into your psyche. Highly skilled coaches know that behavior is ingrained and intentional; sometimes understanding the source of it is the first step into helping to modify it.

Phase 5. Follow-Up

I believe that coaching is a relationship. As such, you deserve to have access to the coach for some period of time following the specified coaching period. This doesn't mean you should become overly dependent on the coach, but rather that change takes time, mistakes will be made, and the opportunity to discuss what's working and where you may be getting stuck is important. Be sure to ask your coach the procedure for follow-up and what was included in his or her original proposal to your company.

COMPANIES OFFERING PUBLIC WORKSHOPS OR TRAINING PROGRAMS

There are numerous companies that offer public (as opposed to customized in-house) workshops on a variety of topics. As with coaches, the quality of these programs varies greatly from company to company, as does the cost. With the less expensive programs ($99 to $199 for a day-long event), you can expect to sit in a room with hundreds of other people, with little opportunity for interaction with the facilitator. If you're looking to gain a few tips for how to be more effective in a particular area, this may suit your needs.

The more expensive programs last from two to seven days and can cost thousands of dollars. The price is worth it if the group size is small and you are guaranteed individual attention. The companies I've included below are definitely high-end—but they're also high-result organizations. The class size is usually limited, providing you with the chance to receive individual feedback and have your specific questions answered in depth by a seasoned facilitator.

American Management Association
www.amanet.org

The American Management Association (AMA) offers more than two hundred seminars for employees at all levels within an organization. Their programs typically provide participants with hands-on techniques for increasing effectiveness in areas such as communication skills, strategic management, assertiveness, management skills, and accounting.

Center for Creative Leadership
www.ccl.org

The Center for Creative Leadership (CCL) is a non-profit educational institute with branches throughout the country and in Europe. It works to adapt the theories and ideas of the behavioral sciences to the practical concerns of managers and leaders throughout society. Through research, training, and publication, CCL addresses the challenges facing leaders of today and tomorrow. It offers outstanding programs for executives and senior managers as well as an array of publications related to leadership.

NTL Institute
http://ntl.org

NTL, founded in 1947, offers an array of workshops for those who want to develop their interpersonal skills. Its workshops are experientially oriented and provide participants with the opportunity to explore their own values, attitudes, and actions as well as how others perceive them. They create a positive and supportive environment in which participants are free to explore behavior changes. I have attended a number of NTL workshops and recommend them highly. A client who attended one described it as "a life-changing experience." Be aware that because NTL is experientially oriented, its programs can be quite intense and require more than passive participation.

Outward Bound
www.outwardbound.com

Outward Bound courses are designed to help people develop self-confidence, compassion, and an appreciation for selfless service to others. This is not a survival school. Its challenging curriculum enables participants to learn by doing, and personal growth is central to the Outward Bound experience. Programs enable you to realize individual success and encourage you to develop a team spirit that results in the camaraderie and interdependence necessary for your team to achieve its goals. In addition to public programs, it customizes events for individual company retreats or team buildings. I highly recommend an Outward Bound program for anyone who wants to learn to take more risks, develop confidence, and understand the value of teamwork.

MENTAL HEALTH CONTACTS

If you think you might need help that goes beyond the scope of a workshop, coach, or book, you might want to consider entering into counseling with a licensed mental health practitioner. Most business coaches report that up to 75 percent of the people they coach are referred for some kind of longer-term counseling in conjunction with or following the coaching. Counseling isn't for people who are sick, but rather for people who want to lead fuller, more productive lives. Good counseling can help you to understand what part your past plays in the present and how to avoid allowing it to control your life.

Most people will do well with a licensed psychologist or psychotherapist. Psychiatrists are physicians (MDs) who typically use a medical model for the treatment of psychological problems. Psychiatrists can prescribe drugs, whereas the other two classifications cannot. I recommend beginning with a psychologist or psychotherapist; if needed, a referral can then be made to a psychiatrist.

There are many people who call themselves counselors or psychotherapists, and licensing varies from state to state. When seeking psychological assistance, you want to evaluate a number of things: the person's professional credentials and licenses, his or her experience dealing with the problems you want to address, the match between you and the therapist, and the cost. Don't be afraid to ask questions. Remember, you are the consumer.

Depending on the part of the country in which you live, the average cost of therapy can range anywhere from one hundred to two hundred dollars per hour, or more. When you're ready to find a therapist, there are a number of ways to locate someone reputable:

• **Referral from a trusted friend or relative.** This is probably the best way to find a therapist. Be aware, however, that just because your best friend loves his or her therapist, it doesn't mean you will, too. Give yourself at least three or four sessions before you decide a particular therapist isn't for you.

• **Your family physician.** Your own physician can be a good source for a referral. Make certain that you let him or her know what you are looking for in a therapist so that an appropriate referral can be made.

- **Local mental health agencies.** If you look in the yellow pages under Mental Health, you'll find agencies that provide psychological services. These are often non-profit community agencies where treatment is reasonably priced.

- **Your company's employee assistance program (EAP).** Many companies today have EAPs designed to help employees in distress. Some even offer a limited number of confidential therapy sessions paid for by the company. Ask your personnel or human resource manager for more information.

- **The American Psychological Association (APA).** This organization consists of members who are licensed psychologists and psychotherapists. Each state has a chapter of the APA and can refer you to a licensed member in your area. When calling for information, ask for the name of your state's psychological association—say, the Illinois Psychological Association.

BEGIN IT NOW

You've gotten this far by reading this book—why not take it one step farther and actually make a commitment to behavioral change? Go back to your self-assessment and identify the areas that most require your attention if you're going to get and keep the job you want. Then review the coaching tips you checked at the end of each chapter. And finally, use this information to complete the personal development plan that follows. Share it with people you trust, ask for feedback, and review it regularly. Career success lies not in the hands of your boss or management, your mother or father, or your husband or wife, but in the choices you make. You have no control over the past, but you can take charge of your future.

PERSONAL DEVELOPMENT PLAN

Three Things I'm Currently Doing That Will Contribute to Long-Term Success Are:	Three Things I Commit to Doing *More of* to Ensure Long-Term Success Are:	Three Things I Commit to Doing *Less of* to Ensure Long-Term Success Are:

Acknowledgments

The most pleasant part of writing a book is when it comes time to thank those who helped and supported me through the process. My work is enhanced by my unique relationship with each of you:

- Diana Baroni, vice president, executive editor, and editorial director of Warner Wellness; Leila Porteous; Penina Sacks; and the entire editorial team at Warner Books not only for giving me the opportunity to update and re-release this book but for making it even better with your input and guidance.

- Chris Dao, former assistant director of publicity at Warner Books, for helping to put my last two books on the best-seller lists!

- Bob Silverstein, for your unending support, friendship, encouragement, and wise counsel as a literary agent.

- Dr. Kim Finger, for being a terrific first reader, sounding board, colleague, and friend.

- Dr. Pam Erhardt, for being the best muse anyone could ever ask for.

- Jessica Vaughn, for your help with this book's illustrations and every other little thing you do to make things in our office flow like they're supposed to.

- Dr. Karen Otazo, for introducing me to the concept of coaching and changing the direction of my professional life in the process.

- The entire coaching team from Corporate Coaching International, for generously sharing your expertise with me over the years, thereby enabling me to become a better coach to our clients.

To each of you, and the others in my network of extended family and friends, I extend a heartfelt thank-you. I hope that each of you knows how very grateful I am for the gifts you have given and continue to give me.

Index

abrasiveness, 167–169, 272

accents/dialects, 124–126

active listening, 240–241

    obstacles to, 53–56

    relationship building through, 52–59, 199, 295, 311–312

    Rogers' techniques of, 54–59

    workplace example of, 161–162

affinity groups, 137

American Management Association, 329

American Psychological Association, 332

The Apprentice, ix, 171–172

Arafat, Yasir, 169

The Artist's Way (Cameron), 242

Ash, Mary Kay, 231–232

attention to detail. *See* detail orientation

attractiveness, as self-sabotage, 117–118

authority figure

    challenging of, 197–198, 212–213, 215, 216

    deference v. confrontation with, 197–203

authority figure relationship

    as parental relationship, 5, 10–12, 194–195, 211–212

    self-assessment checklist of, 193

bait taking, as self-sabotage, 181–183

balanced skill set, xiii, xv, 27, 68, 232, 235, 246

Bardwick, Judith, 252

Barker, Joel, 90

Bates, Suzanne, 150

behavior

    factors for changing, 25–29, 164

    inappropriate, 10, 11–12, 198–199

    self-assessment checklist of, 19–24

    workplace example of changing, 44–46, 161–162

belligerence, 169–170

blaming, 170, 213

body language, 120–123, 148

Borman, Frank, 229–230

boss

    coaching tips for difficult, 211–214, 217

    managing up with difficult, 209–214, 217

    subordinate challenging of, 197–198, 212–213, 215, 216

boundaries, of corporate playing field, 12–16, 126, 128, 200–202, 243, 255, 293

Bradberry, Travis, 155, 184–185

Brag! The Art of Tooting Your Own Horn Without Blowing It (Klaus), 257

Burr, Donald, 230–231
Bush, George W., 107, 298
Business Class: Etiquette Essential for Success at Work (Whitmore), 147
The Business of Paradigms (Barker), 90

California Pizza Kitchen, 81–82
Calley, William, Jr., 200, 202
Cameron, Julia, 242
can-do attitude
    coaching tips to develop, 275–284
    meeting promises of, 276–277, 285, 287–288
    no-can-do attitude v., 266–267, 269–272
    value-adding of, 261–262, 264–265, 272, 273–275, 279, 284
Canon Business Machines, 228
caring, 63–66
Carnegie, Dale, 59, 72, 151, 295
Carter, Jimmy, 298
Center for Creative Leadership, xi, 329
changing behavior. *See* behavior; self-sabotaging behavior
character traits
    of effective networkers, 302–304
    of emotional intelligence deficiency, 165–172
childhood experience
    career influenced by, xii, xiv, 30–33, 38–39, 45, 176, 192–197, 202, 236–237, 270–271
    manager/employee relationship influenced by, 194–195, 203–205, 211–212, 217
    teamwork resistance influenced by, 84–86, 90, 99–100
Claiborne, Elizabeth, 225–226
Clinton, Bill, 37–38, 153–154
Clinton, Hillary, 297–298
coaching, x–xii, xiii. *See also* professional coaching

on balancing detail orientation v. strategic thinking, 246–250
on body language, 122, 123
on communication style improvement, 133–134, 148–150, 196, 199, 329
on corporate playing field success, 133–134
on developing value-adding brand, 285–289
on emotional intelligence, 184–188
on image improvement, 144–148
on increasing likability, 70, 72–73, 184–188
on manager/employee relationship, 206–220
on managing up successfully, 206–220
on networking, 318–322
on relationship building, 44–46, 69–73, 310–314, 318–322
on self-awareness development, 178–180
on speech patterns, 131–132
on strategic thinking, 240–242, 329
on successful presentations, 133–137
on team player effectiveness, 103–106
collaboration, 2, 84, 90, 95, 280
communication problems, 88, 181–183
communication style
    accents/dialects in, 124–126
    coaching tips to improve, 133–134, 148–150, 196, 199, 329
    differences in, 137–144, 196–197, 303
    self-sabotaging behaviors in, 126–129, 138–144, 181–183
    speech patterns in, 129–132
    success factor of, 31, 37–38, 124, 129, 131

of Western males, 137–140,
142–143
condescension, 166–167
conversation. *See* doorway
conversations
Coping with an Intolerable Boss
(Lombardo and McCall), 211
corporate playing field
boundaries of, 12–16, 126, 128,
200–202, 243, 255, 293
coaching tips for success in,
133–134
competition v. cooperation in, 75,
76
managing up in, 200–202
Costner, Kevin, 173
Couric, Katie, 176
creativity, 13, 223, 242, 244
cultural difference in communication
style, 137–144
customer satisfaction
going extra mile for, 259–261,
264–265, 276–277
success/failure examples of, 262–263
teamwork dynamics for, 80–82,
264–265
"The Customer Is Clueless" (Hall), 286

Danger in the Comfort Zone (Bardwick),
252
defense mechanisms, 3–5, 50
intelligence as, 160–161
perfectionism as, 41, 117–118
The Definitive Book of Body Language
(Pease and Pease), 120, 148
DeLay, Tom, 168
derailment, of career path, xi–xii
DESCript, honest message delivery
model, 174–175, 186
detail orientation
coaching tips to develop, 244–246
self-sabotage in, 238–240, 271,
277–278

detail orientation, v. strategic thinking
can-do attitude and, 277–278
coaching tips to balance, 246–250
continuum of, 227–228
imbalance in, 238–240, 242–244, 271
job satisfaction and, 233–236
self-assessment checklist of, 224
dialects/accents, 124–126
Ditka, Mike, 1
doorway conversations, relationship
building through, 59, 69, 317
downsizing, xii, xiii, 243
Drawing on the Right Side of the Brain
(Edwards), 223, 242
dress for success, 111–120, 144
height/youth suggestions to,
119–120
standards in, 115–116, 117–118
dressing standards, 111, 112, 115–118

earnings potential, 109
Eastern Air Lines, 229–230
Edison, Thomas Alva, 225
Edwards, Betty, 223, 242
emotional intelligence (EQ)
Clinton, Bill, v. Nixon, 153–154
coaching tips for enhancing,
184–188
competence types in, 155–157
deficiency character traits of,
165–172
development, 161–163
likability quotient and, 157, 159
proficiency in, 151–156, 172–182
self-assessment checklist of, 158
*The Emotional Intelligence Quick Book:
Everything You Need to Know
to Put Your EQ to Work*
(Greaves and Bradberry), 155,
184–185
empathy, 180–181, 302
employee satisfaction, 80–82, 191–192,
233, 235–236

employee/manager relationship
  childhood experience influencing, 194–195, 203–205, 211–212, 217
  coaching tips to improve, 206–220
  deference v. confrontation in, 197–203, 212–213
  expectations in, 190–192, 206, 213–214
  tolerating inappropriate behavior in, 197–199, 214
Enron, 170, 221–222
EQ. *See* emotional intelligence
exchange relationship. *See* quid pro quo

facial expression. *See* body language
failure
  childhood experience influencing, xii, xiv, 30–33, 39, 45, 176, 202, 270–271
  signs of, xi–xiii
Field, Sally, 66
Fiorina, Carly, 189–190
first impression, 111, 113, 115, 116
Four Seasons Hotels, 273
Frankel, Lois P., ix, xv, 67, 137, 176
Freud, Sigmund, repetition compulsion theory of, 3–4

gatekeeping, 99, 103–104
gender difference
  in communication style, 137–144, 303
  in self-confidence, 275
  in workplace boundaries, 14
The General Managers (Kotter), 293
generosity, of spirit, 48, 173, 279, 295
genuineness, 177–178, 302, 312
gestures. *See* body language
Gingrich, Newt, 151–152, 168
goal achievement, in career, xv, 2–3, 116, 125–126, 290, 324
von Goethe, Johann Wolfgang, 323

golden handcuffs. *See* job dissatisfaction
Golden Rule, 172–173, 188
  of management, 206, 215
Goleman, Daniel, 155
Greaves, Jean, 155, 184–185
Greenleaf, Robert K., 263–264

Hall, Doug, 286
Harkins, Jim, 228
Hawking, Stephen, 116
Headline Communication Model, 133, 134–137
Heller, Bruce, 290
Helmsley, Leona, 168
Henschel, Tom, 108
  Headline Communication Model of, 133, 134–137
honesty, 60–61, 174–175, 303, 312. *See also* DESCript
Howard, Jane, 290
humility, 175–177, 304

image, 159
  body language forming, 120–123
  characteristics perceived from, 111, 113, 121, 123, 129
  coaching tips to improve, 144–148
  message v., 108–109
  self-assessment checklist of, 110
  self-sabotage from, 113–115
information access, 52, 98, 291, 298
insensitivity, 170–171
integrated teamwork. *See* teamwork
International Coach Federation, 185, 324–326
interpersonal skills, self-assessment checklist of, 43
investment, in career, 39, 45, 52
It's All Politics: Winning in a World Where Hard Work and Talent Aren't Enough (Reardon), 305

Jackson, Phil, 82–83, 92

job dissatisfaction, 222–223, 233, 235–236, 270, 280–284
Jones, Jim, 124
Jump Start Your Career (Frankel), ix

Katzenbach, Jon, 84
Kennedy, John F., 52–53
Kerry, John, 107
kindness, 172–174, 304, 312
Klaus, Peggy, 257
Knight, Bobby, 152–153
Kotter, John, 291, 293

Lao-tzu, 66, 183
Lay, Kenneth, 221–222
likability, 157–159. *See also* need to be liked
    coaching tips to increase, 70, 72–73, 184–188
    emotional intelligence v., 157, 159
likability quotient, 31–32, 37–38, 122, 151–188
The Likeability Factor: How to Boost Your L-Factor and Achieve Your Life's Dreams (Sanders, T.), 187–188
Lindbergh, Anne Morrow, 53, 181
listening. *See* active listening
Lombardi, Vince, 175
Lombardo, Michael, 211
Los Angeles Lakers, 82–83, 92
loyalty
    as self-sabotaging behavior, 200, 201
    as success factor, 195, 232–233

MacKenzie, Gordon, 247
manager/employee relationship
    childhood experience influencing, 194–195, 203–205, 211–212, 217
    coaching tips to improve, 206–220
    deference v. confrontation in, 197–203, 212–213
    expectations in, 190–192, 206, 213–214
    tolerating inappropriate behavior in, 197–199, 214
managing up
    apple polishing v., 190–191
    in corporate playing field, 200–202
    secrets of success in, 206–209
    for success, 189–220
    workplace example of, 195
Mandel, Debra, 12, 217
Manigault-Stallworth, Omarosa, 172
manipulation, quid pro quo v., 48, 50, 297
Mary Kay Cosmetics, 231–232
matrixed team, 79, 92–95
MBTI (Myers-Briggs Type Indicator), 87
    communication problems identified by, 88
    preferences measured by, 87–89, 222–223
McCall, Morgan, 211
micromanaging, 5, 17, 236
Montoya, Peter, 251, 252, 289
Myers-Briggs Type Indicator. *See* MBTI

National Training Laboratory. *See* NTL
Navratilova, Martina, 159
need to be liked, 66, 67. *See also* likability
Netanyahu, Benjamin, 37, 38–39
network reciprocity, 45, 305–309. *See also* quid pro quo
networking. *See also* relationship building
    coaching tips on, 310–314, 318–322
    effectiveness in, 302–304
    importance of, 37, 39, 44–45, 290–291
    opportunities for, 314–318
    organizational chart v., 293–294
    politics and, 305, 308–309

networking (*con't.*)
    quid pro quo in, 298–301, 305–309
    resistance to, 295–297
    self-assessment checklist on, 292
    types of, 296–297
Networking for Job Search and Career
    Success (Tullier), 320
new job, 7–8, 9–10, 46–47, 219–220,
    233
Nice Girls Don't Get the Corner Office
    (Frankel), 67, 137, 176
Nixon, Richard, 153–154, 170
Nordstrom, retail chain, 274
NTL (National Training Laboratory),
    106, 179, 187, 329–330

offensive behavior, valued by
    organization, 165–166, 195
Orbiting the Giant Hairball: A Corporate
    Fool's Guide to Surviving with
    Grace (MacKenzie), 247
Outward Bound, 330
Overcoming Your Strengths: 8 Reasons
    Why Successful People Derail
    and How to Remain on Track
    (Frankel), ix
Owens, Terrell, 74–75

paradigm shift, 90–91, 286
Paradigms: The Business of Discovering
    the Future (Barker), 90
Pease, Allan, 120, 148
Pease, Barbara, 120, 148
pecking order, in organizations, 264,
    293
People Express, 230–231
people skills, 30, 38
    importance of, 37, 44, 50
    quid pro quo as, 46–52, 301
    self-assessment checklist of, 43
perfectionism, 39–41, 117–118, 177,
    204–205, 242
personal development plan, 323–334

Philadelphia Eagles, Owens, Terrell,
    teamwork failure with, 74–75
Picascia, Susan, 203–205
posture. *See* body language
Powell, Colin, 121, 130
power of perception, success from,
    107–150, 252–253
preferences, MBTI measurements of,
    87–89, 222–223
presentations, coaching tips for
    successful, 133–137
pretension, 177–178
professional coaching. *See also* coaching
    fees for, 325
    finding coach for, 324–328
    International Coach Federation,
        185, 324–326
    mental health contacts for, 330–332
    public programs for, 328–330
    steps in process of, 326–328
program administrator, 180–181
pseudo-listening, 53–54, 100, 187

quid pro quo. *See also* networking;
    relationship building
    business referral as, 48–49, 291,
        298–299, 307–308
    developing currency in, 191,
        305–308
    manipulation v., 48, 50, 297
    in networking, 298–301, 305–309
    reciprocity in, 61–63, 305–309
    relationship building through,
        46–52, 298–301, 305–309
    self-disclosure in, 61–63, 70

Reardon, Kathleen Kelley, 305
reciprocity. *See* networking; quid pro
    quo; relationship building
relationship building. *See also*
    networking
    active listening in, 52–59, 199, 295,
        311–312

coaching tips for, 44–46, 69–73,
310–314, 317, 318–322
doorway conversations for, 59, 69,
317
essential ingredients of, 59–66
failure in, 38–39, 181–183
importance of, 37, 44, 290–291
information access in, 52, 291, 298
interpersonal v. team, 75–76
quid pro quo in, 46–52, 298–301,
305–309
reciprocity in, 61–63, 305–309
self-assessment checklist for, 43
self-disclosure in, 61–63, 70
skills for, 43, 45, 53, 59
success in, 37–38, 173, 185,
257–258
360-degree, 37–73
360-degree feedback survey on, 178,
185, 257–258
trust in, 60–61
repetition compulsion, 3–10
example of, 8–9
self-sabotage from, 3–7
staff resistance to, 7, 10
theory of, 3–4
Ritz-Carlton, hotel chain, 80–81,
264–265
Rogers, Carl, 54–59
Roosevelt, Eleanor, 205

Sacred Hoops: Spiritual Lessons of a
Hardwood Warrior (Jackson),
82
Sanders, Frankie J., 82–83
Sanders, Tim, 187–188
Schwarzkopf, Norman, 176
seamless service, of matrixed team, 94
The Secret Handshake: Mastering the
Politics of the Business Inner
Circle (Reardon), 305
self
awareness, 178–180

confidence, 275, 311
disclosure, 61–63, 70
esteem, 194–195, 203–205, 210, 214
self-assessment checklist, 19–24, 43, 77,
110, 158, 193, 224, 254, 292
self-sabotage, 1–2, 25–30
attire as, 112, 115–116
attractiveness as, 117–118
behaviors of, 16–19
body language as, 121–123
character traits for, 165–172
communication style as, 126–129,
138–144, 181–183
in corporate playing field, 12–16
in detail orientation, 238–240, 271,
277–278
emotional intelligence deficiency
as, 167–169
examples of, 8–9, 66, 74–75, 82–83,
96, 151–153, 189–190, 200,
202, 221–222, 297–298
facial expression as, 121–122
first impression as, 113–115
image as, 113–115
need to be liked as, 66–68
network limits as, 297–298
in new job environments, 7–8
personal development plan v.,
323–334
from repetition compulsion, 3–7
resistance to networking as,
295–297
resistance to teamwork as, 86, 90
self-sabotaging behavior
challenging manager as, 197–198,
212–213, 215, 216
changing, 25–29, 44–46, 161–162,
164
of communication style, 126–129,
138–144, 181–183
intelligence as, 160–161
inventory of, 19–24
joking as, 162–163, 184

self-sabotaging behavior (con't.)
  loyalty as, 200, 201
  perfectionism as, 39–41, 117–118,
      177, 204–205, 242
  rewarding, 165–166
  self-assessment checklists of, 19–24,
      43, 77, 110, 158, 193, 224,
      254, 292
  social climbing as, 51–52
  speech patterns as, 128, 130–131
  standoffishness as, 39–41
  strengths as, 26, 34, 86, 163,
      196–197, 200, 202, 243
  table manners as, 127
  team role disinterest as, 102
  technical competence as, 18, 39–41,
      277
  thought patterns as, 129–132
  turning up/down volume of, xiii,
      7–10, 118, 128, 198
  value-adding failure as, 268–269
  workplace example of, 16–17,
      39–41, 159–161, 181–183
Servant Leadership: A Journey into the
    Nature of Legitimate Power
    and Greatness (Greenleaf),
    263–264
service orientation. See can-do attitude;
    value-adding
shyness, 310–314
skill set balance, xiii, xv, 27, 68, 232,
    235, 246
skills gap, 1, 2, 8
skills repertoire, xv, 35, 118–119, 162,
    172, 272, 323–334
Smith, Douglas, 84
social networking. See networking;
    relationship building
Speak Like a CEO: Secrets for
    Commanding Attention and
    Getting Results (Bates), 150
speech patterns
  coaching tips on, 131–132
  of communication style, 129–132
  self-sabotage in, 128
sports teams, 74–75, 82–83
standards of dress. See dressing
    standards
Stewart, Martha, 152
strategic thinking
  coaching tips to develop, 240–242,
      329
  failure to develop skills in, 238–240,
      271
  overdevelopment of, 242–244
strategic thinking, v. detail orientation
  can-do attitude and, 277–278
  coaching tips to balance, 246–250
  continuum of, 227–228
  imbalance in, 238–240, 242–244,
      271
  self-assessment checklist of, 224
success. See also dress for success
  active listening for, 52–59, 161–162,
      199, 295
  balancing strategic thinking/detail
      orientation for, 221–250
  behavior assessment for, 19–24
  behaviors promoting, xvi, 103–106
  body language for, 121–123
  career transition for, 28, 219–220,
      233–235, 245–246, 270,
      282–284
  challenging manager for, 197–198,
      212–213, 215, 216
  childhood experience influencing,
      30–33, 38–39, 45, 176,
      192–197, 236–237
  emotional intelligence skills for,
      151–188
  examples of, 37–38, 80–81, 121,
      130, 153–154, 176,
      225–226, 231–232, 256,
      264–265, 274, 298
  fast track to, 44, 104, 179
  first impression for, 111, 115, 116

Headline Communication Model
    for, 133, 134–137
likability quotient for, 31–32,
    37–38, 122, 151–188
managing up for, 189–220, 206–209
people skills v. technical
    competence in, x, 44, 50,
    52, 68, 79, 277
power of perception on, 107–150,
    252–253
recognizing boundaries for, 15–16,
    200–202, 293
relationships importance to, 37–38,
    39, 50, 52, 102
risk taking for, 16–17, 26–27,
    196–197, 214, 219, 225,
    310, 330
team membership for, 74–106, 102
technical competence and, 18, 42,
    52, 68, 96
360-degree relationship building for,
    37–73, 178, 185, 257–258
success factor
can-do attitude as, 261–262,
    264–265, 272, 273–275,
    279, 284
communication style as, 31, 37–38,
    124, 129, 131
emotional intelligence as, 151–188
likability as, 31–32, 37–38, 122,
    151–188
networking as, 290–291, 294–295,
    297–298, 300–301
people skills as, 30, 37–38
team working as, 30–31, 100,
    279–280
value-adding as, 102, 216–217, 241,
    253, 261–262, 264–265,
    274, 285
Summitt, Pat, 74
survival skills, 4–5, 78–79

table manners, 127

team
functions of, 96–98
member roles, 95–102
team building
behaviors, 279–280
examples of, 64–66, 87–90
self-assessment checklist of, 77
team player, 258–261
coaching tips for, success, 103–106
individual contributor v., 79–80, 90,
    92, 101
teamwork
examples of, 74–75, 78–79, 82–83,
    92–95, 264–265
member roles in, 95–102
overcoming resistance to, 82–86,
    100
skills required for, 45, 76, 90
as success factor, 30–31, 100
value of, 76–83
teamwork dynamics
customer/employee satisfaction
    through, 80–82, 264–265
roles in, 96–99
sports teams examples of, 74–75,
    82–83
star v. team player in, 82–83
teamwork resistance, 83–86, 100–101
behavior examples of, 90–91,
    99–100
childhood experience influencing,
    84–86, 90, 99–100
cross cultural example of, 84–85
technical competence
in career success, 18, 42, 52, 68,
    96
as self-sabotage, 18, 39–41, 277
Thatcher, Margaret, 8–9
360-degree feedback survey,
    relationship building
    assessment with, 178, 185,
    257–258
Toastmasters International, 148

Tomlin, Lily, 159
trust, in relationship building, 60–61
Tullier, Michelle, 310–314, 320

United Parcel Service, 262–263
US Postal Service, 262

value-adding
    can-do attitude as, 261–262,
        264–265, 272, 273–275,
        279, 284
    coaching tips for, 275–284
    customer service example of, 80–82,
        259–262, 264–265, 274
    failure to add value, 268–269
    no-can-do attitude v., 266–267,
        269–272
    to organization, 102, 216–217, 241,
        253, 279, 285
value-adding behaviors, self-assessment
    checklist of, 254
value-adding brand
    characteristics of, 252–253
    coaching tips for developing,
        285–289

marketing of, 256–257
WALLET steps to define, 253–262

WALLET steps, for defining value-
    added brand, 253–262
Wal-Mart, 262
Walters, Barbara, 119
Whitmore, Jacqueline, 147
win–win situations, 186, 190–192, 276,
    288–289
The Wisdom of Teams (Katzenbach and
    Smith), 84
Wooden, John, 157
Woods, Tiger, 256
workplace behavior repertoire, 34,
    44–46, 64–66
workplace relationships. See
    networking; quid pro quo;
    relationship building

Your Boss Is Not Your Mother: Eight Steps
    to Eliminating Office Drama and
    Creating Positive Relationships at
    Work (Mandel), 12, 217

About the Author

Lois P. Frankel is a licensed psychotherapist with a PhD in counseling psychology from the University of Southern California and author of the international best-sellers *Nice Girls Don't Get the Corner Office* and *Nice Girls Don't Get Rich*. As president of Corporate Coaching International, a Pasadena, California–based consulting firm, and a keynote speaker, Dr. Frankel has traveled the globe serving such diverse clients as Amgen, ARCO, BP, Cedars-Sinai Medical Center, City of Hope, McKinsey & Company, KPMG, Lockheed Martin Corporation, Miller Brewing Company, Natural History Museum of Los Angeles County, Northrop Grumman, Procter & Gamble, the Walt Disney Company, and Warner Bros. She has appeared on the *Today* show, CNN, and Fox News, and has been interviewed by *The Wall Street Journal*, *USA Today*, *The Washington Post*, and *People* magazine. Dr. Frankel can be heard daily in Southern California on KNX 1070 with her coaching tip of the day. To learn more about Dr. Frankel, to schedule her to speak to your organization, or to receive her free monthly e-mail career coaching tips, visit her Web sites www.drlois frankel.com or www.corporatecoachingintl.com.

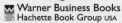